BASEBALL COP

BASEBALL COP

THE DARK SIDE OF AMERICA'S
NATIONAL PASTIME

EDDIE DOMINGUEZ

WITH

CHRISTIAN RED & TERI THOMPSON

NEW YORK   BOSTON

Hachette Books
Hachette Book Group
1290 Avenue of the Americas
New York, NY 10104
hachettebookgroup.com
twitter.com/hachettebooks

First Edition: August 2018

Hachette Books is a division of Hachette Book Group, Inc.
The Hachette Books name and logo are trademarks of Hachette Book Group, Inc.

The publisher is not responsible for websites (or their content)
that are not owned by the publisher.

The Hachette Speakers Bureau provides a wide range of authors for
speaking events. To find out more, go to www.hachettespeakersbureau.com
or call (866) 376-6591.

Interior design by Timothy Shaner, NightandDayDesign.biz

Library of Congress Control Number: 2018935830

ISBNs: 978-0-316-48397-1 (hardcover), 978-0-316-48399-5 (ebook)

Printed in the United States of America

LSC-C

10 9 8 7 6 5 4 3 2 1

This book is dedicated to my family and friends.

Thank you for all your love and support.

CONTENTS

BASEBALL COP

PROLOGUE

In 1994, Eddie Dominguez, a seasoned detective in the Boston Police Department with fifteen years on the job, was assigned to the Major Case Unit at BPD headquarters, working alongside state troopers and the rest of the MCU squad. Dominguez lived in Braintree, Massachusetts, and coached his young sons, Andrew and Christopher, and their Little League team. As a boy, the Cuban-born Dominguez had learned to love the game of baseball on the rock-strewn sandlots of Havana, and he brought that love to his sons on the playing fields of Boston. The Little League travel season was heating up, and Dominguez and his sons watched the Red Sox on television on a nightly basis. Sometimes they were fortunate enough to catch a game at Fenway Park. The Dominguez boys loved Roger Clemens and Mo Vaughn from those early-'90s teams. The Sox even had a Cuban player, the left-handed pitcher Tony Fossas, with whom Eddie had grown up in Jamaica Plain, the gritty Boston neighborhood where Dominguez settled with his family after they fled Cuba.

The baseball season ended prematurely in August 1994 due to a players' strike, making for a long, dispiriting close to the summer and fall. But only four years later an exciting, unprecedented chase for the single-season home run record made fans forget all about the strike as they flocked to the ballpark in record numbers. Even the most casual observer watched in awe as Mark McGwire and Sammy Sosa blasted baseballs over outfield walls with the ease of Babe Ruth.

What Major League Baseball didn't want advertised was how McGwire and Sosa, among others, could achieve those superhuman feats. To someone like Dominguez, the Cuban refugee and decorated cop, the answer seemed plain as day. During the following season, 1999, when he was hired to work in conjunction with Major League Baseball as the resident security agent (RSA) overseeing all manner of security issues for the Red Sox, Dominguez would see the scourge permeating the game firsthand.

In 2001, two years into his work as an RSA, Dominguez was at a rookie career development conference when he was invited to an informal gathering in the hotel room of Kevin Hallinan, a former New York Police Department lieutenant who was head of MLB's security department and Dominguez's boss. Hallinan asked a hypothetical question of his Boston RSA: What would happen if Dominguez were to investigate drug use in the Red Sox clubhouse? Dominguez was still somewhat new in his role, but the exchange that followed Hallinan's question was telling.

"So Dominguez, what do you think?" Hallinan began. "People are up in arms about this steroid stuff, thinking the commissioner's office and the rest of us were asleep at the wheel. If I wanted you to really investigate what was going on in the clubhouse in Boston, what would happen?"

Dominguez, who was keenly aware of baseball's unofficial drug use policy at the time—"Don't ask, don't tell"—had never been a fan of Hallinan and demurred, "I don't know, Kevin. It's getting late. I'm going to head up for the night."

Hallinan persisted. "I want to know what you think," he said. "What would happen? Would we find anything at all? A couple Dominicans with a few syringes?"

"Are you talking about just steroids?" Dominguez asked.

"Steroids, uppers, downers, and whatever else," Hallinan replied. "Open season. What would you find if I let you loose in there?"

Dominguez answered slowly, measuring his response, "I think half of them would be in handcuffs."

Hallinan was incredulous. His two underbosses in the room, Tom Belfiore and Marty Maguire, were speechless.

"Are you kidding?" Hallinan asked.

"No," Dominguez said. "You asked me my opinion, and I told you what I think."

Dominguez, who continued to work for the Boston Police Department while serving as an RSA, had based his answer on what he had observed during his first two years in the Red Sox clubhouse. He was a twenty-two-year veteran of the Boston PD and had been a case agent working undercover on dozens of drug cases. He had cultivated informants and befriended mob bosses. He relied on his instincts and simple common sense, tools that translated well to a major-league clubhouse.

Some of the signs of drug use were subtle, others not so much. Players would head toward the training room, slap their own butts, and make a motion with their fingers as though they were going to be injected. There were hangers-on with fake names and IDs— red flags to an experienced narcotics detective because drug dealers wanted elsewhere were known to purchase and assume another person's identity. There were specific instances that led Dominguez to believe that Hallinan and MLB were either clueless about or willfully blind to what was going on under their noses.

Before MLB vowed to crack down on the player entourages that frequently clogged clubhouses—personal trainers, gofers, valets— even employees of the team weren't subjected to background checks. The underpaid clubbies depended on the big tips doled out by the players and would carry out any task asked of them. Dominguez's targets included clubhouse attendants in Boston and other cities, as well as all the other barbers, assistants, bodyguards, and hangers-on. As history would reveal, players such as Clemens, Barry Bonds, and Alex Rodriguez relied heavily on those confidants and associates, some of them family members, as crutches and front men for their alleged drug needs.

Those were the years before a drug-testing program was negotiated between MLB and the players' union, when there were players who would return from the off-season looking like ultrabuff cartoon characters. Speculation among fans and the media about many of the players—McGwire, Sosa, Bonds, Brady Anderson, José Canseco, and others—was that they were getting pharmaceutical "help" for their performance on the field. One of those transformed players was Nomar Garciaparra, the phenomenal Red Sox shortstop from 1996 to 2004. "No-mah," as he was known in Boston, appeared on a March 2001 *Sports Illustrated* cover transformed from a skinny, wiry kid into a muscle-bound superman. Under the headline "A Cut Above: How Baseball's Nomar Garciaparra Made Himself the Toughest Out in Baseball," Garciaparra was shirtless and looked as if someone had injected him with helium, or, as was speculated in the media, something else, even though he had never tested positive for or otherwise been connected to performance-enhancing drugs.[1]

Baseball's obstructive, head-in-the-sand approach to its burgeoning steroid problem would abruptly end in 2005, when Congress began to ask what the professional leagues—baseball in particular—

were doing about doping and called for a hearing on performance-enhancing drug use in sports. Subsequently, MLB commissioner Bud Selig and his labor chief, Robert Manfred, who would succeed Selig as commissioner, were hammered by members of the House Committee on Oversight and Government Reform for ignoring the drug scourge for years. As early as 1994, baseball, and specifically Hallinan, had been warned by an FBI agent about the game's growing steroid problem, a problem MLB adamantly denied for years.

Only a month before the 2005 congressional hearing, the New York *Daily News* reported that Michigan-based FBI agent Greg Stejskal had told Hallinan during a 1994 FBI agents' conference in Quantico, Virginia, that a three-and-a-half-year-long federal steroid investigation known as Operation Equine had revealed evidence of heavy steroid use by star players, including Canseco and McGwire, as far back as the late 1980s.

"It did not happen," Hallinan told the *Daily News* after the story appeared. "Not with this guy [Stejskal]. Not with anybody else."[2]

Stejskal's partner, FBI agent Bill Randall, told the *Daily News* and other media that the FBI had records of the meeting between Stejskal and Hallinan. "The fact is, Greg met with Hallinan and MLB, and told him about Canseco and other names," Randall said.

Another *Daily News* report published days before the congressional hearing described an Operation Equine informant's account of having injected McGwire at a gym in southern California with an array of hard-core steroids, including testosterone, Equipoise, and Winstrol. Operation Equine was the federal probe into steroid dealers that Stejskal oversaw, with Randall acting as the undercover agent. Even after McGwire admitted in a 2010 interview with NBC broadcaster Bob Costas that he had used steroids throughout his career, MLB continued to equivocate.[3]

"We overcame many obstacles to develop an unprecedented UC [undercover] operation that is still the most successful case of its kind," Stejskal wrote in a 2012 FBI publication. "I often wonder how things would have been different had MLB acted on our warning. (In 2005 MLB even denied we warned them, and they have never unequivocally admitted that we did warn them.)"[4]

Eleven years after the 1994 warning, Henry Waxman, the highly respected Los Angeles congressman and then the ranking minority member of the committee, bluntly summed up the congressional view: "We're long past the point where we can count on Major League Baseball to fix its own problems."[5]

The message from the committee members was clear: clean up your game, or Congress will. A full-blown federal investigation, and perhaps even a change of status to baseball's vaunted antitrust exemption, were the unstated threats. His legacy at stake, Selig commissioned his good friend, former Senate majority leader George Mitchell, to carry out an independent investigation into doping in baseball with the hope that the congressional watchdogs would be appeased. The result was a lengthy report released in December 2007 detailing extensive drug use by players, cover-ups, lax oversight by the game's overlords, and a shadowy underworld of drug peddlers—from trainers to clubbies to agents—who had infiltrated baseball.

Clemens and Andy Pettitte were the biggest names to surface in Mitchell's report, but it was a little-noted section of the document near the end that would have the most impact: the portion that recommended that MLB establish an in-house investigative unit. Mitchell stressed that the unit should comprise former law enforcement members, be autonomous, and, most pointedly, receive no interference from MLB's Labor Relations Department. The unit's members would report only to the commissioner and MLB president Bob DuPuy. The report stated that the MLB Labor Relations Department's "principal responsibility is to oversee the collective bargaining relationship with the Players Association," leaving little room or time for Labor to investigate potential player transgressions. The report further stated:

> That primary responsibility, however, also complicates the ability of the labor relations department to meet another of its responsibilities, to investigate allegations of player wrongdoing. The department must maintain good relations with the Players Association; but aggressive, thorough investigations of the alleged possession or use by players of performance enhancing substances may be inconsistent with that objective. . . .
>
> The senior executive should have sole authority over all investigations of alleged performance enhancing substance violations and other threats to the integrity of the game, and should receive the resources and other support needed to make the office effective.[6]

It went on to say that the commissioner's office should adopt a written policy requiring all information received by a team or the commissioner's office about possible performance-enhancing substance use, other than the collectively bargained drug-testing program, "must be reported immediately and directly to the senior executive in charge of the Department of Investigations."[7]

For Eddie Dominguez, a man who throughout his law enforcement career had worked hand in hand with the DEA and FBI in taking down mobsters and drug lords, becoming a member of MLB's new Department of Investigations seemed like a dream job. His family had fled Fidel Castro's Communist Cuba in 1966. Nine-year-old Eddie had arrived in Boston as a kid who had played baseball in the streets of Havana, hitting a crumpled can or rock with a broomstick. He was a Minnesota Twins fan; his favorite players were the Cuban outfielder Tony Oliva and the Red Sox great Luis Tiant. He met Oliva years later when Oliva was a Twins coach and Dominguez spoke at a spring training presentation. Tiant, the Cuban-born right-hander and a star of the epic 1975 Cincinnati Reds–Boston Red Sox World Series, had lived in Dominguez's Jamaica Plain neighborhood, and Dominguez got to know Tiant well when the Sox hired their former pitcher as an ambassador. "The only player," Dominguez says, "I would ever call my friend." Dominguez coached Little League for thirteen years. His sons would play college baseball, and Andrew would even go on to play in the Red Sox organization for three years.

Twice Dominguez had turned down Hallinan's offer to join MLB's security department, but this opportunity, working in a proposed autonomous unit, was different: Hallinan was out—he had retired in 2007—and Dominguez's friend Dan Mullin, a retired NYPD deputy chief, had been promoted to vice president of the newly established Department of Investigations.

"For me, the whole reason I jumped ship to join Dan Mullin and the other DOI agents he hired was because of the appeal of maintaining the integrity of America's pastime," Dominguez would say. "In fact, that is the exact way Mullin pitched the job to me."

"We could clean up the game," Mullin told Dominguez in a text when the department was formed in early 2008.

Dominguez had known Mullin for more than twenty years, going back to a summer night in 1981 outside Fenway Park when two of Mullin's NYPD colleagues had left a memorable imprint on Lansdowne Street, behind the famed Green Monster. Suffice it to say, two of New York's Finest had drained more Budweisers than all the frat boys in Boston. When Dominguez addressed the officer sitting in the driver's seat of the police cruiser—the one with his police cap turned backward—the officer muttered a slurred "Ehhs tthisss Fehhnway Puh-ark?"

Dominguez helped get the NYPD boys onto their feet, dressed in fresh clothes, and into the Fens to watch the Red Sox game. The episode sparked a long relationship with Mullin's peers from Midtown South in Manhattan, the beginning, as Humphrey Bogart said in *Casablanca*, of a beautiful friendship.

Not only was Mullin a decorated NYPD veteran whose heroic efforts on 9/11 were well documented—a harrowing still photograph taken by *New York Times* photographer Ruth Fremson showed Mullin, covered in ash and soot, leaning against a deli case moments after he and Fremson had found refuge from the collapse of the South Tower of the World Trade Center—he also held a law degree from New York University. He had served as the commanding officer of Manhattan district attorney Robert Morgenthau's detective squad, was the head of Staten Island's detective operations, and then became the executive officer of the NYPD's narcotics division, where he oversaw more than three thousand detectives.

"What's there to think about?" Mullin texted Dominguez.

The truth? There were a few things to consider in taking on a new job: uprooting from Boston to New York; Dominguez's first marriage, which was crumbling, but there was no fixing that, and his sons were done with high school; and four more years on the Boston PD would secure his full pension.

But the pull was there. The DOI was to be an independent unit, at least on paper. It would have a clean slate to carry out its own investigations, with no interference. That meant digging deep into more than just the drug mess. The Dominican Republic—from which a large portion of MLB's players originated—was an island with myriad problems throughout the baseball business, including age and identity falsification, bonus skimming, and the exploitation of teenage prospects. Players were trickling in from Cuba, some trafficked, others defecting.

Dominguez read the Mitchell Report again. In MLB's structure, DOI and Labor would be separate. With Mullin in charge, great change would be possible. Mullin was tough enough to stare down a pampered millionaire and hold him accountable if there was evidence to suggest wrongdoing. He had the balls to drop the hammer. Dominguez picked up the phone and dialed the Irish cop whom he later nicknamed "El Guapo"—"The Handsome One."

Mullin answered on the first ring. "Hey, Dan. Yeah, I'm in," Dominguez said.

The DOI was born in January 2008 with the blessing of the government but died quickly and quietly in 2014, the victim of the very same forces that had led to its formation. Baseball may have declared the Steroid Era dead and buried, but as the summer of 2017 wound down, a new record hit the books: on September 19, Kansas City's Alex Gordon hit Major League Baseball's 5,694th home run of the year, breaking a season record set in 2000, which had been, as news reports noted, the height of what would become one of the most controversial periods in baseball history.

Dominguez joined what at the time was an unprecedented experiment in self-policing: the DOI's announced mission was to expose individuals and entities that would corrupt the game. Mullin had assembled a dream team of investigators: five former FBI and DEA task force members, high-ranking detectives skilled in undercover stings and narcotics busts. They would hit the ground running and use the law enforcement techniques they had spent years honing to tackle any corrupting force. Dominguez had a front-row seat for some of the most groundbreaking investigations in base-ball's history—some shocking, some farcical. But each case repre-sented a beneath-the-surface threat to the billion-dollar industry that is Major League Baseball. If steroids, gambling, and human trafficking were poxes on the game, baseball's bosses would find that the cure for those ills was, in their eyes, even worse.

Dominguez had barely started the job when he was approached by an executive at baseball's pristine Park Avenue offices in New York City. He told Dominguez that no one—no one!—wanted him or any of the DOI members around.

"You made a huge mistake taking this job," the executive said.

"Excuse me? What are you talking about?" Dominguez asked.

"The owners don't want you, the commissioner doesn't want you, Labor and Manfred sure as hell don't want you," the executive said. "You guys are internal affairs, and if baseball can do anything about it, you won't last long."

There had been an equally sobering exchange in the Dominican Republic with a team's international scouting director during Dominguez's first year on the job.

"We had knocked back a few Presidentes in old town Santo Domingo, at a bar near the Caribbean surf. It was the first and last time I would ever set foot in the place," Dominguez said. "The guy looked at me and said, 'Your mind and heart seem like they're in the right place, but what you don't understand is that this industry is like the Mafia.'

"I had actually been involved in undercover operations with real Mafia hoods, and now a baseball scout was making compari-sons between baseball and organized crime? I laughed it off at the time. So did my superiors, Dan Mullin and former FBI agent George Hanna, after I rehashed the conversation with them. I guess I should have run right then and there, run straight back to Boston and the law enforcement career I had ditched, run as far away from baseball as I could."

"Nobody wants you cleaning up any dirt," the guy said, tipping back the green beer bottle.

How do you like that? Dominguez thought. The recommendation by Selig's handpicked investigator, former senator George Mitchell, was off to a beautiful start.

That dream job? Turned out it was too good to be true.

CHAPTER 1

THE BEGINNING OF THE END

I had already received three phone calls on Monday, April 28, 2014, from a familiar 212 area code, although the extension at MLB's offices wasn't one I immediately recognized. The Red Sox were off that day after getting creamed by Toronto 7–1 a day earlier, so I was preoccupied with work, revisiting some loose ends in a couple investigations, going over reports in my home office.

Alex Rodriguez, the player Major League Baseball had relentlessly pursued and demanded that the DOI nail at all costs, was somewhere—perhaps in Miami? L.A.?—serving his season-long suspension for his years-long association with Anthony Bosch, the founder of the Biogenesis antiaging clinic. And Bosch himself? Who knows? Maybe he was snorting coke somewhere, after baseball had paid his way—room and board, lawyers, fancy New York restaurants—to be its star witness in A-Rod's bruising arbitration the previous fall when the fallen Yankee star had contested his historic 211-game suspension for doping. Bosch's day would come down the road.

My cell phone lit up again. This is it, I thought.

When I answered the call, the man's voice on the other end blurted out that he was in Payroll at MLB. I had dealt with that department for fifteen years, and this had to be the most bizarre conversation I had ever experienced.

"We just need the name and number of the person with the car service you used," said the voice. He was hurried, curt, maybe purposely unfriendly. I realized he was asking about the car service and how I had been having members of my family pitch in to drive. I'd stopped using car services after a drug dealer I had busted years earlier had shown up at the end of my driveway early one morning in a limo owned by a service recommended by MLB. That had unnerved me a bit, to say the least.

On too many occasions in my previous line of work as an undercover detective purchasing or selling narcotics to middle- to upper-level drug dealers, I had received threats on my life. I had once put a cocaine dealer in jail who had then hired someone to find out where I lived. According to a source, the dealer wanted me dead. The threats were always there, but this was the first time I learned that one of those thugs was looking into where I lived. Now you're talking about my family. The result was round-the-clock surveillance of my home until I paid the drug dealer a visit and let him know I was onto him.

That was why it was more than a bit disconcerting to see that the driver for the car service MLB had recommended, who showed up to deliver me to the airport, was a guy that I had previously arrested. It was 4 a.m., late 2010, and it was dark, so I kept my head down and hoped he didn't recognize me. But I was not about to chance that again. Being picked up at your home by a total stranger is not a healthy practice for someone who did what I did for a living.

So after that incident, I paid my sons, Andrew and briefly Chris, the market rate to drive me to the airport or the nearest train station. When my sons weren't available, sometimes my mother, or my wife, Donna, drove me. It wasn't as though MLB recommended that our unit use a specific service—it simply asked that we use the

cheapest one available. It was up to us to figure it out, and I estimated that I had been paying the previous service about $100 for a
trip from my house to Logan International and $40 to the closest
Amtrak station.

Now this MLB payroll guy was barking for a name and phone
numbers and saying that he had to run the information through the
system. Even though I had been handling my car service like this for
three or four years, with no questions asked, no flags raised, every
expense approved in a four-step process, there was no way I was
getting my sons involved, so I left their names out of it. The conversation ended abruptly. I immediately called my bosses, Dan Mullin
and George Hanna.

No answer. Nothing.

Outside my home, I must have paced up and down the driveway the equivalent of a mile, parsing my thoughts. Up and down.
Up and down. The great DOI experiment was over, and for the first
time in my life I was about to be fired. I knew it. Donna knew it. The
phone call about the car service made that clear. I knew they were
capable of playing hardball and I barely had enough money to even
start to think about mounting a defense.

While I was waiting for the phone to ring again, I put the question to Donna: "I want you to know that it's going to get ugly. Are
you in?"

"I'm in," Donna said.

I circled back through my garage and went to the office.

I tried Mullin and Hanna again. Still, no answer. Shit, I thought.
We're history. Then came Dan Halem's call, his extension lighting
up the digital display on my phone. The chief lieutenant in the Labor
Relations Department, Halem had been one of the DOI's main
adversaries.

I ignored it.

I reached out to Nancy Zamudio, the lead assistant at the DOI, and she confirmed that Mullin and Hanna were gone. (Tom Reilly, my DOI partner during the Biogenesis case, would be terminated days later.) I held the phone for a couple seconds, thinking back to those heady days in early 2008. What was it Mullin had said? "We could clean up this game."

I finally reached Mullin and Hanna. They told me that MLB was already digging deep into our emails and text messages, presumably trying to find a reason to fire us. Baseball was also leaning on us to sign confidentiality agreements, and I knew the people there would try to use the car service issue as leverage to get me to sign.

But despite the significant hurdles that lay ahead, I was ready to take on MLB and expose the bullshit behind the Mitchell Report, the DOI, and the dissolution of our unit.

Even before 2012, when the Biogenesis investigation began to heat up, it was becoming clear to me after four years with the DOI that the warnings I'd heard about MLB were accurate. I became convinced that baseball's lords were going to get rid of us for doing the job we had been charged with after Congress, revelations in the media, and the Mitchell Report had embarrassed them for their years of neglect.

From the very beginning, we had followed George Mitchell's edict: to work hand in hand with law enforcement. Mitchell had made it clear that the unit's success would depend on that interaction. "The Commissioner's Office should establish policies to ensure the integrity and independence of the department's investigations, including the adoption of procedures analogous to those employed by the internal affairs departments of law enforcement agencies," he wrote. "The adoption of and adherence to these policies can serve to ensure public confidence that the Commissioner's Office is responding vigorously to all serious allegations of performance enhancing substance violations."[1]

But as we would later discover, Manfred and his Labor Relations Department would put up walls almost every step of the way—everything from preventing us from interviewing players under investigation or, as was the case in the Biogenesis investigation, hiring an outside contractor and retired law enforcement to shadow us and undermine our work. That we would later be blamed for many of the actions of that shadow group was especially galling.

Though Mitchell had pointed to the need for MLB to cooperate with the Major League Baseball Players Association in implementing his edicts, I never bought the theory that Manfred and Labor's interference with our mission was somehow justified by restrictions in baseball's collectively bargained relationship with the players. We followed protocol in our dealings with players and never unilaterally pursued a player's cooperation. The fact was, if a player violated baseball's rules, he had to meet with MLB representatives. He could be accompanied by his attorneys and didn't have to incriminate himself, but he had to meet with baseball representatives. We should have been present at those meetings, too. We simply wanted a seat at the table.

Mitchell even underscored in his report how important it would be for the newly established DOI to forge strong relationships with law enforcement agencies, since, as he wrote, "Law enforcement officials, of course, have a broad array of investigatory powers, including search warrants and subpoena power." He cited one law enforcement official he and his investigators had spoken to who had expressed frustration that there was no specific contact at Selig's office to whom to relay important information. "The senior executive in charge of [DOI] would be that person," Mitchell wrote.[2]

Mitchell referenced the case of former Mets clubhouse attendant Kirk Radomski, who had been a key witness in the Bay Area Laboratory Co-operative (BALCO) steroids trafficking case out of the US Attorney's Office for the Northern District of California.

When Mitchell and his team were compiling the report, they wrote, "the Radomski investigation yielded information regarding performance-enhancing substance use by major league players, much of it corroborated by documentary or other evidence."[3] In fact, in the eyes of many, it was BALCO prosecutors Matt Parrella and Jeff Nedrow, along with then-IRS investigator Jeff Novitzky, who provided the bulk of the information in Mitchell's report and two of its most crucial witnesses. Without the cooperation of Radomski as well as trainer Brian McNamee, who told Mitchell that he had provided performance-enhancing drugs to former Yankees Roger Clemens, Andy Pettitte, and Chuck Knoblauch, Mitchell's report would have been about ten pages long.

We were more than willing to cooperate with any agency that could help us—there were no strict rules per se. We all had experience working with other law enforcement agencies, and we had contacts with, sources in, and relationships with a wide range of authorities.

I had worked on a joint Boston PD–FBI task force for ten years and had worked closely with the Drug Enforcement Administration and local and federal prosecutors; Mullin's law enforcement experience was steeped in narcotics investigations, among his many other accomplishments; George Hanna was a former FBI agent who served thirty years in the bureau, and was the lead agent in the case that brought down the DeCavalcante crime family, the model for the HBO hit series *The Sopranos*. Hanna received several distinguished service awards during his career; Tom Reilly, who would join us in 2010, had retired from the NYPD as a detective first grade and was a member of the Joint Terrorism Task Force, the Rapid Deployment Team, and a DEA task force. Reilly and Joseph V. Mazzei were recognized as Top Cops in 2011 at an event in Washington, DC, sponsored by the National Association of Police Organizations, for the arrest of would-be Times Square car bomber Faisal Shazad. Reilly,

Mazzei, and Special Agent Brian O'Rourke were the lead investigators on the case and managed to arrest Shazad fifty-three hours after the incident. Shazad pled guilty at his arraignment, and according to the FBI, the agents' interview of Shazad had resulted in more than three thousand intelligence reports resulting in numerous FBI and CIA cases. The Top Cop award is considered one of the highest honors that can be bestowed on a law enforcement officer. Victor Burgos, another original member of the unit who would be forced to leave in 2012, had been a member of a DEA–NYPD–state police joint drug task force.

The DOI took a number of cases to the DEA around August 2012. Most had to do with wellness centers, many of them in Florida. We dealt primarily with Joseph Rannazzisi, the head of the DEA's Office of Diversion Control, who was responsible for cracking down on doctors, pharmacies, drug manufacturers, and distributors who failed to follow the country's drug laws, along with DEA deputy administrator Thomas Harrigan and Penny Payne-Korte, an investigator assigned to us through the DEA Diversion unit.

Rannazzisi would be featured on *60 Minutes Overtime* in October 2017 in a powerful segment on the war against opioids called "The Whistleblower," in which he described being thwarted by Congress as he led a long investigation into the complicity of drug companies, manufacturers, distributors, and chain pharmacies in the epidemic. Rannazzisi was articulate, compelling, and outspoken in his interview, no surprise to those of us who had worked with him on baseball's drug issues. His comment, "This is an industry that allowed millions and millions of drugs to go into bad pharmacies and doctors' offices, that distributed them out to people who had no legitimate need for those drugs," was classic.

Dan and George were friends with Tom Harrigan, and he and Rannazzisi assigned Payne-Korte as our contact person. Penny worked in Joe's unit and would refer the cases we sent her to an agent who was either already working on some aspect of the case or who was assigned to the area where the case was developing. In instances where one of us knew a law enforcement person who could help us, we dealt directly with that investigator and his department in the city where the case had originated.

By the time Tom Reilly and I were ready to go to the DEA's Weston, Florida, offices in the summer of 2012 to present our findings on a number of ongoing investigations, including the one that would mushroom into Biogenesis, George and Dan had briefed Rannazzisi and Harrigan in Washington. Our relationship with the DEA was solid.

Validation of our work would come from Kevin Stanfill. The DEA's assistant special agent in charge (ASAC) of the Biogenesis investigation would say years later in a conversation with two reporters, "I can tell you, there would have not been a case had it not been for those guys. It was like they handed over the whole [Biogenesis] case on a silver platter."[4]

In January 2013, Selig and Manfred had managed to undermine both our investigation and the DEA's, too. It had begun with a *Miami New Times* report published on January 29 that had detailed A-Rod and other baseball players' ties to Anthony Bosch and Biogenesis. Even though the *New Times* had sent letters to MLB and players' representatives asking for comment for the bombshell story revealing the names of Bosch's clients, the drugs they had purchased, and the amounts of money they had paid, we were unaware that the report was coming until a few days before it was published. Once the story ran, the pressure Selig and Manfred heaped on us was nothing short of biblical. Both were aware that only six months earlier we had presented the DEA with our case against Bosch and his Biogenesis accomplices and that the DEA had opened its own investigation.

With our continued assistance, it had gathered enough evidence to conduct a wiretap on key figures and were focusing on more.

Several weeks of conference calls directed by Manfred followed, punctuated by orders to "Get A-Rod and the Levinsons"—the two agents who had founded the powerful Brooklyn-based ACES sports agency—or else. The brothers Seth and Sam Levinson represented Melky Cabrera, the San Francisco Giants outfielder who had tested positive for testosterone in 2012 and then attempted to cover it up by creating a phony website. A-Rod, by then, was baseball's public enemy number one.

Manfred would often put "Al from Milwaukee" —his name for Selig—on the line.

"Al from Milwaukee" would then repeat all the threats Manfred had already hit us with, and then he would say, "Gentlemen, I want A-Rod and the Levinsons and I want them now. I don't want to wait thirty, sixty, or ninety days, I want this solved now! I don't want to hear stories about it's going to take time because of the DEA investigations. We are Major League Baseball, and we want results now. If you can't get us those results, we will find someone who can."

Tom Reilly and I would just look at each other as we listened to those two heads of a multi-billion-dollar corporation sounding like a couple of petulant children. After the call we would laugh ruefully. When we were in uniform and pulled someone over for a motor vehicle infraction, every once in a while we'd get someone who thought they were important, and they would say, "Do you know who I am?"

"Yes, sir, I do. You're the guy who's getting a ticket."

The call from Selig was obviously choreographed, and it came across that way. Once Al from Milwaukee was off the line, Manfred would reiterate the threats, completely ignoring the tedious reality of what it takes to obtain a wiretap and the time it takes to gather evidence. It was as if Manfred thought we could twitch our noses like in *I Dream of Jeannie* and make the DEA and the US Attorney's Office complete the investigation ASAP.

We were pretty sure by then that George Mitchell's recommendations were being flushed down the toilet. Selig had announced his retirement, effective at the end of 2014, and didn't want to go out with the "Steroid Era" tag attached to his legacy, and Manfred was angling to replace him. Labor had begun running the show, and once that happened we were undermined, compromised, and marginalized every step of the way.

Manfred informed us in no uncertain terms that Halem would lead the Biogenesis investigation. Manfred and MLB threatened to fire us not only if we failed to nail A-Rod and the Levinsons post-haste but also if we continued to share information with the DEA, an order we found incomprehensible. Without telling us, MLB hired private investigators and retired law enforcement agents to work the case. Those investigators and former agents started interviewing witnesses on their own, flashing badges at them and threatening them. The federal agents involved in the case were incredulous.

"We kept on getting reports, we were talking to witnesses, and they're saying, 'Major League Baseball is doing surveillance on these people,'" Stanfill would say. "And people were knocking on doors saying they're investigators with MLB. I picked up the phone. I would call [Dominguez]. 'Eddie, what the fuck?' And he's like 'Dude, it ain't me. It's not us.' I'm like 'Dude, you got somebody from MLB down here [in Florida] knocking on people's doors.'" For my part, I kept telling Tom, "This is just not right."[5]

By that point it had become clear that baseball was going to terminate us or dismantle our group in some capacity, and I was preparing myself for that.

There it was again: Halem's office number lighting up my phone. "Hey Ed, it's Dan, Ray [Ray Scott, VP of Human Resources], and

Steve [MLB Labor lawyer Steven Gonzalez]. We're doing a reorganization and, you know, to cut to the chase, you know, your employment is being terminated," he said. "Steve will send you an agreement."

He brought up the car service and said I was being fired for cause. Aside from when Gonzalez mentioned that I would be getting a COBRA health insurance notification, Halem's was the only voice the entire conversation. He spoke in a measured tone. "You know we'd just rather, you know, kind of part ways amicably and, you know, without having to dig further here . . . "

The echo from the speakerphone warbled over the receiver.

"Okay, so Steve will send you the agreement," Halem said of the separation agreement and general release they would send me. "Steve will be getting in touch with you."

"Okay," I said. "I'm sure you will be getting a call." Then I hung up.

I spent that first month after Halem's call searching for legal help. My brother, Carlos, briefly discussed representing me, but he was a one-man legal office who would be going to battle against an army of lawyers. I next reached out to Tom Frongillo, a former prosecutor in Boston whom I had known for years when I was with the Boston PD and who had prosecuted many of the cases I had investigated, and he agreed to represent me. A day before the deadline MLB had given me to sign the separation agreement expired, I received a text from Steven Gonzalez, the MLB labor lawyer. "Hey Eddie. Just realized that your agreement, if you want it, is due back tomorrow. Haven't heard from you about it, so just wanted to give you that reminder," it said.

I was at Frongillo's office when I got the text, and needless to say, I conveyed to MLB through Tom that I wasn't signing anything and that all further communication should be directed to him.

Once I got the call from someone whom I had never heard from in the MLB Payroll section, I was immediately suspicious that something wasn't right. I had been using the car service for years without ever having been questioned by anybody.

I had spent fifteen years in Major League Baseball, years in which I had done everything I could to conduct my work in a timely manner and in as cost-effective a manner as possible, and baseball was stooping to this?

I felt like if I signed that agreement, I would have been giving their trumped-up allegations some sort of credibility. I thought about the long hours I'd spent taking care of players, their families, owners, front-office people, the commissioner and his wife, even Manfred and his wife; the security I had arranged for events in places like Cuba, Mexico, and Venezuela, where I dealt with kidnappers and crooked cops; the fifteen- to sixteen-hour days investigating cases; the meeting and questioning of scouts accused of malfeasance in the middle of God knows where, and then being threatened by them.

The crazy thing was, once they fired Mullin, I was gone. All MLB had to say to me was that they were going in a different direction and I would have understood. We had just taken down fourteen players, including the one—A-Rod—that the commissioner viewed as the face of performance-enhancing drugs in baseball. The writing on the wall could not have been clearer: Mitchell's report was seven years old and they wanted it in the rearview mirror.

I never contemplated negotiating with MLB. If I'd thought I had done something wrong with the car service, it would have been easy to negotiate a settlement for more money than was being offered to me to sign the agreement, including whatever amount MLB claimed I owed it. The separation agreement stated clearly that if I signed the agreement, MLB would not go after me for the car service. Gonzalez was incredulous when he learned of our position. He told me that we'd never win if I decided to take any kind of legal action against Major League Baseball.

I was the only one let go from the DOI who declined to sign the separation agreement, and I heard through someone in the MLB offices who said they could hear Manfred yelling in the corridors, *"What do you mean, he didn't sign?"*

Two and a half years later, an unmarked NYPD car was parked in the wooded driveway of my suburban Boston home, right next to our garage, which is about seventy-five yards from the street. My stepson Kevin came upon the car and the unexpected visitors after work late one night. Donna and I were in Florida, so Kevin called me in a panic. One of the officers had checked out the garage, he said. When he had told the officer we weren't home, the cop had replied, "Their car is in the garage." The officer had thought Kevin was lying. Kevin read me the officer's name on the business card, and I called him immediately. The officer told me that the NYPD was investigating my use of a fictitious car service.

"I would think, since you knew I am a retired Boston cop, you would have the decency to have called me," I said. "You mean to tell me, with all crime going on in New York City, you have the man-power to come investigate something that allegedly happened three years ago?"

The cop stammered, "Well, you've got to understand—"

"I understand," I said. "But if I were in your shoes, I would have done the decent thing and called me directly. If you come back again, you better have a warrant. Please leave. My eighteen-year-old stepson had to find you, which is more than disturbing."

It was clear to me that the baseball bosses were sending me a message: we have powerful friends in New York. The Manhattan District Attorney's Office had already initiated the "car service" investigation before the unmarked car with its detectives showed up in my driveway. Maybe it was a coincidence or maybe not, but around that same time I had appeared in the two doping documentaries, prompting MLB to send additional threatening letters to my attorney. Manfred's office also sent a statement to a *Daily News* reporter in response to a question about remarks I had made in one of the documentaries about the percentage of players who I believe continued to use performance-enhancing substances. I had told the filmmakers I believed conservatively that 20 percent of players on each team's forty-man roster were still using PEDs, despite baseball's claims that it had cleaned up the game. That didn't sit well at 245 Park Avenue. "Mr. Dominguez is a disgruntled former employee who was terminated for cause," the MLB statement said. "He has not been involved in the game for approximately two years and during his employment he never provided us with any credible information that would support that number."[6]

The statement pointed out that as of September 2014, DOI was under the new leadership of a former assistant US attorney. "The skill sets of the members of DOI fits the group's current needs," the statement said.

But I wasn't the only one convinced that MLB's drug-testing policy remains woefully ineffective. A few months before the single-season home run record was obliterated in 2017, *Sports Illustrated* baseball writer Tom Verducci wrote a piece detailing the reasons home runs were flying out of ballparks at the highest rate in the game's history. Verducci's story, which included a quote from a former player who said he thought players were "back up to large scale use again," also featured a chart that showed virtually no decline in drug policy violations from 2005 through early in the 2017 season. As the player Verducci quoted said of PED use: "It's all over but folks don't want to see it."

It occurred to me, too, that following the Biogenesis indictments and player suspensions, there didn't seem to have been serious investigations into performance-enhancing drug use by either baseball or law enforcement. Even the media had seemed to back off.

I based my estimate that 20 percent of players still use PEDs on a time-tested theory I used over the course of my career in law enforcement: If you want to know what bad people are doing, you have to ask bad people. I became acquainted over the years with many individuals that society considers undesirables—criminals, drug dealers, organized crime figures—the lowest of the low. I tried to treat them all as I would hope they would treat me if my path in life took me in a different direction, and many of these undesirables became my sources. I used these sources because I needed them to help me catch other undesirables. Who would know best where to find a major drug dealer but another major drug dealer? Sometimes defense attorneys and even prosecutors or judges would ask me why I used such vile individuals as informants. I answered them by saying, "Well, I tried to ask the local priest about the defendant, but he didn't even know him."

Three trusted baseball sources I talked to in 2017—one an informant close to the game, one a baseball coach who had been part of the Biogenesis investigation, the third a doctor who had done time in prison for PED distribution—all said the game remains as dirty as ever. Their estimates were wildly disparate based on their individual experience, but each of them was unequivocal in their judgment that baseball remains affected by performance-enhancing drugs. My 20 percent estimate was the lowest in the range. The coach guessed that at least 30 to 35 percent are on some type of performance enhancer; the doctor said that in his professional opinion, 70 percent of players today who've been in the majors for at least a year are using performance enhancers of some type; the informant, who regularly deals with professional athletes, estimated that 90 percent of current base-ball players "use something." The doctor, who has done research on the use of peptides, a popular banned substance among athletes that is a building block for protein, also pointed to the 2017 season total for home runs, which had broken a seventeen-year-old record.[7]

Even Biogenesis founder Anthony Bosch, who became MLB's star witness during the Biogenesis investigation and whom George Mitchell would later speak up for once Bosch pleaded guilty to con-spiracy to distribute performance-enhancing drugs, estimated that 80 percent of all major leaguers had used PEDs at some point. "If I had a dollar and you had to bet a dollar and you asked me that question [now], I would comfortably say at least fifty percent, and I would be comfortable knowing that I would make a dollar," Bosch said during a 2017 interview.

"Think about it, how would so many guys [have been] using anabolic steroids and now they beat that home run record, beat the pants off of it?" the doctor asked. "How does that happen? Did they change the trajectory of the ball? Did they do something to the inside of the ball? There's definitely something going on. I would say 70 percent of players who have been in the league a year are using upper-echelon PEDs that can't be detected. The word has floated downstream, and they're on them. Things like this, they trickle down. I've worked with this stuff for thirty-five years."

Perhaps even more troubling to MLB than my documentary appearances questioning how baseball is handling drug issues was that the US Attorney for the Southern District of Florida had sub-poenaed me to testify in a 2017 human-trafficking trial against the Cuban sports agent Bart Hernandez. I had developed Hernandez as a source during my DOI days, and my dealings with him and other Cuban agents were revealing, to say the least.

CHAPTER 2

CUBAN ROOTS

In 1999, thirty-three years after my parents and my brother and I fled Cuba, I was headed back to the island in my new role as a resident security agent for Major League Baseball, working security during the Baltimore Orioles' historic trip there to play the Cuban national team. I was handpicked by Kevin Hallinan for the assignment— the MLB security chief and his staff would pick RSAs for certain assignments such as the All-Star Game and playoff series—and Hallinan, for some reason, had chosen me to accompany him on this trip. That would be the first of many special assignments I received as an RSA.

The one thing I promised my mother, Raquel Dominguez Fraguela—Tata is her endearing nickname—before leaving the United States was that I would not shake hands with Fidel Castro should the occasion arise, and it was certain to, given the magnitude of the event.

Tata had visited me in Miami prior to my departure for Cuba, and she was racked with fear and paranoia that I was going to be detained by Castro once I touched Cuban soil. All of her long-ago plans and preparations would be for naught, she said. I assured her that it was virtually impossible for me to get into any sort of international incident since it was a government-sponsored trip. Tata did not buy my logic in any way, but she acquiesced—with the proviso that under no circumstances would I shake Castro's hand.

"*No te preocupes, Tata, te prometo,*" I told her. Don't worry, Tata, I promise.

But even I wasn't fully prepared for the impact the trip would have on me once we touched down in Havana. This was the first time any US professional baseball players had been to Cuba since the embargo had been put into place in 1962, and the first time a US professional team had played the Cuban national team on the island since Castro's overthrow of the Fulgencio Batista regime. Kevin Hallinan was a fish out of water in Cuba if there ever was one. The moment we arrived, it was clear that his power as MLB's head of security would be nonexistent. Colonel Mario Ferron Mirabel, the Cuban military official in charge of our delegation, communicated with either me or Miami–Dade County detective Tomas Reilly, the other Cuban RSA on the MLB security detail, whenever Mirabel needed something done. Hallinan, who had begun to refer to himself as "The Talent" during spring training presentations to players during which he would discuss a hot topic, sometimes bringing in a supporting actor such as ex–New York Mafia boss Michael Franzese to address the evils of gambling, did not take kindly to his demotion, but with no Spanish-speaking skills he was helpless in the presence of Cuban authorities. I had found the presentations to be much like a Broadway play—we would check for lighting, sound, the perfect staging area—and God forbid if someone didn't know who The Talent was. Halfway through the spring training tour, The Talent told me that MLB had received clearance from the US government to take the Orioles to Cuba for an exhibition game, and he wanted to know if I was available to travel. I was beside myself at the possibility of going back to my home country. I called work and home and got the green light—off to Cuba!

The day the Orioles and the Cuban national team were scheduled to play, rain was threatening and there was some concern that the game would be postponed. Several of the Orioles players were in the visiting dugout, chirping about the weather or some nonsense while I was surveying the field. I felt someone's presence and turned to see a man wearing a red polo shirt with the Cuban flag stitched on the chest.

"Looks like we'll get this game played," the man said in broken English.

I replied in Spanish, which caught him off guard, and told him I was Cuban.

"Your first time back?" he asked.

I told him yes. "You must have been on one of Johnson's flights," he said, referring to former president Lyndon B. Johnson's "Freedom Flights," which had liberated 300,000 anti-Castro Cuban dissidents from 1965 to 1973.

"I take it you chose to stay," I said with a smile.

He nodded. "That we did."

When I introduced myself, he responded, "I'm the Cuban team doctor, Tony Castro. Welcome back."

That was the start of a long friendship with Fidel's son, one that exists to this day and has benefited me greatly. In 2006, I was assigned to the Cuban national team that competed in the World Baseball Classic from beginning to end, starting out in Puerto Rico and finishing in San Diego for the championship game against Japan. Cuba lost in the finals, but the night before, Tony asked me if he and his bodyguard could go out with us on the town. I asked him if the head of the committee would be mad if he found out, and he gave me a smirk, as if to ask, "Do you realize who I am?" I told Mullin, who said, "Sure, let's do it."

That night Tony and I sat by ourselves at a local pub. He asked for a tall glass of beer, and as the baseball talk dwindled, he looked at me and said, "*Somos Cubanos y vamos a estar de acuerdo que no vamos a estar de acuerdo que lo que mi padre a hecho para nuestro País es bueno.*" Translated, he was saying, "We are Cuban and we are going to agree to disagree that what my father has done for our country is good," to which I nodded my head. And then he said something that caught me by complete surprise: "*Pero si vamos a estar de acuerdo que es hora que nuestro país cambie*"—"But we are going to agree that it's time our country changed."

We raised our glasses and toasted to change.

That friendship, of course, is one that eternally pains my mother. A promise to Tata not to shake Fidel's hand was one thing; forging a friendship with one of his children was against everything my mother had fought for when we left.

While I was at the stadium overseeing security measures, several Mercedes limos—an oddity in Havana, whose streets are cluttered with vintage 1950s Fords and Chevys—pulled up and came to a halt. It was the presidential detail with a heavy Cuban law enforcement escort. Out stepped Fidel, dressed in his green military fatigues and what I was certain was a Kevlar jacket. I was stunned. Even that glimpse of Castro caused me to sweat through my shirt. He made his way into the Orioles' clubhouse, walking right past me but our eyes didn't make contact.

Following the game, Castro announced that he would host a reception at the Presidential Palace. Colonel Ferron relayed the message to me that Castro wanted our delegation to attend. The blunt translation was that if we didn't accept El Presidente's request, things could get ugly quickly. I conveyed the invite to Hallinan, who advised the commissioner, Bud Selig. When I boarded the team bus with the Orioles players, my stomach was already in knots. My head was spinning thinking about my mom's plea and all the assurances I had given her in Miami. Let's just say the odds on my keeping my promise were not good.

I also helped handle the satchel—a suitcase MLB had stuffed with $1 million in US currency. The money, used in part to pay for our accommodations, food, and transportation, was to be split between MLB and ESPN, which was broadcasting the game. But it was also used to deal with any problem that surfaced.

When we arrived at the palace, the players, who were still in uniform, and other guests lined up as if they were going to see Santa Claus at the mall—Santa in military fatigues. Security checked and frisked each person in a way just short of a full cavity search. There was no way the satchel was going to get by without being searched. I contemplated hiding on the team bus until the reception was over. Ed Petersen, Hallinan's second in command, admonished me for even considering ducking out on the occasion.

"You're Cuban, Eddie," he said. "You have to go."

I told Petersen, who was holding the satchel that day, that an explanation would have to come later but that I was taking the satchel back to our hotel. When I got to my room, Tomas Reilly (who had almost the same name as my future DOI partner) called and begged me to return to the reception.

"It ain't happening. Tell them I'm sick, anything, but I'm staying here."

If there was hell to pay later, so be it. I had honored Tata's wish.

A few days before the game, I made my way back to my family's old apartment in Havana, accompanied by the Cuban official who was at my side the entire trip. But when we arrived at Posos

Dulce 1113, Apartamento 6, that morning, the official let me enter the building alone. The saying goes that visiting Cuba is like walking back in time, and when I started to make the ascent to the apartment, I was transported back to my childhood days. Dust covered the stone steps. Heat choked the stairwell. When I knocked on the door of number 6, two boys greeted me. Both were about the same age as my brother and I had been when we had left Cuba in 1966.

The boys' mother invited me into the apartment for a visit and coffee. Once inside, I had to keep myself from bursting out in laughter or tears or both. Nothing had changed inside those walls. The same TV, the same couch, the same tile floor. It was all there, just as when I had walked out the door for what I had thought would be the last time.

The four of us had lived in those cramped conditions: one bedroom we had all shared and another room. The building was in a gritty part of Havana, not far from José Martí Memorial Park, renamed Plaza de la Revolución after Castro took over on January 1, 1959. My pets were black Molly fish that I stored in an old car battery casing. A kid who lived down the street had real fish tanks. His family, I believe, was connected to the Cuban government in some manner, and they seemed to be affluent. I had seen those fish tanks and was fascinated by them. The family gave me two fish, but the only thing I had to store them in was the battery casing. I scrubbed it a million times and plopped the Mollies into the darkness. You could barely see them swimming around in the cloudy water, black ovals dashing back and forth in a space not unlike the cramped quarters my family lived in. The fish were visible only in daylight or if you shined a candle near the water's surface.

My maternal grandfather, Andrés Fraguela, had the biggest influence on me, not my father, who was deeply affected by the Cuban revolution, a stretch of time that had left him mentally and physically scarred. When we finally escaped in 1966, I was forced to say good-bye to my grandfather—twice—before leaving for good. I was only three years old when Castro toppled the Batista regime, and the next seven years of my life, before my family escaped, was a catch-as-catch-can existence. My younger brother, Carlos, was born in 1960, and the two of us did our best to torment my mother, which caused her to beat on us pretty good. Unlike my brother, who would run anytime there was even a hint that an ass kicking was coming, I would stand there and take the punishment. No questions asked. My mother's instruments of discipline were anything she could get her hands on: a broom, a pan, a bat. Not that the two of us didn't deserve it. My father worked for General Electric, an American company that ceased to exist in Cuba after Fidel took over. It was nationalized, and he lost his job to a Castro loyalist. That devastated him, and my mother became the dominating presence in the family.

As my father became more distant and reclusive, Andrés helped raise me. He was a tough working-class dockhand who had sailed from Galicia, Spain, to Cuba at age fifteen in search of a new life. There he would meet my grandmother, Leonor Sánchez, and have two daughters, Evangelina and my mother, Raquel. A hulking man, Andrés stood six feet two and weighed about 260 pounds, all of it muscle. A reserved and respected man, he was known by seemingly everyone in Havana. Once, at an open-air bar across the street from where he lived, a guy was giving the bartender a hard time. My grandfather glanced at him, and the man asked, "What are you going to do about it?" My grandfather slowly walked over to him and, with one hand, picked the guy up and held him over his head. The guy's shoes fell off, and he pissed himself. Andrés would later join an anti-Castro group and become a staunch activist. I was part of his underground, even though at the time I was too young to understand what was happening. When he met with other anti-Castro dissidents during clandestine meetings in and around Havana, he would take me with him. He would lead me through the narrow streets of the city, and all of a sudden we would duck into a residential building and wend our way through an open balcony or part of someone's apartment before settling into a corner room. There my grandfather would tell me, "Just sit here for a few moments," and he would then join the other activists. I wouldn't pay attention to what they were saying as much as just stare at the different faces.

Andrés was eventually thrown into jail for his activism, and he asked that I not be told the truth about where he was. His personal business had taken him out of Havana to another part of the country, my mother told me. But one day she received a message from him. He wanted us to visit. I was told we were going to see him in the countryside, and I was so happy as we headed out. We entered the stone building and were placed in a waiting room. Having never heard of jail, I had no idea we were in one. A few minutes later a guard opened the door, and behind him my grandfather entered in handcuffs. When he saw me, he yelled and cried and tried to run back into the hallway. "*No, no, ¿porqué lo trajiste, porqué?*"—No, no, why did you bring him, why? The soldiers beat him up and sat him on a chair across from us. It all became clear to me. He had begged my mother and the guards not to let me see him that way. Now I was witness to one of his lowest points—a man in tears, broken, vulnerable, collapsing before his own grandson. His clothes were filthy, and he was disheveled. The Castro thugs had thought that bringing me in would soften him up and he would betray his friends. They were wrong. My first thoughts were of those clandestine meetings, and I knew I had to believe they had never happened. I believe he was detained for six months, but to me, it seemed more like six years.

My father was also jailed, but his crime was far less egregious. He was selling red plastic bread baskets on the black market after he lost his job at General Electric. My mother saw that the situation in Cuba was getting worse. Fulgencio Batista was no angel, but within his corrupt government you could find work and live a comfortable life. The promises Castro made quickly vanished, and soon children were being taken away from families and sent to government institutions where they would be indoctrinated in the ways of the Communist system. My mother decided that this was not the life she wanted for her two boys. To leave the country, we had to denounce Castro's government, which we did in 1962. But it was four years before we could finally leave, and there were more than a few hurdles along the way. We were soon labeled *Gusanos*—worms—by the local leader of the government-run neighborhood watch, and at one point, a picture of a worm was glued to our apartment door. The government didn't allow my parents to work or me to go to school for a year.

Thanks to my grandparents, who gave us what they could, we survived. Many days my mother and father went without food so my brother and I could eat.

On the early afternoon of July 24, 1966, two armed soldiers knocked on our apartment door. My mother wasn't home, and my father answered the door. The soldiers told him to pack one bag and leave the apartment.

"You are leaving Cuba on July 26," they said in Spanish. "When you leave, we are locking and placing a government seal on the door. If the seal is broken, you won't leave."

Luckily my mother had thought ahead and had already packed the bag. The soldiers searched the bag, and we left. My most vivid memory of that day is begging the soldiers to let me take the Mollies with me because otherwise they would die.

"Too bad, get out," they said.

They handed my father a piece of paper with instructions, sealed the door, and on we went to our grandparents' house.

At the time, I thought the morning of July 26 was the saddest day in our lives. My parents would be saying good-bye to their parents, siblings, nieces, nephews, and friends for the last time. We were headed to a place we knew nothing about other than the fact that it was called "The Land of Opportunity." Families like ours were bused to a small lake—"El Lagito"—near the airport in Matanzas and then processed in preparation for departure. I had already said my painful good-bye to my grandfather prior to boarding the bus to "El Lagito," and when we arrived at the processing center, we slept on the floor. No beds. No air-conditioning. No food. It was the equivalent of prison, without the bars. But there was another hitch, an unexpected delay for no other reason than to let us know who was in charge.

Around 4 a.m., bleary-eyed and aching from lying on a concrete floor, we learned that we wouldn't get onto the airplane and were being sent back home. We returned to my grandfather's a second time, but that visit crushed him. The first good-bye had been a wrenching encounter in its own right—my mother had led the charge for our leaving Cuba, but her own father and mother were staying behind. When I hugged him at his apartment the first time, the tears from his face soaked my hair and face and my tears left a wet spot on his shirt. That we had to return to him was almost more than he could bear. He refused to see us at first, but he relented, and we said a second painfully crushing good-bye. Later in life, I would name my son Andrew after him and use the name Andres Fraguela as my undercover name.

Three days passed before we were back at "El Lagito" and the austere processing center. We were again awakened around 4 a.m., and this time I had to pitch in and carry whatever meager supplies we had. When we finally boarded the prop plane on July 29, 1966, and took off toward Miami, we had nothing—nothing—but the clothes on our backs. My face pressed against the airplane window, I watched the swath of land below fade farther away, until it was a speck in the distance. And then gone.

Those images filled my head as I sat at the table at Posos Dulce 1113, Apartamento 6, more than three decades later. When I concluded my visit, and without the woman or the boys watching, I slipped a hundred-dollar bill under my coffee cup.

Later, I made my way to the main cemetery in Havana— Cementerio de Cristóbal Colón—a vast patch of real estate with most of the grave sites aboveground because the area often flooded. I asked the official to wait on the outskirts of the section where my grandfather was buried. There were no other visitors within a stone's throw, and I walked slowly among the headstones, looking for the familiar name. My shirt was drenched in sweat, the temperature close to 100 degrees. The humidity choked the air. Then I saw it. Tears welled up in my eyes. I was back in my grandfather's arms, saying good-bye in the quiet of his apartment all those years ago, his body shaking uncontrollably against mine. I guided my hand over the gravestone and whispered good-bye once more before turning back into the sunlight.

CHAPTER 3

BPD

We arrived at the Opa Locka Airport on the outskirts of Miami on July 29, 1966—my father, my mother, my younger brother, Carlos, and me. As part of the process, someone in the United States had to claim us upon arrival and, by doing so, take responsibility for us. That person was Gladys Gil, my mother's childhood friend from Cuba, and we were turned over to her soon after being questioned, documented, and vaccinated in the immigration center. Gladys's husband, Chiqui, had made his fortune in Cuba as the owner of movie theaters around Havana. Their wealth hadn't carried over to the United States, but, like a lot of wealthy Cuban families, they could afford to leave in the early years of the Castro regime.

My mother was so overwhelmed that she passed out at the immigration office. My brother and I spoke no English, and of my parents, only my father had learned some English words back in Cuba, studying textbooks written by Leonardo Sorzano Jorrin. The English coming from the mouths of the staffers at the center sounded flat. We had no money, no food, and no friends, save Gladys, who was my godmother, and two aunts—my father's sisters, Zenaida Penedo and Sonia Dominguez, who had arrived in the United States shortly after the Castro takeover—who lived in Boston. Gladys kindly took us to her Miami-area home, fed us, and housed us.

After a month or so in Miami and with no job prospects materializing for my mother, she decided we would take our chances in Boston. She had heard that the school systems were better there, and my aunt Zenaida thought she would find work there more easily. The four of us boarded a train to Boston, and to a nine-year-old, it felt as if we were on that train for a month. We never left the train the entire trip, which in reality took only about two days. Once we got to Boston, we lived in a halfway house before my mother found an apartment above a Spanish grocery store in Jamaica Plain, a gritty Boston neighborhood. Our hardships and struggles were plentiful: the language barrier, my dad's inability to keep a job, no money, and little of anything else. My mother worked two jobs to help us make ends meet. Both were grueling: she worked backbreaking hours at the Garland Sweater Company. When she was done with her seamstress job, she cleaned dorm rooms at Boston University. The money from those jobs helped put Carlos and me through Don Bosco Technical High School, an all-boys Catholic school that was located near the red-light district in Boston until its closure in 1998. We led peripatetic lives, moving from one apartment to another, all over the greater Boston area, each home and neighborhood an improvement over the previous ones. Eventually Tata would work for the Boston Gas Company and retire from there after almost twenty-five years on the job.

By the time Carlos and I were preparing for college, we figured we had asked enough of Tata, so we both paid our way through Boston State College by working at a Spanish restaurant, La Iruna, in Harvard Square. Carlos later attended law school and became an assistant district attorney before opening a private practice. I took classes in criminal justice, prelaw, and history at Boston State with aspirations of going to law school, but a friend I met playing basketball at the Cambridge YMCA encouraged me to take the civil service exam. I had no idea what that was, but I took the test. Nine months later, at the beginning of 1979, I got a call from the Boston Police Department offering me a job. On May 29, 1979, I entered the BPD, my home for the next twenty-nine years.

Even though I had encountered injustices and the pain of being an outcast during my childhood and adolescence—being called a *Gusano* in Cuba after my mother had denounced the government, feeling alienated in the United States because I couldn't speak English and didn't know the culture—my first taste of an offensive comment working for the Boston PD was sobering. I was sitting outside the doctor's office waiting to take the Boston PD psychological exam required to attend the police academy, along with two other candidates who were waiting with me—an African American and a white guy. When the African American was called into the office, the white guy, who appeared to be a few years older, turned to me and said, "Can you believe all these niggers and spics getting on? I've been a cadet for three years, and I can't get on because of them."

I looked at him and smiled. Several minutes later my name, Eduardo Dominguez, was called. As I got up, I glanced at my neighbor, who clearly could not believe what he had just heard. I wished him good luck.

I never used race as a tool of any kind in my career, good or bad. It goes against all I was taught and believe in. I taught my kids that hard work outweighs everything else.

I was at the top of my class in physical training, so I was supposed to have the choice of the district where I would be stationed. District 4 was where all the cops, including me, wanted to go. That district had everything: crime, ghettos, wealth, Fenway Park, nightlife, and the "combat zone," which was where the strip clubs were and where the pimps, hookers, and drug dealers hung out all night. D4 was the place where you could make money working details (side jobs), meet influential people, enjoy the nightlife and the restaurants, and apprehend criminals as well. But in what would be my first taste of office politics, someone made a call to City Hall on behalf of another rookie and I wound up starting my career in District 13—good ol' Jamaica Plain, my childhood stomping grounds. I learned that this was the district where they sent the drunks and the "problem children" of the Boston PD. I never found out who had decided there was no place for me in District 4.

My first tour of duty was scheduled to start at 11:45 p.m. Slightly nervous, I arrived early and introduced myself to the lieutenant at the front desk, who promptly asked me a pointed question: "Why the fuck are you here so early?" He then told me to go to the guardroom and wait. As I walked around, I heard strange noises from the bathroom. I looked around the corner and saw something I will never forget: a man in his underwear with a holster and a gun, practicing his draw in the mirror—just like Robert De Niro in *Taxi Driver*.

As he drew his gun, he stared at the mirror, smiled, and said, "You're dead." I ran back to the front desk and, much to the lieutenant's dismay, refused to move.

I was assigned to ride with Danny Ramirez, the first Cuban Boston police officer I'd ever heard of while I was growing up. I'd read about him in the newspapers and followed him wherever he went. In an era when cops used to take their gun belts off and settle differences with their fists, he was an aggressive cop who stood his ground against anybody, including other officers. He once offered to have a duel, with guns, against a cop who had made racial remarks about him. He was so hated by the Puerto Rican community that he was burned in effigy at Hyde Square during an antipolice rally.

The majority of the Spanish-speaking population of Jamaica Plain was Puerto Rican, and Ramirez had built a reputation for eradicating the drug problem—and that meant plenty of locals getting cuffed. Since he spoke Spanish, the suspects often didn't know what to make of an arresting officer who communicated with them in their native tongue. He also got them to rat out others.

That night, Ramirez and I abruptly left in the middle of roll call to respond to a stolen car chase three miles away. Ramirez had fun with that one: he blew through red lights doing about 100 mph, while I turned a sickly white. I think he was secretly hoping I would puke. The perps got away, but unless we had been in a rocket ship, we couldn't have caught up to them.

Later, I ended up chasing two men on foot into the Heath Street projects after a 3 a.m. break-in. Usually, such calls were false alarms or the suspects had long since left by the time we arrived. But not this one. As soon as we walked past the open front door, Ramirez pointed to a pile of smoking feces in the middle of the floor. It was a cold winter night, and the perps had relieved themselves right there. Danny smirked as he took out his gun. I was soon chasing the suspects, jumping over fences and leaping from rooftop to rooftop.

Finally, with early morning bleeding into sunrise and the shift almost over, Danny and I used a speed gun to ticket people. Danny had stolen the device from a captain's office. I went home around 8 a.m. and told my mother that I was going to sleep and might never go back to work. Danny would break my balls about that first night for years to come, but as he lay dying of cancer years later, he told me I had passed with flying colors. "You took it in stride," he said, "didn't say a word, just as I thought you would."

The first six years of my career, I was on patrol with my partner, Robert Tully, in what they called a "rapid car," a two-man vehicle that responded to emergency 911 calls. One night we were involved in a car chase through the South End where the occupants had just robbed an elderly couple. Bob, my Boston PD partner for thirteen of my twenty-nine years there, was driving, and as we were going down Washington Street, all of a sudden Bob took a turn into a side street. Next thing I know, I was on the hood of the cruiser, spitting glass out of my mouth. I had gone through the windshield, and Bob was yelling "What happened?" It turned out we had driven into a three-foot ditch while going 60 miles per hour.

We did everything imaginable in those six years, from chasing two store robbers on their motorcycle while they fired back at us to finding disturbing and unexpected things during motor vehicle stops. Early one morning, for instance, Tully and I pulled over a van on a ramp near the Massachusetts Turnpike. There were three men inside, and what had caught our attention was the driver's-side window—or rather, what had been the window. It was clear that someone had recently smashed the glass. Tully approached the driver's side, but all three men acted as if they spoke no English. I overheard one of them say in Spanish something about the back of the van. I asked the men if the van was stolen and what was in the back. Some nervous shuffling. No papers. Tully and I asked them if we could search the van. One of the men opened the side door, and while Tully watched the three men, I used my flashlight to peer into the dank rear space. There was an old, worn rug rolled up, but there didn't appear to be much else. I was leaning in against the rug to inspect the van more closely when suddenly I felt what appeared to be a human knee jutting into my midsection. I leaned back out of the van, walked over to Tully, and said, "We have to arrest these desperados."

The knee belonged to an African American male whose body was ravaged by bullet holes and trauma. The investigation revealed that the man was a Boston PD informant who had been tortured and executed in the basement of a nightclub by a drug dealer from Roxbury.

During six years in uniform, Bob Tully and I testified in every court in the Commonwealth of Massachusetts and received recognition for numerous arrests we had made, including the seizure of thousands of Quaaludes found in a suitcase that belonged to a man we apprehended in an early-morning motor vehicle stop as he was leaving the Peter Pan bus terminal in Park Square. That case, coupled with the fact that we had some good sources and that I was fluent in Spanish, led to our being transferred to the Drug Control Unit, a stepping-stone toward becoming a detective. Assigned to Sergeant Detective Gil Griffiths's squad, we had the opportunity to learn from two of the top drug detectives in the city, Joseph Driscoll and Arthur "Skippy" O'Connell. They soon had us making heroin buys in the projects, harrowing work since I was sent into those situations with no training and absolutely no knowledge of what heroin even was.

As we built our sources, Tully and I were soon executing search warrants regularly, as many as five a week. Most of our informants and dealers were Dominicans and Colombians, but we did not discriminate. Our squad handled a wide spectrum of traffickers. During that six-year stretch, I would experience a kaleidoscope of different cases, ones that put the fear of God into me, others that had me in tears from laughter, and ones that were emotionally crushing.

In one instance, a young officer, Timothy Duggan, had just gotten his first search warrant. I had left court and checked up on my warrant, and I drove by the home Tim had targeted. We later met in Dorchester, where Sergeant Griffiths went over the warrants we both had and asked which one was ready to be executed. I told Tim that I had driven by his house earlier and the place was running hot, police jargon for saying the house was steaming with drug activity—clients, dealers, users. I wanted to mess with him a little bit. As Tim drove away to set up at his house so we could hit the door, I started laughing.

"Dominguez, what are you up to?" barked Griffiths.

Soon we heard Tim over the radio: "Sergeant, we will not be doing my warrant. Dominguez was right, the house is smoldering. It burned down earlier today. The fire department is here." Tim never let me forget that one.

DCU's Joe Driscoll had freckles, so the Dominicans we arrested called him "*Cara de Huevo de Guanajo*"—"Turkey Egg Face." On average, we had several search warrants to serve each night, and a particular one was for a stash house where Dominicans were allegedly running a cocaine ring.

We had different ways of gaining entry into residences: either we would wait for one of the targets to walk out of a house, approach the person, and walk back in, or sometimes I would go to the door and sweet-talk my way in, especially if we knew I would encounter someone who spoke Spanish. If it was an apartment building, we would gain entry by waiting for someone to come out, and then we would shift inside and ring the doorbell as if it were broken until somebody buzzed us in. We would break down a door only as a last resort because of the danger it presented. Most of the doors were fortified with two-by-fours, and even though O'Connell was a horse of a man, it would have been impossible to knock down the door while the people inside were going to either flush the drugs down the toilet or, worse, shoot at us.

But with this particular coke house, there was going to be no other option—we had to go in the hard way. We approached the second floor of a three-story home, waited in the hallway, and listened before deciding to hit the door. Since the occupants were Spanish-speaking, I did the eavesdropping. Something wasn't quite right. My heart started pounding. I whispered to Joe that we should go to the back side of the house and peer in any way possible to see what was going on inside.

When we arrived at the rear entrance, we gave the signal up front, where the other officers were stationed. They started yelling "Police! We have a warrant! Open the door!"

As the yelling and commotion drowned out everything else, I turned the back doorknob, and it gave way easily. Driscoll and I rushed in and moved to the front of the house, our guns drawn. There we spotted three males, all with assorted weapons drawn—but aiming at the front door. "Put your guns down!" Driscoll and I screamed. "Down! Down! *Abajo! Abajo!*" God was watching over us that night because they dropped their guns. We ended up finding several kilos of cocaine and arrested all the occupants.

CHAPTER 4

THE FBI DRUG TASK FORCE

I was assigned to the Boston PD's Major Case Unit in 1996, and in '98 I was asked to join an FBI drug task force. Though I was flattered, there was one major drawback: working alongside the FBI's Boston agency, which in the past had had corrupt agents involved in the notorious Whitey Bulger case, including the disgraced agents John Connolly and John Morris, the head of the FBI's Boston organized crime unit. Granted immunity from prosecution in a 1998 federal court hearing, Morris confirmed scathing allegations of FBI misconduct involving Connolly, Bulger, and Bulger's cohort, Stephen Flemmi. He admitted that he had told Connolly about an informant who had implicated Bulger and Flemmi in a murder, knowing full well that the information would get back to the mobsters. The informant, Edward "Brian" Halloran, wound up dead.

Those corrupt FBI agents were known to have compromised cases brought by other agencies as well—including the Boston PD— by lying for Bulger and his Winter Hill Gang or tipping them off to investigations. The FBI had incarcerated six Boston detectives for infractions and crimes that paled in comparison to what the bureau's agents were doing during the Bulger case.

After I joined the Red Sox as a resident security agent (I was given the position in late 1998 but didn't start working until 1999), my boss, Kevin Hallinan, told me that the first choice of the Red Sox organization to become the team's first RSA had been none other than John Connolly, who would be sentenced to ten years in prison for writing a letter on stolen Boston Police Department stationery falsely accusing BPD Detective Frank Dewan of fabricating evidence against Bulger. Hallinan claimed that he had nixed the idea because he had heard rumors about Connolly, who would be put on trial in 2002 on charges that he had tipped off Bulger in 1994 that he was about to be arrested on extortion and racketeering charges, a warning that had resulted in Bulger going on the lam for sixteen years. In something of a twist, Hallinan would eventually hire Dewan as one of the first Red Sox RSAs.[1]

Morris also accepted $7,000 in payoffs from Bulger. He retired from the FBI in 1995 and now lives in Florida.

Nonetheless, by 1998 there were new agents, most of whom had nothing to do with Whitey Bulger. I pondered the new assignment and was eager to start a different chapter in my law enforcement career. It was a decision that I never regretted. I worked with a young FBI agent named John Woudenberg, and I was welcomed by all of his peers. We handled large-scale cases involving wiretaps, undercover operations, and international crimes. An older police officer had once told me, "Kid, don't make a federal case out of this," and I soon learned what he had meant: cases at the federal level take time, money, and endless hours of writing reports.

I had had plenty of small undercover assignments while at the DCU, but the stakes were now higher. Soon after I arrived at the FBI drug task force, an older agent, a guy we called Mucko—real name: Mike McGowan—transferred into the Boston FBI office from Philadelphia. He sat across from me in our office, which at the time had more than twenty agents; I was the only task force officer. Mucko was a cagey veteran who had been a cop before joining the FBI, and from what I was hearing, he was, and still is, one hell of an undercover. The younger agents were terrified of Mucko. He rarely spoke to anyone, even to say hello. For some reason, he and I hit it off.

Tony Dillon and his partner, Donald Nelson, were two of the other older agents, and they had a great source who had worked with them for years. He was a middle-aged Colombian who had a nondescript look about him but had brought down half of Bogotá. Dillon, whose parents were Spaniards, asked me if I would be willing to work undercover cases with him and the source, whom I will call Homero Santiago—not his real name, but he's still alive and still working cases.

I said yes, and that brought me to the undercover world of recorded telephone conversations, audio and video recording devices, fake identifications, make-believe businesses, and lots of paperwork. I completed undercover training and had to be cleared by the FBI undercover unit before I could take part in an FBI operation. At the time, Mucko was a regional FBI UC board member, and he took me to Quantico to take part in one of its two-week UC training courses as an observer.

I also took several psychological tests that would be repeated every six months to see if I was still mentally prepared to continue in whatever UC role I was participating in. At times undercovers get so caught up in their characters that they actually become the character. As you can imagine, nothing good comes of a once clean-cut agent transforming himself into a narco trafficker selling and using drugs, driving fancy cars, and having women all around him. The psych checkup was supposed to alert the bureau about an undercover who might be in danger of going over the edge. After you took the written test a psychiatrist would speak to you, and if you cleared that interview, a member of the FBI UC unit would go over your case with you to see if you had a good plan and were prepared to follow through with it. That was a long way from "Hey, kid, here's $50, go buy some heroin in the projects." Sometimes you might get a "Good luck, kid" from the supervisor who was asking you to stick your neck out. After several years, Mucko asked me if I would be interested in setting up a shorter version of the Quantico school for the Boston PD's potential UCs. I thought that was a great idea. I kept thinking of all the things my surveillance team and I had done wrong over the years and wished I had attended such a school before I grabbed the $50 and ran into the projects to buy heroin, a product I had never seen. I went to BPD chief of detectives John Boyle, and we got approval. The class is still in operation, and my son Christopher is a recent graduate.

In the meantime, Mucko started his own undercover operations, which were mostly organized crime cases, and on several occasions I was privileged to help him in his UC roles. He is one of the most respected undercover agents in the history of the FBI. He has mentored most, if not all, FBI undercover agents throughout the United States. Mucko is no joke.

Another operation included a Colombian brown sugar company owner who was bullied by drug traffickers into packaging their cocaine and heroin in his heat-sealed brown sugar packages. The owner contacted Tony's source, Homero Santiago, and he in turn contacted us. The owner had been told that if he didn't allow the traffickers to ship their cocaine in his packaging, they would kill him and his family. We agreed to get the owner and his family to the United States, and Tony and I assumed an undercover role as the heads of a drug-trafficking import and export business. The owner, now a source as well, introduced us to the traffickers.

As soon as Tony got the family out of Colombia, we began to meet the distributors who would receive and distribute cocaine in the United States. They came from all over the New England and New York area. The traffickers in Colombia pay a visit to the distributors' homes and families, a sign that unless they pay up, their families will pay with their lives. The trick was to get the distributors to enter into negotiations and pay for the delivery of the coke and heroin so that we could get enough audio and video to put them away. In an office in an old brick building in Providence, Rhode Island, equipped with a secretary and all the trappings of an import-export company, I sat behind a big desk and welcomed the distributors.

The entire office was wired for sight and sound, and we would begin by negotiating the cost of transportation, usually a couple thousand dollars per kilo. I would reach out to law enforcement contacts and sources to get the most current cocaine and heroin prices and the going rate for transportation. That was especially important not only to convince the distributors that I knew what I was talking about but to make sure when the case went to trial that defense counsel would have no shot at getting a dismissal on entrapment allegations.

The FBI arranged to rent a local auto body shop, and we wired that, too, testing the equipment the night before the sting to make sure we positioned ourselves at the right angles so as not to block the cameras. The techies had to choose a location inside the garage where they could sit and monitor the situation.

In that room would be a handpicked Spanish-speaking agent who listened to what was going on and had enough experience and common sense to send in the SWAT team and stop the operation if he thought the UCs were in trouble. FBI special agent Michael De La Peña was the guy Tony and I trusted for those operations. We were then met by the SWAT team, which would choose and set up the takedown room. The room had to be big enough to house at least a half-dozen fully armed agents who would be dressed head to toe in bulletproof equipment, even helmets. I referred to those guys as the "Ninja Turtles."

On the Sunday the product was to be delivered, we met the distributors at a prearranged location, and they followed us to the auto body shop. They drove their vehicles, which were equipped with hidden hydraulic compartments to store the cocaine and heroin, and showed us how to open the compartments, usually by touching a combination of electric window openers, the radio, and the heater in a specific order. They gave us the agreed-upon transportation fee, and we gave them heroin in the brown sugar packages. Once the exchange was finalized, we gave a signal and the troops came in to handle the arrests.

The "Ninja Turtle" takedown was a scary thing every single time. After the signal was given, the agents would burst into the room we were meeting in as if they had been shot out of a cannon, brandishing automatic and semiautomatic weapons like those you see in video clips of war-ravaged battlefields. It was controlled chaos. Even though we practiced the takedown every time we executed one of those operations, sometimes things went wrong. On one of our first busts, a young Turtle got so excited that he put an automatic to the back of my head during the takedown.

Because we would execute up to five of those takedowns in one day, about one every three hours, we were always concerned about one group of distributors warning the next group. We would time the takedowns and coordinate with authorities in Colombia, who would then bust the drug lords back in their own country. Sure enough, after the fourth takedown of one operation, we received a weird call from the last group. We thought they had figured out what was going on, and we could not get in touch with the Colombian agents in Medellín. We decided that I would drive out in one of the last group's vehicles to see if I would be followed. We figured if they knew what was happening, they would be waiting for us to come out and would take us down.

I drove out, and sure enough there was someone parked just down the street watching the garage. As I continued down the street, the vehicle pulled out and started following me. I called the Ninja team waiting outside the garage and gave a description of the vehicle and the single occupant.

About a mile down the road, I looked in my rearview mirror and saw two vehicles full of Ninjas block the suspect car and proceed to do their thing.

It was a false alarm—a local police officer who had been monitoring his radio had decided to join the party without telling anyone from his department. He was lucky he didn't get shot.

Those arrests received major media coverage in Colombia, with television stations showing perp walks, armored vehicles, weapons, bank accounts, and tons of seized cocaine.

Back here, it was just another day's work.

There were undercover cases involving organized crime families in Rhode Island, national wiretaps, and coordination with departments and agencies all over the country. I also did a few investigations where we seized steroids, but those cases had usually been initiated as heroin or cocaine investigations. Unfortunately, because of the opioid epidemic in this country, there is little time to pursue steroid cases.

On another UC case, Mucko asked me if I could help out in an organized crime case he had been working for a couple of years in Rhode Island. It involved the Patriarca crime family. Mucko had talked it over with his case agents and the US attorney's office, and they wanted to see if the Patriarca family would fall for securing loads of cocaine that were going to be distributed in their area. It's common for organized crime families to allow those outside their family to make illegal money on their turf as long as they are paying a tariff. Otherwise, the crime family will come knocking at your door and you will either pay rent for working in their area, or you will pay with your life.

Mucko said that I would be the boss of the drug group and I was to meet with one of the underbosses to set up the security detail. We met that overweight thug at a Dunkin' Donuts in Providence and set up the job. The second time we met, this time at a Marriott hotel, I brought along a young Spanish-speaking Boston police officer we called "Pito," a big boy who had just graduated from our UC school. We thought Pito would put a little bit of fear into the minds of those thugs.

Unfortunately, the two boys who showed up made Pito look like a midget wrestler. About forty minutes into the meeting we had Tony and another UC check in with two huge suitcases on wheels. We opened them and showed the thugs the 50 kilograms of cocaine we were allegedly distributing in the area. Tony was to receive a call on his cell and would conduct a conversation in Spanish. He would then fill a smaller bag with up to 10 kilos and would let me know to whom he was delivering the drugs. That would repeat until the coke was gone and we let the thugs go.

The third time we met with only one of the thugs. He was a red-haired, athletic-looking young man who claimed he had played hockey at Northeastern University. Just prior to the meeting, I received word from Mucko that the assistant US attorney needed to see the weapon the kid was carrying to be able to charge him with a more substantial crime. I hesitated about doing the gig since the request seemed so out of place for the scenario; as an undercover, I rarely wore a gun. I talked it over with Mucko, and we came up with a way that might work. That time I was packing, and so was Pito.

We began a conversation with the redhead, and after hours of small talk we got around to talking about guns. I asked him what gun he preferred, and sure enough he took his out and showed it to us. It was a .45-caliber magnum. The assistant US attorney was pleased, and we didn't get killed. A successful day.

After the redhead was sentenced, I asked his attorney if I could interview his client for the undercover school, and he allowed me to do so. In the jailhouse interview, which was solely for teaching purposes and is still shown in classes, the redhead said he had handed over the gun only because I had surprised him with my question. He also said that the thought of robbing us had crossed his mind but the fact that he hadn't known when we would be coming into the room kept him from doing so.

He knew that if he decided to rob us he would also have to kill us.

CHAPTER 5

OPERATION BARBERSHOP

Kevin Hallinan founded the resident security agent (RSA) program at Major League Baseball in 1986, but I knew nothing about it until November 1998, just as I began to adjust to working on the federal side of the law.

All the while, I was still handling BPD cases and helping out with my own kids' sports teams. In the middle of that chaos, the FBI special agent in charge (SAC), Charles Prouty, asked me to drop by his office. Prouty explained that BPD detective Charlie Carroll, who had been assigned to the FBI-BPD bank robbery task force, was retiring.

As he spoke, I thought, I'll hear him out, but if he thinks I'm leaving narcotics to work on the bank robbery task force he's nuts. I was still eager to uncover major drug dealers who worked under the radar, and the thought of chasing bank robbers left me cold. Maybe Prouty could read my mind, because he told me that Carroll was also working as a consultant for Major League Baseball. His title was resident security agent. Prouty explained that every MLB team had a police officer from the team's jurisdiction working as an RSA. Prouty knew little else about the RSA program but asked if it would be all right for him to enter my name as a candidate for the job. Being incredibly honest, he told me that he would also be submitting the name of a second RSA candidate. I thanked Prouty but explained that I couldn't see how I could add another job to my schedule. He said that at the very least I should meet with the head of the MLB security department, Kevin Hallinan, who would be interviewing all the candidates. I realized that Prouty would not take no for an answer, so I agreed to meet with Hallinan. That same day I received a call from BPD commissioner Paul Evans, who advised me that he would also be submitting my name as a candidate for the RSA program.

At the beginning of that day, I hadn't known the job existed, yet now I was being entered as a candidate by both the FBI SAC and the BPD commissioner.

On the day of the interview at the Park Plaza Hotel, I called Hallinan's room from the house phone, but after dialing I glanced up and was surprised to see many familiar faces around the lobby. They were all BPD detectives and bosses dressed in suits. What the hell had I gotten into? I later learned that more than forty candidates had been interviewed.

When I entered Hallinan's room, I was greeted by Ed Petersen, Hallinan's second-in-command, who introduced me to Hallinan, who did most of the talking during the thirty-minute interview. Petersen sat mute, as if we were playing in a high-stakes poker game. Hallinan mostly told me stories about himself while briefing me on the RSA program.

"An RSA is the eyes and ears of MLB," he said. He kept on repeating, "Think of this as an internship in baseball."

I would hear those words a thousand times during my eight years as a member of Hallinan's security team. The MLB security department and the RSA program were the watchdogs of the integrity of the game, he said.

If chosen, I would have to get permission from the BPD on a yearly basis to participate in the program. Hallinan explained that an RSA would wear many hats. The police hat came first, followed by the many other roles an RSA was expected to take on, including security officer, investigator, consultant, clubhouse attendant, travel agent, driver, and anything else that came with a particular job. There were special assignments such as the All-Star Game, the playoffs, the World Series, and international events. Hallinan and his staff would choose the agents who worked those assignments, and I would be asked to participate in many of the events.

As I left the room, my view of the job had not changed. I went back down to the lobby of the hotel and ran into an overly confident young detective who thought very highly of himself. I knew he was also politically connected. "What's up, Ed?" he asked. "I heard you were interviewing for the job. I can tell you that it's between you and me."

Maybe for the wrong reasons, I was now interested.

Another interview came months later, and this time I was told it was down to three candidates: me, a BPD boss, and the overly confident young detective. On Christmas Eve, I got a call from Hallinan and Petersen, who told me I had the job. "Looking forward to working with you," they said.

The first week in January, I received another call from Hallinan and Petersen. I could tell from their tone that something was wrong.

"Ed, we have a problem," said Hallinan.

I stopped him right there and said, "Mr. Hallinan, I have a feeling I know what your problem is, and I'll make it easy for you. Give the job to the other guy. We have met, and you know who I am and what I'm about. When it's the right time, you'll call me back. No harm, no foul."

There was silence on the other end; then Hallinan said, "That's why we chose you, because we knew this is the type of guy you are."

They called again later that day to tell me that for the first time in their program they were going with two primary RSAs in the same city.

I found out later that Joe Moakley, a US representative for South Boston, had called in a favor from the Red Sox and been very upset when he received information that his guy hadn't gotten the job. He had threatened the Red Sox, and the rest was history.

Hallinan assembled some of the best law enforcement people in the United States, the Caribbean, and Latin America for his RSA program. Many were police commissioners, chiefs, or, like me, old-school gum-chewing detectives. The strength of Hallinan's program was that he demanded that every RSA be an active law enforcement member with knowledge of the communities where the ballparks were located. By no means was it an easy program to implement: the ball clubs, certainly in the beginning, understandably resisted having cops looking over their shoulders.

Senator George Mitchell addressed the security issue in his 2007 report, saying that many of MLB's investigations involving performance-enhancing substances had not been aggressive or thorough enough.

"Before this investigation, with few exceptions, the Commissioner's Office had not conducted investigative interviews of current major league players regarding alleged possession or use of performance-enhancing substances, by that player or by others," Mitchell wrote. He also noted that MLB's security department's primary function was to provide security for players, teams, and families. "That also places security officials in a difficult situation when they are asked to investigate the very persons they are responsible for protecting."[1] Translation: Security was there to protect players; Labor was there to negotiate with the Players Association and enforce the collective bargaining agreement. We were there to get the dirt out.

Mitchell cited Robert Manfred, then MLB's executive vice president for economics and league affairs, otherwise known as the Labor Relations Department, and Labor's handling of the Manny Alexander case, which had involved Red Sox clubhouse attendant Carlos Cowart. Cowart was stopped by Massachusetts State Police officers on June 30, 2000, driving Alexander's car. They found hypodermic needles and anabolic steroids in the car's glove compartment. Following a police investigation, Manfred and union official Gene Orza negotiated a deal in which Alexander was not tested until forty-five days after the incident. Predictably, the test was negative.

When I accepted the RSA position with the Red Sox, I indeed became the eyes and ears of Major League Baseball in Boston. The job entailed abiding by some general rules, but in reality, each RSA shaped the day-to-day policing of the club however he or she saw fit. I chose to work as an MLB employee who would help the Red Sox and report any perceived wrongdoing to baseball's Park Avenue headquarters in New York.

At that time, the late 1990s, the Red Sox had no real security department. The guy in charge of security was a high school principal by the name of John McDermott, whose security staff consisted mainly of high school– and college-age kids. He answered to Joseph McDermott (no relation), who was the team's executive assistant for stadium and security operations and vice president of property management. Joe McDermott, a nice man who seemed to be everywhere but had no real security background, handled all the stadium and security issues and reported directly to John Harrington, the president of the Yawkey Trust. The traveling secretary, Jack McCormick, was a former Boston PD detective who knew me from his previous job, and once the Red Sox–Yankees rivalry started to heat up in the late 1990s and early 2000s, former Red Sox general manager Dan Duquette asked me to accompany the team on all away series in New York and sometimes other places if they expected trouble. I was the first RSA to take on that role.

The assignment put me right smack in the middle of scores of emotionally charged circumstances, including the terrorist attacks of September 11, 2001. The Sox had played the Yankees at Yankee Stadium before leaving for Tampa on September 10. I remained in my hotel room at the Grand Hyatt adjacent to Grand Central Station for a scheduled flight back to Boston the next day, and as I got out of the shower in the morning I was suddenly glued to the television watching news anchors go speechless as images of a burning tower flashed on the screen.

I watched in horror as the second plane plunged into the South Tower of the World Trade Center. Duquette reached out to me from Boston and asked if I was safe and had been able to get in touch with my family. Needless to say, my flight never left. I walked over to 245 Park Avenue, where Tom Belfiore, who worked on Hallinan's team, and a secretary were the only two employees who had made their way into the commissioner's office that day, and was immediately put to work. The White Sox, who had arrived in New York to begin the next series with the Yankees, were desperate to flee the city the day of the attacks, and I was brought in to try to help those efforts.

The White Sox, who were also staying at the Grand Hyatt and acting as if they were the only people affected by the attacks, were looking to get away. They wanted the impossible, to be honest.

I met with Ed Cassin, the team's traveling secretary, and tried to explain that the city and country were in chaos, that thousands of people were dying, and that my best advice was for the players to stay in their rooms until things were sorted out. All the bridges, tunnels, airports, and trains in New York were shut down, I said. He didn't like my answers, but I reiterated that we were powerless to get the team out. I told him I was also staying at the hotel and for him to call me with any concerns.

The next day, September 12, the team managed to get onto a bus and leave the city. I took the train back to Boston and went directly to the FBI office, which was organized chaos. Our work was both challenging and sad. War rooms were set up, and we were all running around confirming the identities of the passengers on American Airlines Flight 11 and United Airlines Flight 175, the two planes that had departed Logan Airport for Los Angeles and had been flown into the towers, and trying to identify the hijackers and their accomplices. We were receiving hundreds of leads on our tip line and had to run them all down, never knowing which one would lead us in the right direction. One of my assignments was to locate one of Osama bin Laden's twenty to twenty-six children, who was attending school in Boston.

After we identified the terrorists who had hijacked the planes, we had to try to put the pieces together. How had they gotten into the country? Where had they been living? Who was financing the operation? Who were their family members? Where had the terrorists learned to fly? And all the while we wept for the thousands of innocent people murdered in the cowardly attack.

The events of 9/11 forever changed the FBI. Our drug task force unit consisted of more than twenty FBI agents, but after 9/11 all but a few were reassigned to the Joint Terrorism Task Force. The drug unit is now made up mostly of special task force officers, which is what I was. Local police officers were sworn in as federal special task force officers and built cases, which we took to the US Attorney's Office for prosecution.

Even without tragedy, passions ran high between the Red Sox and the Yankees. During the 2003 American League Championship Series (ALCS), there was the notorious on-field tussle between Red Sox pitcher Pedro Martinez and Yankees bench coach Don Zimmer, during which the seventy-two-year-old Zimmer was thrown to the ground by Martinez. That bench-clearing brawl, on October 11, had huge fallout, and no player took more abuse than Pedro, who received death threats prior to the series shifting back to New York for Games 6 and 7.

Martinez told me he had received phone calls from unknown numbers saying the callers were going to get him when he went to New York. I contacted everyone—the NYPD, the baseball commissioner's office, the Yankees, the Yankees' RSA—and they set up a twenty-four-hour-a-day security team at the hotel. We also had police escorts to Yankee Stadium.

I was Pedro's personal security in Gotham. He loved to go into the New York projects to visit his Dominican friends, but during that trip he stayed in his hotel room. He had never taken the team bus to Yankee Stadium, but he did following the threats. He was always laughing, but not so much this time. I accompanied him to the stadium bullpen prior to Game 7, and on the walk there we were assaulted by vile, hateful, obscenity-laced threats and insults hurled at us by the angry fans. In the moments before he took the mound, Pedro was visibly shaken.

Pedro was always a cocky player. In 2001, Joe Kerrigan took over as manager from Jimy Williams and tried to run the team like a marine drill sergeant. The players hated him for it. We were at Yankee Stadium, and Kerrigan was upset that Pedro wasn't obeying him. When Pedro failed to show up on time for a team meeting, Kerrigan locked the clubhouse door. He asked me to tell Pedro that he wasn't welcome in the room. I thought, This is not going to end

well. Ten minutes later, Pedro came walking down the hallway sing-
ing and all smiles.

"*¿Qué pasa, Eddie, cómo estás?*"

I told him that I was fine and that Kerrigan was having a team
meeting but he wasn't welcome. Pedro smirked and said, "Is that
right." Then, without hesitation, he lifted his right leg and kicked
the door so hard that it burst open and then back shut, broken. He
walked into the locker room, looked around, and casually asked,
"What's going on, boys?" It was almost as if he had been anticipating
the showdown and felt that now was a good time to get it over with.

Kerrigan was stunned; his face turned beet red, and everyone
in the room could almost see the steam pouring from his ears as
he glared at Pedro. The other players, whose backs had been to the
door, all turned in their chairs and tried to keep from laughing.

Kerrigan immediately ended the meeting, marched into his
office, and slammed the door behind him. Five minutes later, he
came out, made a beeline to me, and said, "Didn't I tell you that he
wasn't allowed in?"

I said, "Yes, you did, and I told him."

Kerrigan said he had wanted me to physically stop Pedro from
coming in.

I said, "Joe, are you serious? Let me get this straight: You wanted
me to tackle him, handcuff him, or kidnap him? You certainly
couldn't handle him, and you're his manager. If I was predisposed
to put my hands on him, and I did, I would have been in a fight with
Pedro Martinez. How do you think that would read in the newspapers or in front of a judge?"

Kerrigan managed for about another two months, then was
fired before spring training in 2002.

The Red Sox shocked the Yankees in the 2004 ALCS in seven
games, coming back from a three-games-to-none deficit, and

would go on to defeat St. Louis in the World Series, ending the Sox's eighty-six-year World Series drought. But there was tragedy along the way.

Although Game 7 was in the Bronx, an estimated 80,000 Red Sox fans gathered outside Fenway Park on October 21, 2004, to celebrate the ALCS victory over the Yankees, and when the situation turned dangerous, with revelers throwing projectiles at cops and lighting fires in the streets, additional police officers were summoned to the area. An emergency truck with FN 303 projectile launchers on board was on scene, and a special operations commander, Robert O'Toole, ordered the issuance of the launchers, which dispense pepper spray on impact. Three officers, including Boston PD officer Rochefort Milien, were armed with the device. All three, including O'Toole, who was not certified to use the weapon, fired shots.

A stray bullet, fired by Milien, hit twenty-one-year-old Emerson College student Victoria Snelgrove in the eye. The bullet caused massive bleeding and required immediate attention. But ambulances were blocked by the crowds, which refused to clear the area, and Snelgrove didn't make it to a medical facility in time.

Though the Boston PD accepted responsibility for the incident and paid a $5 million wrongful death settlement to Snelgrove's family, none of the officers faced criminal charges. O'Toole, a thirty-seven-year veteran of the police department, retired.

The tragic incident caused the new Red Sox head of security and former Boston PD captain Charles Cellucci to stay back at Fenway for Game 4 at St. Louis in case the Red Sox swept the series and the fans back home swarmed the stadium. That left me in charge of Red Sox security at Busch Stadium. The Sox swept the series, and there I was allowing John Henry, Tom Werner, Larry Lucchino, and Theo Epstein onto the field. It was tough holding in my joy, but professionally I had to, and I did. The smile was there, though.

MLB asked me to attend the 2005 congressional hearings on performance-enhancing drug use in the game held in Washington, DC. I was there with other RSAs as security for Commissioner Bud Selig, as well as for the players who testified—the 1998 home run chase *Sports Illustrated* cover boys, Mark McGwire and Sammy Sosa, self-admitted "Godfather of Steroids" José Canseco, Red Sox pitcher Curt Schilling, and Rafael Palmeiro.

The atmosphere was surreal: the same congressmen who crucified the likes of McGwire and Canseco in the hearing were drooling over the players behind the scenes, posing for photos with them, and asking for autographs. Selig and Manfred were hammered on Capitol Hill, and Selig saw no choice but to launch the Mitchell investigation.

It would have been difficult to find anyone with any inkling of sports knowledge who didn't suspect players like Sosa and McGwire. In the 1999 Home Run Derby at Fenway, one of the most memorable in baseball history, McGwire hit thirteen homers in the span of a few seconds, including one that went over the Green Monster, over the street, and over a parking garage and bounced off one of the billboards that line the train tracks alongside the Massachusetts Turnpike.

During that congressional hearing, my frustration was rooted in all the information I had turned over to baseball in my time as an RSA, information that had been either ignored or buried. The Manny Alexander incident, when steroids had been found in his car by the state police in 2000, was an especially troubling case.

Carlos Cowart, the nineteen-year-old batboy who was arrested driving Alexander's car, had asked Manny if he could use the car while the team was on the road. Cowart later told the *Boston Globe* that a friend had been behind the wheel when Cowart went into his apartment on Blue Hill Avenue in Dorchester to drop off his baby daughter.

When he came out, an unmarked cruiser was there. State police were patrolling the area as part of an antitheft unit, and the trooper suspected that the Mercedes might be stolen. Cowart didn't have a valid driver's license and was wanted on a previous charge of driving without a license and failing to stop for police, so he was arrested.

A search of the glove box revealed an envelope containing needles and a vial of Dimetabol, a mixture manufactured in Mexico that contained the steroid nandrolone. No complaint was filed against Cowart, but it's safe to say he took the fall for the incident. Cowart also told the *Globe* that MLB had tried to keep the whole thing quiet. Alexander and his lawyers went to Cowart's house, he said, and "wanted me to testify. To tell them our story. They felt like there was no reason for [police] to search the vehicle. He never told me to say they were my drugs. Never."[2]

I spoke to Alexander when the team got back to town, and he all but admitted it had been his package in the car. He said something like, "It was in my car, so who do you think it belongs to?" I stopped the inquiry at that point and called Hallinan. He went ballistic and told me never to do anything like that again. He said that baseball would handle it. I was surprised and confused by his response because it was one of the first times I had heard him lose his composure, although it certainly wasn't the last. Why wouldn't we be interested in what had really happened? I was later told by Hallinan to monitor the court case but not to talk to the state police or anybody else about the matter. It was one of many instances when the RSA role crossed paths with the police role, and it was truly a glimpse into the future. I decided that when I saw something I believed should be handled by the authorities, I would not only pass it on to MLB but also alert one of my brother officers.

Years later, in 2006–07, when Mitchell was preparing his report, I received a call from his investigator about the Alexander/Cowart incident. All I said was that I had been told by Hallinan that MLB would handle the matter and that I was to follow the court proceedings and report to them.

Mitchell concluded in his report that Cowart and his friend had never been interviewed about the incident by anyone in the commissioner's office and that Labor had made no effort to interview Alexander because, I assumed, the collective bargaining agreement required that the Players Association be notified and present for an interview of a player on the forty-man roster. As Manfred said in the report in reference to negotiations with the union on how to proceed in drug investigations, "this was the price of reasonable cause testing."[3]

The case involving former slugger and two-time American League MVP Juan Gonzalez, which took place in 2001 at the Canadian border, was another incident with puzzling results. Steroids and needles were found in an unmarked suitcase among the Cleveland Indians' baggage at Toronto Pearson International Airport during a series between the Indians and Blue Jays three weeks after the 9/11 attacks. The Indians' RSA at the time, Jim Davidson, tipped me off to the incident, one of the early doping scandals involving PEDs before baseball instituted a drug-testing program.

But it wasn't until five years later in a *Daily News* report that the Gonzalez unclaimed baggage incident came to light.

The article detailed how Canada Border Services Agency officials had searched the suitcase that was part of the Indians' baggage and found—according to a CBSA seizure report—five ampules of anabolic steroids, needles, and clenbuterol. The Canadian officials had allowed the unmarked bag to be delivered to the Indians' hotel, the Westin Harbour Castle, to see if anyone would claim it.

A Dominican trainer named Angel Presinal, who was part of Gonzalez's entourage, picked up the bag and was stopped and questioned by authorities. Presinal said the bag belonged to Gonzalez. The trainer and the slugger were both questioned by agents for about four hours, then told they were free to go. There wasn't enough evidence to link the bag to either man, according to the seizure report. The bag was confiscated.

Presinal, who eventually took the fall for the Toronto incident, was never seen around the Indians again that year and was eventually banned from all MLB stadiums. Gonzalez, meanwhile, was never disciplined. Presinal would later latch onto pitcher Bartolo Colón in the mid-2000s and then was in the spotlight in 2009, when he was linked to Alex Rodriguez. Presinal was not an official member of the 2006 Dominican World Baseball Classic team, but he trained players on the Dominican squad and for many years operated a gym in Santo Domingo near the Palacio de los Deportes Virgilio Travieso Soto, where he continued to train players after he was banned.[4]

Baseball's drug policy wasn't in place in 2001, but Gonzalez was one of the principal names later mentioned in José Canseco's 2005 steroid tome, *Juiced: Wild Times, Rampant 'Roids, Smash Hits, and How Baseball Got Big.* Canseco wrote that he had personally injected Gonzalez and other players with steroids. Gonzalez last played in the majors in 2005.

"The Canadians [said] they don't have enough information to proceed criminally, for reasons that still escape us," Rob Manfred told the *Daily News* in the 2006 report, referring to MLB's reaction to what transpired with Canadian law enforcement in the Presinal-Gonzalez matter. As for MLB's position, Manfred described it this way: "Remember, at the time we don't have a steroid policy."

After the sometimes unpleasant interactions Hallinan and I had over my first seven years of working in baseball, I finally had a good laugh at his expense during the inaugural World Baseball Classic in March 2006.

Part of the early-round play took place in San Juan, Puerto Rico, and the Cuban national team was in that pool. We had anticipated that the Cubans' presence there would draw some protests, and the Puerto Rican police made it very clear to us that its department and Puerto Rican officials respected freedom of speech. They also stated that any protesters holding signs that denounced Fidel Castro or the Cuban government were to be left alone, even though MLB and the Players Association had guaranteed the Cubans that no signs against Castro would be allowed. Well, the man who referred to himself as "The Talent" had other ideas.

No sooner had protesters flashed signs outside Hiram Bithorn Stadium than the Cuban team was complaining, and that's when Hallinan took it upon himself to snatch posters from two of the protesters. Big mistake.

Puerto Rican officers arrested Hallinan on the spot and locked him up in a makeshift detention area. Hallinan even had to do a perp walk to the police station—a camper that was parked outside the stadium near a security fence along the third-base line. Paul Padilla, an MLB security employee who was part of the detail during the WBC portion in San Juan, came up to me after Hallinan had been arrested and asked what was going on. Barely able to get the words out because I was laughing so hard, I told Padilla that Hallinan was in the clink.

Padilla eventually had Hallinan released from his "holding cell," but I thought the experience would humble him a little bit, maybe even teach him a little lesson. Didn't happen.

There were cases of domestic violence—again years before that issue torpedoed Roger Goodell and the NFL and before MLB decided to implement its own policy. Just as it is my belief that MLB was not the only culprit back in 2005 for the PED accusations, I believe that the NFL was not the only culprit in the domestic violence accusations that surfaced years later. Baseball had its own issues, including one memorable case in 2006 when Phillies pitcher Brett Myers punched his wife on a street corner not far from Fenway Park, a case my brother, Carlos, and I were involved in.

On Friday, June 23, 2006, I got a call from the Phillies. "Are you the RSA in Boston? I'm the traveling secretary for the Phillies, and we have a problem." He went on to tell me that Myers had been arrested on domestic violence charges in Boston and was being held downtown.

Soon after, I got a call from Myers's lawyer, who asked me if I knew a local attorney who could represent Myers at his arraignment the following Monday. I knew the only lawyer who would pick up the phone at that time on a Friday night would be my brother, Carlos. I called MLB and told the people there about the incident, and they told me to follow up on it. I also asked if it was okay to get my brother involved, and they said it was. I called Carlos.

I was still a Boston police detective at the time, and I headed downtown to pick up Myers, who was waiting for my arrival. The six-foot-four, 240-pound pitcher from Jacksonville, Florida, whose wife had posted bail for him, still reeked of alcohol. He got into my car and told me, "I don't get what the big deal is. My wife and I beat the shit out of each other all the time."

I advised him that I wasn't his lawyer and perhaps he should consult with him before saying anything. I dropped him off at the Sheraton Hotel in the Back Bay and headed home.

The next morning I contacted MLB again and told the people there what had happened and that Myers had admitted to me that he had hit his wife. They told me not to investigate the matter but to stay informed as to what was happening with his case.

Months later, Carlos managed to pull a rabbit out of his legal hat by using a little-known statute intended for minor altercations to get the case dismissed. Despite horrific accounts of the assault by witnesses who said they saw Myers dragging his wife by her hair and slapping her across the face, it helped, too, that Kim Myers said she did not want her husband prosecuted for the attack. Myers was never punished by baseball either.[5]

Eight years later, when the NFL faced its own dramatic domestic violence issue after a video showed Baltimore Ravens running back Ray Rice knocking his fiancée unconscious in an Atlantic City hotel elevator, not much had changed on that front.

NFL commissioner Goodell initially suspended Rice for two games for the incident. It wasn't until the elevator video surfaced on TMZ that the Ravens cut Rice from the team and the NFL suspended him indefinitely. An arbitrator overturned Goodell's suspension, saying it had been arbitrary and in conflict with the case, but Rice has not played in the NFL again.[6]

In the middle of all that, the Associated Press reported that an unnamed law enforcement officer claimed he had sent the NFL a video of Rice punching his fiancée and played a voice-mail message from an NFL office number confirming the arrival of the video. Goodell and the NFL said it had no knowledge of anyone in its offices having received the video. Nonetheless, Goodell hired former FBI director Robert Mueller, the same Robert Mueller who would go on to serve as a special investigator into allegations that Russia had meddled in the 2016 presidential election, to investigate the league's handling of the Rice case. Mueller's investigation found no evidence that the NFL had seen the elevator video before it became public or that anyone had acknowledged receipt of the video, but Mueller did conclude that there was "substantial information about the incident—even without the in-elevator video—indicating the need for a more thorough investigation. The NFL should have done more with the information it had, and should have taken additional steps to obtain all available information about the . . . incident."[7]

Within the report, Mueller also advised the NFL to create a special investigations team to handle domestic violence and sexual abuse cases, and he recommended that the league adopt investigative guidelines for its investigations, expand its security department, and provide training for a performance review process for investigators.

Echoes of the Mitchell Report? Kind of. But in my experience, the leagues' commissioners all speak to one another, and I imagined that, if asked, Manfred would have told Goodell something along these lines: Whatever you do, make sure Mueller doesn't recommend that you adopt an independent investigative unit.

"I would say what it tells me is that they didn't want to see their warts," Joe Rannazzisi, the head of the DEA's Office of Diversion Control, would say years later, referring to the lords of each sports league and their fear of uncovering malfeasance in their own backyard. "Major League Baseball [DOI] investigators were out there exposing their weaknesses and potential problems, and they did their job so well that [MLB] decided maybe they're doing their job so well that we don't want to know any more. That's just crazy."

Sometime in the summer of 2005, two and a half years before Mitchell's report and while I still was working as an RSA, allegations began surfacing that a member of Red Sox slugger David Ortiz's entourage was suspected of being involved in betting on baseball games. I investigated the matter in the same manner I would handle any law enforcement investigation, but the information I gathered was brushed away as if nothing had happened.

His nickname was "Monga," and from the moment I laid eyes on him, I knew there was something wrong. It's one of those things that comes to most working cops after a while. Call it intuition, experience, a hunch, or whatever, but it's a feeling you get, and if you know what you're doing, you follow that feeling and you start the hunt.

By then I had repeatedly informed MLB that the locker rooms were as porous as ever. Players and clubhouse attendants were allowing people into their private area without criminal background checks, passes, or even IDs. The hangers-on, the gofers, and those posing as "barbers" were meeting in a back room of the clubhouse, out of sight of the media and security. My informants and sources were telling me that the "barbers" had assumed identities and that some members of the players' entourages were known drug dealers, while others were bookies and gamblers. I ran background checks that supported those claims and forwarded the results to Major League Baseball.

I told Charlie Cellucci, the Red Sox security chief, that Monga had to get a pass and that he needed proper identification. I soon found out that Monga had submitted several versions of a name: Edwin Manuel Cotto, Edwin Manuel Cotto Garcia, or was it Edwin Garcia Cotto?

Monga seemed confused about his own name, and the reason was obvious—none of the names was his. The hunt had started.

Poor Monga was dealt a bad hand, or at least a bad ID. Turned out Edwin Manuel Cotto . . . or Edwin Cotto Garcia . . . or Edwin Garcia Cotto . . . was a convicted drug dealer serving a federal prison sentence in Puerto Rico. Even though there was no evidence that Monga himself was a drug dealer, he had somehow assumed a drug dealer's identity.[8]

I summoned one of my informants and told him to try to get into Monga's inner circle. That was not an easy thing to do since Monga was Ortiz's top aide-de-camp. He was a big, muscular Dominican and was always by Ortiz's side. Every time the player showed up at

Fenway or appeared at an event, Monga was there, too. If Ortiz's wife and kids were around, Monga was, too. Ortiz even referred to Monga as his half brother.

I suspected that Monga was using PEDs just by the way he looked: his muscle mass. The informant eventually came back to me with more information: Monga was frequenting a Dominican barbershop located on Blue Hill Avenue. The informant said that he had seen him frequently at the shop and that the barber had a gambling parlor in the basement. While Ortiz was with the Red Sox in Chicago for a series against the White Sox, Monga was betting thousands of dollars on baseball games at the Blue Hill Avenue address as well as at other shops, including at 371 Centre Street in Jamaica Plain, where my informant said he had witnessed Monga placing a bet on a game in Chicago between the White Sox and Red Sox on July 24, 2005. Monga placed one $1,000 bet on the White Sox to win—Chicago went on to beat the Astros in the World Series that fall of 2005—and also placed a $1,000 bet on the "over," meaning that Chicago and Boston had to score a combined total of at least nine runs. The White Sox beat the Red Sox 6–4 on July 24. Monga hit on both bets.

It also isn't uncommon for Dominican bodegas and barbershops to serve as fronts for gambling parlors. Drug dealers hang out in those parlors, which was somewhat of a concern to me.

All along, I was sending information to MLB concerning Monga and other suspicious types unrelated to Ortiz who were entering the clubhouse, as I was sure the news would pique some interest. I heard nothing for months. I would send my reports to a supervisor, LeRoy Hendricks, who would acknowledge receiving them, but I knew that all final decisions were made by Hallinan, or at least he told us he made them. In retrospect, I think most final decisions of a sensitive nature were made by Selig or Manfred and Labor, even back then.

Eventually the office got back to me and said that it would tell the Red Sox that Monga would not be allowed in the clubhouse without credentials. Charlie Cellucci wanted no part of it since Ortiz did not take kindly to being told what to do, so I was made the bogeyman, which was fine with me.

Ortiz and I had a somewhat cordial relationship—I made myself available to handle issues the players might have had—but I kept my distance. Ortiz knew I had helped supply security for him and his family on several trips to Yankee Stadium. The incident with the barber damaged that relationship, but that was part of the job.

Big Papi's entourage included several colorful characters, including two Dominicans nicknamed "El Petete" and "Flaco" ("Skinny One"), and Ortiz was upset that he was being told that his boys could no longer flywheel into and out of the clubhouse as they once had, and he let that be known. He approached me once about the issue, and I told him I was doing my job and that if he gave it some thought he would understand that it was for his and the other players' protection. He wasn't buying it.

The clubhouse attendants weren't happy with me, either, since they also caught Ortiz's wrath for obeying MLB's orders and keeping the likes of Monga out, at least most of the time. I say "most of the time" because if I wasn't at the ballpark, it was as though the doors to Disneyland had opened and all were welcome.

The gambling issue with Monga continued, and I kept on reporting my findings, but by then Hallinan was saying he needed time to figure out the best way to handle the situation.

I believed Hallinan might hire a private investigator to look into what I discovered.

The All-Star Game was at PNC Park in Pittsburgh in 2006, and I was sitting at home watching the Home Run Derby when I saw Monga on the field—along with several barbers I had identified to

MLB as shady characters—toweling off Ortiz and other Dominican players. For God's sake, they were practically getting at-bats. My phone rang, and it was Charlie Cellucci on the line. Then it rang again, and it was Sox clubhouse attendant Joe Cochran. And then again, and it was visiting clubhouse attendant Tom McLaughlin.

The message was the same: "Nice going, Dominguez. We can't let these guys in the clubhouse, and MLB has them in the Home Run Derby."

I took the heat and called Dan Mullin, who was second-in-command under Hallinan in the security department at the time, and was at the game. He told me they had tried to keep them out but Ortiz had said, "If they don't come with me on the field, I don't participate." Selig and Manfred had given in and said, 'Let them on.'"

I thought to myself, This whole security thing is a joke.

Later on in the season Hallinan told me he was flying to Boston. I picked him up, and we made small talk on the way to Fenway. As we arrived, he told me we were addressing the gambling issue involving Ortiz's assistant.

I followed Hallinan into manager Terry "Tito" Francona's office, where Hallinan proceeded to tell Francona that he wanted to have a talk with Ortiz with the manager present. I was dumbfounded. I thought Hallinan would have hired an investigator to follow Monga around. Francona looked as confused as I was. I was used to all bark, no bite from MLB, but this was just crazy. To be clear, I had no proof that Ortiz was placing bets through Monga—or had ever done so—but Monga, who was hanging around the clubhouse, was betting thousands of dollars against the Red Sox. At least take a look at it.

Ortiz walked in, sat down, and said hello to Hallinan, stared at me, and asked Francona what was going on. Hallinan then told Francona and Ortiz what we had found, from soup to nuts. Ortiz claimed it was all a lie.

"I don't know what you're talking about," he said.

Hallinan and Francona warned Ortiz to be careful about whom he associated with, and Ortiz said he would speak to Monga. "I know it's not true," he said.

When we got back to the car, my cell chirped. It was my informant.

"¿*Oye, Dominguez, qué pasó?*" asked the informant. "What happened?"

"What do you mean?" I asked.

"I just got a call from the barber, and he said that the gambling parlor is shut down immediately."

I told Hallinan and he didn't flinch, didn't say a word.

I had already started a police investigation into numerous Dominican bodegas and barbershops, and I passed the information on to Juan Seoane, my Cuban sidekick on the FBI task force. Approximately a year later, on April 8, opening day at Fenway, we executed numerous search warrants throughout the state and, in conjunction with the FBI, Immigration and Customs Enforcement (ICE), and other agencies, arrested store owners and seized money, ledgers, and names. Operation Barbershop involved trash pulls, bank accounts, surveillance, and informants. The barbershop on Blue Hill Avenue was no longer one of the targets. I knew why: by the time the warrants were issued, the barber had long stopped taking bets and moved out. Hallinan's warning to Ortiz had worked.

I gave ICE the Monga information, and it eventually arrested him in July 2007 and charged him with nine counts of making false claims of US citizenship.[9]

ICE agents picked him up at Ortiz's home just as the two were headed to the ballpark. A team spokesman claimed to have been only "vaguely familiar" with the Monga case and cited MLB's beefed-up rules banning anyone but close relatives of players from entering clubhouses. Ortiz, of course, was furious. He wasn't the only one. I was following a drug dealer on St. Botolph Street in Roxbury when I got a call from GM Theo Epstein, who was none too happy, either.[10]

"Eddie, I thought you were with us. What the fuck are you doing?" Epstein asked. "Ortiz is upset the police went to his home and arrested his guy. What are you doing?"

I paused and asked, "Are you done, Theo? I'm going to tell you this once. I'm a Boston police detective. I don't work for you or the Red Sox. I do some contract work for MLB. The player was warned about Monga, who is NG [no good]. Ortiz is not above the law. Don't you ever call me again yelling at me. Do you understand?"

"I thought you were one of us" was all he could say.

"Not sure what you mean by that, but I'm a Boston police detective. Don't forget it."

I remember the first time I met Epstein, he looked more like the team's batboy than its general manager. He had come over from the Padres with Larry Lucchino, who had joined the John Henry–Tom Werner group as president and CEO after Henry and Werner had purchased the team in late 2001 and had been promoted to the GM job in November 2002. No matter what time of day or night I went by Fenway, Theo was there. I swear he slept at Fenway. Most everybody in Red Sox Nation, at least at first, saw his hiring as Lucchino bringing along a sidekick who would do his bidding, but as time went on, you could see Theo's confidence growing, and he began distancing himself from Lucchino.

Then came 2004. Right at the trade deadline, and in one of the boldest moves in Boston sports history, Epstein traded Nomar Garciaparra. The city was stung. Nomar was everybody's favorite. Of course the trade and the season ended with the Red Sox becoming

World Champions for the first time in eighty-six years, and Epstein was the golden boy.

I was in charge of on-the-field security at Busch Stadium when the final pitch was thrown. I had asked John Henry whom he wanted on the field, and he told me he wanted only a handful of people for the first few minutes and that Theo was in that handful, which must have irritated Lucchino.

By 2005, the tension between Lucchino and Epstein had grown to the point that you would often see the two walk past each other without saying a word. Then came the bizarre incident on Halloween 2005, when Epstein resigned from his post, citing differences with management—i.e., Lucchino—and left Fenway Park dressed in a gorilla suit to avoid reporters. The suit was later auctioned off for $11,000 for charity, and Epstein returned to the Sox just a few months later.

John Henry had stepped in and given Epstein what he wanted: to get out from under Lucchino's wing. From then on the lines were drawn and on most subjects it was John Henry and Epstein versus Lucchino and Tom Werner. One incident I had investigated made that crystal clear. The Red Sox had traded Manny Ramirez in 2008, and Lucchino asked MLB to look into how Manny had forced the Red Sox to trade him. Lucchino felt that Manny's agent, Scott Boras, had orchestrated a trade by telling Manny to start complaining about injuries and to instigate a fight with traveling secretary Jack McCormick, actions that would leave the Red Sox with no way out other than trading Manny.

I went to Fenway and interviewed Tito Francona and then Epstein. Tito told me what I already knew: he doubted Manny could stick to a script like that if his life depended on it. In other words, if Boras had been whispering in Manny's ear to take a right, he most likely would have taken a left.

Theo said almost the same thing, adding that he had a great relationship with Boras and couldn't see him making that kind of move with Manny.

Lucchino was next. I walked into his office, and he proceeded to tell me what he thought had happened between Manny and Boras and the Red Sox. He then asked me who else I had interviewed. When I told him I had spoken to Francona and Epstein, he asked me what Epstein had said. As I related the interview, Lucchino's face started getting redder and redder. I hadn't gotten the entire story out when he said, "What the fuck, stop there. I'm calling Tom. I want him to hear this." He proceeded to call Werner, who was in his plane flying somewhere. "Werner, listen to what Theo told Dominguez." As I retold the story, Lucchino kept on asking "Can you believe this shit?"

Werner was not happy and said as much. I assumed that Epstein threw a monkey wrench into their theory that Boras had manipulated his client and that they were looking to get Boras sanctioned and Manny fined for the way they had forced the Red Sox to trade him. Lucchino and Werner agreed to talk about the matter further after Werner landed and decided they would then approach Henry. I spoke later to Henry, whose story was not much different from Epstein's.

Epstein and I had a couple of scrapes, especially after Monga was arrested, but as soon as we had words, things usually went back to normal. Epstein would call me a couple of years later for help on a different issue regarding the signing of Dayan Viciedo.

Theo went on to greater things in Chicago with the Cubs. His sidekick, Jed Hoyer, was a Wesleyan graduate, and we often talked about my son Andrew, who attended the same school and, like Jed, played on the baseball team. By the time Epstein and Hoyer left the Red Sox after the 2011 season, I was already working full-time with the DOI and didn't have a pulse on what was going on with the team and its executives that season, including whether starting pitchers drank beer and ate fried chicken in the clubhouse during games, as the *Boston Globe* reported, or whether front-office tumult had led to Epstein's departure. But I imagine things hadn't changed much since that 2005 season. Not surprising to me, Epstein and Hoyer led the Cubs to their first World Series win in 108 years in 2016. Both are very smart, talented, hardworking, and obsessed.

Meanwhile, Monga's real name, or as close as we ever got to it, was Felix Leopoldo Marquez Galice. He had entered into a sham marriage with an American woman and had submitted a birth certificate and Social Security documents to the Registry of Motor Vehicles claiming to be Edwin Manuel Cotto Garcia. He had even checked the box saying he wished to vote. Monga was deported for his immigration violations and continued to work for Ortiz in the Dominican Republic.

A few years later, I went undercover for the FBI posing as Ortiz's agent to trace a man who was trying to extort Ortiz. The suspect was arrested, and although Ortiz's agent, Fernando Cuza, thanked me, I got the cold shoulder from Ortiz.

CHAPTER 6

"STAND DOWN!"

Patrick Arnold was the first case we brought to the DEA. Arnold was the chemist who had created the designer steroid "the clear" (THG) and had worked with BALCO mastermind Victor Conte years before, when that doping scandal had rocked the sports world and ensnared the likes of Barry Bonds and Olympic track star Marion Jones. Arnold had pled guilty in 2006 to conspiracy to distribute steroids following the federal BALCO investigation and served three months in prison. His name surfaced again when Phillies southpaw reliever J. C. Romero tested positive during the summer of 2008, prior to the Phillies' playoff run that October.

We were only ten months into the DOI stint, and right away we began applying our law enforcement tactics. We made several purchases of the supplement in question, tested it, and did our homework and background checks.

Our investigation led to Arnold, who owned two companies— ErgoPharm and Proviant Technologies—that were manufacturing 6-OXO Extreme. Romero appealed his fifty-game suspension and was twice offered a reduced suspension of twenty-five games if he admitted his guilt, but he refused and was able to play in the World Series, where he earned two wins when the Phillies beat Tampa Bay in five games to win the title. Romero served his fifty-game doping ban starting in 2009, but he later filed a civil suit against the makers and distributors of 6-OXO Extreme—including GNC—and in 2012 reached a settlement for an undisclosed amount.

With all the cases we took to the DEA, the FBI, or any other law enforcement agency, we gathered evidence and presented it. The agency would then make its own call as to whether it wanted to pursue the case. The feds would eventually subpoena Arnold at ErgoPharm, and agents would seize numerous boxes from company headquarters.

I got a lead on a possible new case in late 2008, near the one-year anniversary of the formation of the DOI. We had worked on several investigations already—including the J. C. Romero positive test— but this had the makings of the kind of case I'd used to get when I worked with an FBI drug task force late in my Boston PD days, complete with an adrenaline rush. It appeared to be a solid lead, maybe the door to learning just how involved teams were with the traffickers of Cuban players.

It was late on the night of November 21, 2008, a Friday night, and I had just returned home after a three-and-a-half-hour Acela ride from New York—another long week at 245 Park Avenue.

I was just getting settled with a Bacardi and Coke and lime, a "Cuba Libre" or "La Mentirita" ("The Little Lie"), what we Cuban-Americans who had fled Castro's regime called that drink, even though we were well aware that Cuba is not "Libre" ("free") at all. My phone was going off again in my pocket. I was physically spent and thought of letting the call go to voice mail but reluctantly answered. It had already been a pain-in-the-ass day, but I shaded the phone with my hand to see the caller ID. Interesting, I thought. Been a while. I wonder what he wants?

"Ed Dominguez."

"Eddie, it's Theo. There's something fucking shady going on here," he said.

He sounded harried and frustrated, unlike the calm tone I had come to expect, and respect, from the young Red Sox GM, although at thirty-five, Theo Epstein wasn't all that young anymore.

"What's going on, Theo?"

"Fucking Dayan Viciedo," Epstein replied, in reference to the Cuban phenom. It's as if he has a prearranged deal with the fucking White Sox. This stinks real bad. You have to do something about this. We want this kid!"

While I was an RSA from 1999 to 2007, I accompanied several US baseball teams playing in international tournaments in South America and Cuba. I had been the primary security officer for USA Baseball at an eighteen-and-under international tournament in Cuba in 2006, and it was during that tournament that I saw Dayan Viciedo play.

Viciedo, in my opinion, was head and shoulders the best player in the tournament, and I wasn't the only one who felt that way. Two MLB scouts, Paul Mirocke and Marv Thompson, who had traveled to Cuba under the guise of being team trainers, thought Viciedo was the crown jewel of the tournament. He was the starting shortstop and the closer for the Cuban national team; in reality, he was the best player at every position. The ball made a distinct sound when it jumped off his bat. The scouts believed that even at seventeen he could definitely be in the starting lineup of any MLB team.

"The Cuban kid," I said. "Sure, I remember him, and he will definitely remember me."

I had first seen Viciedo play in Mexico in 2004, when he was only fifteen, and after the Cubans won the tournament there, Viciedo, accompanied by a very talented shortstop by the name of "Candelita," aka José Iglesias, approached me and asked if they could use my phone to call their families back in Cuba. I was more than happy to oblige, and Viciedo and Iglesias, in turn, would remember my gesture of kindness for years to come.

"It's been pretty obvious since the beginning of the negotiations that his agent wants Viciedo to sign with the White Sox and nobody else," Theo barked on the other end of the phone. "I called Dan Halem [Manfred's second-in-command in Labor], earlier today, and he said nobody has filed an official contract with MLB.

"The White Sox only have a verbal agreement, and there is definitely something very wrong going on here. What can you do to get to the bottom of this?" Epstein wanted to know.

"Do you have the kid's cell number, Theo?" I asked.

He gave me the number, and I said I would make a few calls.

The whole business of signing players from Cuba was very much infused with backdoor deals and uncomfortable interactions. Cleaning up the Cuban baseball pipeline process was one of our goals, but shady dealings persisted.

Cuban players had for years been involved with unsavory characters and endured harrowing trips off the island. Often their only way out was to sell themselves to the Devil. The Devil took on the appearance of Cuban and Mexican organized crime figures who trafficked in everything from drugs to human beings. Of course, MLB is culpable, too. Team personnel identify the players they want and reach out to agents, who in some cases reach out to smugglers, who contact the players. The plan begins.

In September 2006, at the eighteen-and-under tournament in Cuba, it was easy to see why Viciedo was at the center of all this activity: his talents were on full display.

I stood at the top of the dugout steps, leaning over the protective fence looking out on the field—José Antonio Huelga Stadium, located in Sancti Spíritus, more than two hundred miles east of

Havana. The rain had slowed to a drizzle, but the tarp was still on the field. The US junior national team was approaching its sixth hour of delay, and the Americans were starting to get a little rambunctious down in the clubhouse.

The American pitcher, Blake Beavan, a tall Texan, had a cool confidence about him, and he was supposed to be the starting pitcher that night. It was a big spot for the kid—an elimination game for the 2006 World Junior Championships against the tournament's top seed, perennial powerhouse, and this year's host: Cuba.

But that seemed to be the last thing on the kid's mind. I had just seen Beavan stroll up to the team's manager—Jason Hisey from Pima Community College in Pima, Arizona—who was looking less calm.

"Gosh, I hope we play today," said Beavan.

Team USA went on to beat Cuba 4–0 in that game. Beavan was transformed from a chill, surfer-cool teenager into a man possessed. The game's highlight came in the bottom of the fifth inning, after one of his teammates was hit with a pitch. Beavan responded by firing a 90-plus-miles-per-hour fastball over Viciedo's head.

Viciedo, who even at seventeen was every bit a man at five feet eleven and 220 pounds, walked out a few steps toward the mound, waving his bat at Beavan. But the pitcher wasn't intimidated. Beavan took a few steps in the Cuban's direction, yelling so forcefully that spit formed on the corners of his mouth. He waved to the crowd with both hands, urging the fans to bring it on, then proceeded to fan Viciedo with three straight fastballs, one of his eleven strikeouts on the night, en route to his complete-game shutout to keep the United States' tournament hopes alive.

During the altercation, while Viciedo waved his bat wildly, I looked across the field at Tony Castro, the Cuban national team's doctor—and Fidel's son—whom I had met back in 1999. Tony responded with a shrug and a mischievous smile. I repeated the gesture after Beavan struck out Viciedo. The game was being broadcast nationally in Cuba, and government officials were unhappy that their undefeated team, which had the number one position in its bracket, had lost to the number four team, which had squeaked into the playoffs. Nonetheless, Tony was impressed with the Beavan kid. Not many people got one fastball by Viciedo, never mind three.

During the game, Marty Rodriguez, the other MLB security officer on the trip, and I had taken bottles of water and thrown them out of the dugout and onto the field. It was a kind of voodoo act that Tony Castro and the other Cubans had used at the WBC earlier that year. Tony smiled.

After the game, he walked over to our side of the field to congratulate the US team. He again took up a post next to me and watched as the American team's pig pile broke up. Beavan emerged somewhere from the bottom.

"Congratulations, looks like you guys will be sticking around for at least a little while," Castro said.

"Looks that way," I responded.

The celebration on the field was losing steam, and the scattered players were picking up their hats and gloves, sauntering back into the dugout and down the tunnel. My attention was on the Cuban dugout. Slumped and dejected, Viciedo was the only player left on the bench.

We had exchanged greetings before the game, but now he was in no mood for pleasantries. I gestured in that direction. "How's he holding up?"

"He's beside himself, feels like he let the whole country down," Castro said. "I tried to tell him it's just a game. I don't think it helped."

I kept my gaze trained on the player. "I'm sure he'll be just fine."

The US team went on to beat Mexico in the semifinals before finally bowing out to the South Korean team in the championship on a ninth-inning run by South Korea to cap a 4–3 victory.

It was a flourish to a tournament that was full of excitement and talent. Beavan's performance against the Cubans solidified him as a shoo-in for Baseball America's 2006 Youth Player of the Year Award. He was joined on that team by a handful of future stars, including Matt Dominguez, who hit a three-run home run against the Cuban team and finished the tournament with 11 RBIs; Mike Moustakas, who drove in five in a game against Italy; Jarrod Parker, who finished 1–0 with a .077 ERA; and a pitcher from Connecticut by the name of Matt Harvey, who was, according to scouts traveling with us, the most talented player on the US team but was underused by Hisey, the hard-nosed Marine Corps–style manager who had made it clear during the tournament that he had no use for, among others, Tony Castro. That uncomfortable moment came when Tony invited us to a cookout at a house he had in the area. Obviously, I was no fan of the Castro regime, but from our days together during the 1999 series between the US and Cuban national teams, I had found Tony to be a gracious host. I accepted the invitation on our behalf.

Hisey refused to attend. "We didn't come here to socialize with Communists," he said.

It wasn't clear if Tony had heard the remark, but I arranged for a car to take Hisey back to Ciego de Ávila while a couple of scouts and I went to the cookout and had a great time.

The list of future big-league talent playing in the tournament was impressive and included Canada's Brett Lawrie, Phillippe Aumont, and James Paxton and Australia's Josh Spence. The Cuban team included the likes of Aroldis Chapman, Leonys Martin, and, of course, Dayan Viciedo.

Epstein's panicked call in 2008 revealed just how sought after Viciedo was, and I would quickly find out the lengths the player and his father had gone to get Dayan out of Cuba and into Mexico, where he would attempt to gain residency. In the murky business of signing Cuban players to major-league teams, Cuban players seek to set up residency in a third country, and once that step is accomplished, they can enter free agency and be on track for a lucrative payday in "Las Grandes Ligas" (the major leagues). If the players enter the US directly, they are subject to the draft and much less money. Viciedo wanted the big bucks.

But what transpired after Viciedo established residency in Mexico was a convoluted morass that looked as if it would be the first big investigation for me and the DOI. When I reached Viciedo via Viciedo's father, Asnaldo, he spoke of his son's predicament. The Spanish was halting at times, and there was a nervous tic in the elder Viciedo's voice. Both father and son were confused, he said. They were afraid that if Viciedo didn't sign with the White Sox, the *lancheros*, or smugglers, would harm him.

"*Está bien, Dominguez, nos mantenemos en contacto,*" Asnaldo said. Sounds good, Dominguez. We'll be in touch.

I then called Dan Mullin, excited about digging into the case immediately. When Mullin answered, I launched into an explanation of how and why we should contact DEA agents in Mexico and start the process of getting the Viciedo family to a safe place. There were also the circumstances surrounding how he had ended up in Mexico, and I had already uncovered some information on the case.

It seemed clear to me that baseball knew, or should have known, that Viciedo, who had obtained his Mexican residency in less than a week, had done so illegally. We were not yet doing age/ID investigations into Cuban players—we would add Cuba and other countries to the list in 2010—but I pointed out to Mullin and George Hanna, who pointed out to their bosses, that the MLB rules governing Cubans led to corruption at every level.

I unloaded the news about Epstein's call to Mullin, talking faster than I normally do. Mullin was enthusiastic as well. The only case up until that point that had generated buzz within our unit involved Atlanta Braves superprospect Jordan Schafer, who had been suspended for a nonanalytical positive drug test for human growth hormone. One of our first moves after our group was formed was to set up a tip line for anyone with information about performance-enhancing drug use to call, and we had been contacted by someone who told us that Schafer was using HGH. We went on to interview over a hundred current and former Schafer teammates. The break came when a former roommate of Schafer told us that his girlfriend had feared that somebody would find the HGH in their common refrigerator and he would be blamed. She demanded that he take photos of the substances and change roommates. The roommate still had the photos, and he and his girlfriend gave us more than enough to suspend Schafer, who did not challenge the punishment. It was the first ever nonanalytical suspension of an athlete for the use of HGH.

But this tip on Viciedo was big. Mullin said he would report back to our superiors.

The next day, Mullin's number flashed on my cell phone screen. I was ready to tell him I had spoken to federal agents who were in contact with their counterparts in Mexico.

"Hello, Dan?" I said.

"Hi, Eddie," Mullin said, but no sooner had my name left his mouth than another voice interrupted.

I had to hold my phone away from my ear, since the voice on the other end was screaming at an ear-piercing decibel level. The screaming came courtesy of Rob Manfred.

"Dominguez, what the fuck do you think you are doing?" he bellowed. "Are you there?"

"Yes, Rob. I'm here."

"Well, maybe you want to tell me exactly what it is you think you're doing?"

"Following up on a tip."

"Don't get fucking cute with me, Dominguez. Stop whatever it is you're doing. Is that clear? Stand down!"

"Sure, Rob."

Click.

Mullin called me back right away.

"I'm sorry. It shouldn't have gone this way, but as you heard he didn't want to hear about anything we had to say," he said.

We had run straight up against Manfred and the Labor Relations Department. Dan knew me well enough to know that my spirits were crushed. Nothing was going to soften the blow, however, and it was only the first of many disappointments to come.

As for Viciedo, he played five years in the majors with the White Sox, putting up modest numbers during his three full seasons. He became a free agent in 2015 and then signed to play for the Chunichi Dragons in Japan.

CHAPTER 7

PLAYER TRAFFICKING

During my tenure with DOI, I was in charge of all investigations that dealt with Cuban players—from age and ID fraud to the basic elements of human trafficking. In 2009, I had the opportunity to investigate the case of Felix Perez, a little-known Cuban player who had escaped Cuba, ended up in the Dominican Republic, and who had eventually been signed by the Yankees.

Along the way, as he was trying to get his visa to travel to the United States, his story unraveled. I was able to interview him and get him to tell me the truth.

It was a harrowing tale, to say the least.

Perez said he had left Cuba at 1:30 in the morning one day in the early spring of 2008, along with two other players, Juan Carlos Moreno and Yenier Corbalan. They waded into the ocean up to their necks and waited for a cell phone call. The call came, and they were told to swim toward a flashlight. They boarded a midsized speedboat that held seventeen other Cuban defectors and a young Mexican boat captain. They set out to sea and traveled until they ran out of gas. Then they waited six to eight hours for another boat.

They cruised for three days before arriving fifty miles off the coast of Puerto Aventuras, Mexico, where they were transferred to a yacht. Perez said they had hidden in a compartment in the base of the boat to avoid Mexican coast guard authorities. Once they reached land, they were transported to a farmhouse where they were kept until their agents, or *buscones*, claimed them. He said they had been fed and given a place to sleep but not allowed to leave the house for fear they might flee. He said that the "mafia" group that ran the operation consisted of Cubans and Mexicans and that they were also engaged in trafficking drugs and arms.

Perez and the other players waited for a month until a *buscón*/agent named Juan Delemos, a Dominican lawyer who had recently become involved in the *buscón* business, came to Mexico to take a look at them. Perez was thin and nervous and said he had worn three shirts under his baseball jersey so he would look bigger when he put on a mini-showcase for Delemos. According to Perez, Delemos was in contact with Manuel Ascona in the Dominican Republic. Ascona was like a comic book character, a well-known, Cuban-born, self-admitted player trafficker who had contracted his crew to get Perez and other players out of Cuba. Ascona had convinced Delemos to take a look at the Cuban players in Mexico, and Delemos was confident, after seeing Perez and the two other players, that this would be a good investment. It helped that Ascona had convinced the three players to give Delemos 50 percent of their signing bonuses in exchange for getting them out of Mexico.

Ascona provided the players with Costa Rican passports and Delemos accompanied them on a flight from Cancún through Panama and on to Santo Domingo, DR. Ascona was waiting for them at the Las Américas International Airport and took them to a house in Santiago where they were all kept and continued to train.

Ascona then introduced Perez to Jaime Torres, who, along with Bartolo Hernandez, was a top agent to Cuban players. In a later conversation during the investigation, Delemos told me that after agreeing to the deal with Ascona, he had found out that Ascona had agreed to a similar deal with a businessman named Tomás Collado involving the same three players. Collado, a used-car salesman who owned Cefisa Motors in Santiago, DR, was also new to the *buscón* business. Delemos described Ascona as a "snake" but teamed up with him nonetheless. Collado and Delemos supplied players with room, board, training, and loans that they agreed to repay once they signed with a major-league club. I found Ascona to be a snake, too, although an interesting one. I interviewed him during the Perez investigation, and he told me some crazy stories. He claimed that he had traveled to Cuba himself to get players and had been arrested. During one of his interrogations, he said, a Cuban soldier had asked him what players he was targeting to take back. "All of them," he said he told the soldier. "If the bearded guy could still play first, I'd take him, too."

Perez hadn't played on the Cuban national team, so not many MLB teams knew his background and Ascona was able to persuade him to change his age from twenty-three to nineteen. Perez said that he didn't know who had been responsible for falsifying his Cuban passport, which I found hard to believe since Ascona told me he had discussed the change in age with Perez and that most everyone involved knew about it. He said that he hadn't seen the actual passport until it was handed to him by Collado so that Perez could show it to Martin Valerio, who was then the director of the Yankees' DR complex. After looking at the passport, Perez said, that was when he knew that the year of his birth had been changed from 11-12-1984 to 11-12-1988.

Torres showcased Perez to teams, and he ended up signing with the Yankees for $3.5 million.

Before Perez went to the US Embassy in the Dominican Republic to apply for a visa, MLB's DR office's lead investigator,

Arlina Espaillat Matos, conducted a residency investigation on Perez as part of the limited investigations the office did on Cuban players. Espaillat was a Dominican lawyer and childhood friend of Rafael Perez, the DR office's original administrator, and soon after DOI came on board we discovered that many of Espaillat's investigations of Dominican and Cuban players had been rubber-stamped or, at a minimum, poorly executed. It was apparent that many if not all of the investigations would have to be conducted again.

Before the DOI was created, the DR office conducted age/ID fraud investigations on Dominican players but not Cuban players, and we would later take on that task. The office investigators' main mission was to make sure that Cuban players had properly established residency in a country other than Cuba or the United States. By this I mean that they merely contacted the country of residency and its immigration department and determined whether the residency document was a true and original copy, and never looked into how it was obtained. That issue would become a key charge in the Miami human-trafficking case.

Espaillat's investigation determined that Perez had legally obtained his residency, but Valerio, who had been made aware of what DOI had found out about Espaillat's investigations, requested that the DR office conduct a second investigation.

By then the DR office was feeling the heat from MLB because of all the corruption DOI was uncovering. Ronaldo Peralta, who had become the head of the office, authorized a second investigation, and the new investigator started asking Perez more pointed questions.

Perez told the new investigator how he had been taken out of Cuba by boat by a Mexican gang and been stripped of his original ID document and held in an apartment with other Cuban baseball players. US Embassy officials who began working on Perez's visa request confirmed that the passport he had presented to them was a false document. At that point Valerio called me and asked DOI to get involved. Perez was hesitant to talk at first, but he eventually told us the whole sordid story about his journey, his passport, and all the people involved. We forwarded our report to the embassy and told the officials there that Perez would come in and cooperate fully. They offered him leniency and another chance in exchange for his cooperation. He agreed and eventually obtained another visa.

MLB's concern in Perez's case—or any other case that involved Cuban players—was never the conditions the player faced as he tried to get into the United States, whether his passport was falsified, or how he had gone about getting his residency, only whether his residency was "legal."

I was contacted by FBI agent Hector Ortiz late in 2013 about trafficking of Cuban players in general and a situation in Haiti in which six Cuban players had been detained because of visa issues, a group that would become known as the Haitian Six. I had met Ortiz, a fellow Cuban, in Boston and at a dinner in DC, where we had both received awards, and he wanted to set up a meeting among me, the US Attorney's Office in Miami, and FBI and ICE agents concerning what I knew about MLB's involvement in how residencies were obtained in various countries.

I agreed to the meeting and communicated the information to Mullin, who reported it to Manfred and Halem. They assigned Labor Relations Department attorney Patrick Houlihan to handle the situation, and he told me not to talk to anyone from the prosecutor's office before speaking with lawyers from the Miami-based firm of Kobre & Kim. I was to meet with attorneys Matthew Menchel and Adriana Riviere-Badell to discuss my involvement.

I flew to Miami and located Kobre & Kim's office downtown. The place had a clean, contemporary look, and after being greeted by a secretary, I took a seat and waited. After a few minutes, Adriana appeared and we moved to a conference room in the front of the office, near the secretary's desk. I was apprehensive about how she might interview me, but in the back of my mind I already knew how it was going to go. She simply asked me to tell her about my dealings with Cuban players, so I explained my duties for MLB, which were to confirm a Cuban player's residency in a country other than Cuba or the United States. All I was required to do was check with the immigration officials of the country of residency to make sure that the player's residency documents were authentic.

I then purposely pushed my luck by telling her that if I had been allowed to dig further into how those residencies were obtained, I would have certainly found that they had been obtained fraudulently. She stopped writing, looked up, and made it very clear that I should stick to describing my official duties and not offer my opinions or beliefs. The trial balloon thus popped, I decided not to share any of my thoughts, including on the Viciedo case, or any of the information I had accumulated from sources and reports that led me to believe that MLB teams were conspiring with human traffickers to bring specific players out of Cuba. I have no regrets about that decision, because if I had told all that I knew, MLB would certainly have known what I was intending to disclose to authorities after baseball let me go.

The second meeting, in early 2014, was on the same day we were to go to the US Attorney's Office. Menchel and Riviere-Badell were both present, and I now understood that they wanted me to tell the authorities only what they wanted me to tell them. I was to follow their lead throughout the interview. It wasn't hard to see that they were there to make sure I didn't leak any information that would cause problems for MLB. I was told flat out not to answer any question unless they directed me to.

As we walked over to the US Attorney's Office, I had a sick feeling in my stomach. The thought had crossed my mind that here was the chance to blow up this trafficking thing. If in the middle of this interview I just started telling the prosecutor everything I knew, two things would happen: Menchel and Riviere-Badell would have ministrokes, and I would be fired not ten minutes after they called 245 Park Avenue. Neither the ministrokes nor the firing would bother me, but I kept thinking of Mullin and Hanna, who still thought we would weather the storm. I don't have many regrets, but the choice not to simply keep talking after the first question was asked is one of them.

At the US Attorney's Office, I was met by Ron Davidson, the prosecutor assigned to the case, Ortiz, and ICE agent Albert Ordonez, the investigators involved. For the first time in my life I felt like a defendant, though one who was muzzled. Menchel and Riviere-Badell answered most of the questions on behalf of MLB, and allowed me to answer only when they deemed it appropriate. When it was over, I felt dirty. There was so much more I wanted to say, but MLB and its hired guns wouldn't allow me to. As I drove back to my condo in Delray Beach, I kept second-guessing myself: I should have blown it up but didn't. I called Mullin and Hanna and told them what had happened. I could sense that they both breathed a sigh of relief. George, who had been physically ill over what had happened throughout the Biogenesis investigation, was silent during the call. He was a man never at a loss for words, and I could almost hear his thought: if this crazy Cuban had said everything he wanted to say, all of us would've lost our jobs. I should have done it.

The next day, I sent Hector Ortiz, the FBI agent, the following text message: "Hector it was nice seeing you yesterday and I'm sorry it was under those awkward circumstances. When this is all over let's have a beer."

The beer would have to wait until I was fired from MLB in April 2014. I spoke with Ortiz and immediately agreed to meet the investigators and the prosecutors. It was a relief to unburden myself. I was finally going to tell Ortiz and the US Attorney's Office all I knew about the Cuban players, human trafficking, and MLB.

Davidson sent my lawyer, Tom Frongillo, a subpoena, and we met in my lawyer's Boston office. This time I turned over documents, including my reports from the Viciedo case, and a report I had entered into the DOI case management system concerning information I had received from Halem in 2012. Halem said he had received a phone call from an owner telling him that an agent for the prized Cuban right fielder Yasiel Puig had contacted his staff and offered them Puig's services if the team fronted the agent $500,000. That, much like the Viciedo case, would have circumvented MLB's free agency rules governing Cuban players, who were supposed to establish residency in a country other than Cuba or the United States before they could enter MLB's free agent market. Puig, who ended up signing a seven-year, $42 million deal with the Dodgers in June 2012, had tried repeatedly to defect from Cuba, and had been embroiled in all kinds of troubles surrounding his defection at the hands of smugglers and Mexican cartel members. I immediately opened a case on the Puig situation in the DOI's case management file but was told by Halem to forget about it once Puig was declared eligible to sign as a free agent. In 2015, a South Florida businessman named Gilberto Suarez, whom Puig had paid $2.5 million to help get him across the Mexico border to the United States, pleaded guilty to violating immigration laws and was sentenced to house arrest and one month in jail.

I told the US Attorney's Office everything I knew.

Ortiz was very excited and told me that the investigation had stalled and that the end goal was to indict anyone associated with the smugglers. A few months after that conversation, Ortiz, Ron

Davidson, and ICE agent Albert Ordonez flew up to Boston, and we met at Frongillo's office overlooking the Boston skyline and Boston Harbor.

I told them that I had informed MLB that its rules governing Cuban players were crazy and that all they led to was corruption on the part of the trainers, agents, and smugglers.

Ortiz, Ordonez, and Davidson were all very interested not only in what I had to say but also in the documents I supplied them, especially since MLB had not submitted many of those documents to the US Attorney's Office in answer to subpoenas sent to them.

Ortiz said that the case, which by now had been in limbo for more than two years, needed a jump start and that my information would help do just that. He also told me that Davidson was doing a great job but they were trying to get Miami assistant US attorney Michael "Pat" Sullivan—who had also prosecuted the Biogenesis case—involved in the investigation.

Sullivan was highly respected and extremely capable. A decorated career prosecutor, he was recognized as one of the best in the country. The case would be the last of his illustrious career.

On February 11, 2016, Bartolo "Bart" Hernandez, an MLBPA-approved agent who represented the vast majority of Cuban-born players who managed to escape the country by boat, was indicted by the US Attorney's Office in Miami on one count of conspiracy to encourage and induce an alien to enter the United States and one count of bringing an alien into the United States for the purpose of private financial gain.

The indictment was superseded two months later, and Hernandez, along with two accomplices, Amin Latouf and Julio Estrada, were charged with one count of conspiracy to commit an offense against the United States and three counts of bringing an alien into the country.

All told, Hernandez was looking at maximum penalties of ten years for the two conspiracy charges and forty years for the four counts of bringing an alien into the United States.

As the trial approached, I was prepped several times, by Sullivan and others, and I have to say, the feeling was strange. For almost twenty-nine years I had been prepped by assistant district attorneys and assistant US attorneys, but that was when I was in law enforcement. The old saying "Once you're gone you're gone" applies to law enforcement in an almost blinding way. I was no longer in the inner circle. When they huddled and talked about what I had just told them, I, of course, wasn't included in the huddle. When they walked me out of the FBI satellite office they waved good-bye as if I were a civilian, which I now was. I understood it, but it was a strange feeling.

Issues also arose concerning my meeting with the feds prior to being fired from MLB and the fact that I had spoken to law enforcement in the shadow of attorneys who had instructed me to only answer questions they approved. Pat Sullivan feared that Bart's lawyers would ask why I hadn't told the US Attorney's Office about this information back in late 2013, early 2014.

The day came, Friday, February 3, 2017, when I would testify in the Bart Hernandez case. A few months before, the Manhattan DA's office had sent police officers to my house in what I believed was an effort by MLB to sully my credibility, not to mention intimidate me.

I had weathered that storm, and now it was time. I wasn't looking forward to testifying against Hernandez for many reasons. First of all, I believed that MLB's rules had left Bart and all other agents involved with Cuban players in a no-win situation, and I believed that everyone who had conspired with the traffickers should be the ones being prosecuted. To achieve that outcome, however, somebody would have to cooperate, and that somebody would have to be Bart Hernandez. The prosecution had almost convinced Bart to cooperate—until he obtained new counsel and abruptly decided not to.

Without Hernandez, or a middleman like him, you have nothing. The traffickers deal with the agents, who in turn deal with the MLB teams. When MLB first heard about the ongoing Cuban trafficking case, I remember that Dan Mullin's phone began ringing off the hook—teams' general counsels were wondering what the feds were really looking into. MLB has said in the past that it fully cooperated with authorities in this case and that it was not a target. I believe neither of those statements.

There is no question that some unsavory details emerged in the trial involving Hernandez and Estrada. Though they claimed they had simply been helping players prepare for tryouts and negotiate contracts through a process that had been accepted by the US Treasury Department and MLB, prosecutors said that players were victimized by thugs such as Joan "Nacho" Garcia, an ex-con who had been kidnapped and murdered in 2009. I had never met Nacho. I had heard his name but had never been allowed to investigate him. Word was that he was one of the traffickers murdered as a result of a battle over White Sox player Jose Abreu between Nacho and the trafficker who had taken over for him. Months later, Ortiz would process four suspects who had been arrested for Nacho's murder.

What only emphasized the dark and troubling nature of the case was the testimony of one player's wife who was told that her husband would be chopped up and sent to her in a box if he fled Cancún and signed with somebody else.

Hernandez and Estrada were portrayed in the trial as the masterminds behind what prosecutors called "The Plan," in which Cuban ballplayers moved through an underground pipeline via third-country way stations onward across the US border. Fraud was integral to the plot because the US embargo of Cuba and immigration laws had to be circumvented to convert the Cubans into free agents eligible to negotiate with teams so they could sign lucrative contracts.[1]

But to be honest, I wasn't interested in seeing Hernandez go to jail. Bart and people like him are the direct result of baseball's rules governing Cuban players signing as free agents with MLB teams and MLB's decision to willfully ignore the human-trafficking aspect of signing Cubans. As Mullin and I had warned our bosses in 2009, when I had gotten involved in the Perez matter, MLB rules governing Cubans led to corruption. I had even spoken to Hernandez about it and asked if he would speak to Selig, Manfred, or Halem about those issues. He had said he would. Whether he meant it or not, only he knows. If you took away free agency for Cubans, they would have to enter the United States, go through the immigration process, and then enter baseball as drafted ballplayers. I understand that smugglers would still be involved, but the payoffs to government officials and the fraud committed to obtain residency in a third country outside of the United States and Cuba would be eliminated. MLB would surely counter by saying it would have to bargain such changes with the Players Association. So what? Bargain. I'm sure there could be a happy medium. After the Viciedo case I never got the green light to fully investigate Cuban traffickers. Manfred's words the day he called concerning Viciedo were clear to Mullin and me: Stand down. When it comes to Cuban players, human traffickers, and all the corruption that goes with that, MLB is not interested.

I had met Bart Hernandez during the Manny Ramirez case and grown to like him. He was a hard worker who filed the paperwork required by MLB on time and correctly. I would call him often to ask him about Cuban players who worked with other agents, and he would give me as straight an answer as he could. I questioned him about players using PEDs and again he would give me answers. I was never sure if he was giving me the whole story, but that's the game you play in an investigation: you take what a source gives you and then try to corroborate the information and build your case.

As a Cuban American born in Cuba, I sympathized with all Cubans who fled, no matter how they got here. I told the prosecutors and the defense attorneys that Cuban baseball players were like prisoners who had to escape one way or another. I also argued with prosecutors about their claim that Cuban players who cross the US border illegally through Mexico have committed a crime. I testified that as far as I knew, the Cuban Adjustment Act allowed Cubans to be viewed as refugees who should be granted permanent residency once they get here. The prosecutors argued that because the players had technically entered the country illegally, their immigration status could only be adjusted after an ICE investigation. It was all semantics to me, and I let them know that.

I began testifying on that Friday, and as I walked to the stand after lunch and turned to be sworn in, I looked back toward the door to the courtroom. To my left sat Hernandez, and directly across from him on my right was Hector Ortiz. Almost as if it had been choreographed, they both winked at me. A Cuban thing for sure. We almost finished direct testimony, and the day ended.

When we reconvened on Monday, Bart's attorney Jeffrey Marcus started the cross-examination. He asked if I had a brother named Carlos Dominguez who was an attorney in Boston. I said yes, and in a cagey old lawyer's move to get my mind off the task at hand, he said, "Okay, we will touch on that later."

Toward the end he came back to the question and asked if I had given Bart my brother's number in an email. I read the email and said, "Yes." He asked sarcastically why I would have given my brother's number to Bart if I knew he was involved in human trafficking. I responded that I hadn't known Bart was involved in trafficking because I had not been given the opportunity to investigate him. I had given the number to Bart in case one of his clients needed a lawyer in Boston. But Marcus had planted the seed in the judge's and jurors' minds that I was somehow condoning Bart's involvement in human trafficking.

Since MLB was not on trial, it was not asked any questions by the prosecution. I had told Sullivan that if, in cross, the defense opened the door to questions about MLB, I was going to walk right in. I never got a chance to talk about Viciedo or the screwed-up MLB rules governing Cubans.

Hernandez was aware of how I felt about those issues, and I thought hearing me say that would have been a good out for him, but his attorney never once touched on MLB. I found that very interesting and troubling at the same time. Why didn't the lawyers try to blame MLB?

The main purpose of my testimony was to link Hernandez with his Haitian contact, Amin Latouf, and I could do that. Bart had put me in contact with Latouf so I could meet the Haitian immigration bosses who were issuing the visas to the Cuban players.

I had traveled to Haiti and visited its immigration department, which was as far as MLB wanted me to go. Sullivan and Ortiz had done some homework on Amin that they did not share with me, and they thought my putting Bart and Amin together would help their case. I wasn't sure how that would help connect the dots, but I guess it did.

During the trial I said I liked Hernandez, and I do. If not for the sketchy MLB rules he would not be in jail now. Bart probably hates me, and I don't blame him. I just wish he had turned evidence against team personnel and anyone else in MLB who was conspiring with him. I think the prosecutors are hoping they will eventually get a cooperating witness.

Hernandez's other attorney, Daniel Rashbaum, approached me months later as I was outside the courtroom awaiting Bart's sentencing and said, "I just want to tell you that of all the people who testified in this case, you were the only one that told the truth, and for that, thank you."

On March 15, 2017, Hernandez was convicted of conspiring with Estrada to deceive the US government into granting visas to two dozen Cuban ballplayers so they could sign with major-league teams. He was also convicted of bringing Leonys Martin, an outfielder who signed with Texas for $15 million in 2011, into the United States after he had been smuggled from Cuba to Mexico. He was sentenced on November 2, 2017, to almost four years in prison.[2]

Estrada was found guilty of conspiracy and three additional counts of bringing Jose Abreu, Omar Luis, and Dalier Hinojosa into the United States illegally. Abreu had signed a $68 million deal with the Chicago White Sox in 2013. Estrada got five years. Latouf remains a fugitive.

At the sentencing, US district judge Kathleen Williams said, "This case is not about the love of the game," echoing the defense team's theme during the sentencing hearing. "This case is about money."

As far as I'm concerned, truer words couldn't describe what MLB is all about.

Hector Ortiz, the FBI agent, would tell me in 2018 that the case was called Operation Sisyphus, because the prosecutors felt, at the outset, as though they were pushing a big rock up a hill for no gain.

"We knew who we were facing, and it took a while, but we finally got Bart," he said. "And we're hoping to get more."

I felt there was much more to Cuban trafficking than was ever revealed during the trial. Interestingly, the case remains open.

CHAPTER 8

BONUS SKIMMING

The problems in the Dominican Republic didn't begin with age and identity fraud or the trafficking issue, and they certainly didn't end with them.

What we unearthed in the Dominican Republic was so big and so corrupt that baseball was forced to let go of almost everyone in the MLB offices in Santo Domingo. For years, players had complained to MLB executive Lou Melendez, the head of MLB International Baseball Operations (OPS), and Joel Araujo, who worked directly under Lou in OPS, about their bonuses and tax returns being stolen, among other things. Melendez told me he had taken the complaints to his bosses in New York, where he was usually told, "You don't have enough." Melendez hired Rafael Perez, the first head of MLB's DR office, then Ronaldo Peralta, who succeeded Perez. They in turn told Melendez about complaints they received.

Sandy Alderson, a longtime baseball executive and the current GM of the Mets, was hired in 2010 by Bud Selig to reshape and overhaul how MLB handled matters in Latin America, a direct result of what the DOI was discovering. Many of the ideas Sandy recommended—and got credit for in the media—were based on what we were discovering and the formulations of Mullin, whose blueprint for reform included the registration of players at an early age to curb age/ID fraud.

Mullin took over the age/ID investigations and sent DOI investigator Nelson Tejada to oversee the existing Dominican investigative team and to analyze the process by which cases were handled. Alderson and Mullin decided that all international players should be investigated, and I was assigned to form an international team of investigators. They would conduct probes according to each country's laws, and before long, we had investigators all over the Caribbean, Latin America, Europe, and Japan.

We investigated US-born scouts working specifically in the Dominican Republic and Venezuela for corruption, and many were fired. A few were even prosecuted, including White Sox executive David Wilder and his international scout supervisor, Jorge Oquendo. Wilder, who was indicted along with Oquendo and another scout, Victor Mateo, in 2010 by an Illinois federal grand jury on mail fraud charges, was accused of getting kickbacks from the bonuses of twenty-three prospects during a four-year stretch. Wilder was sentenced to two years in prison. We investigated some scouts working in the United States as well, including one who was a bookmaker.

We uncovered many age/ID schemes, including that of Venezuelan pitcher Daniel Sanchez, who was being offered millions of dollars while passing himself off as a sixteen-year-old whose fastball was clocked in the mid-90s, when in reality he was twenty-one.

At first there were no impediments to our investigations. After all, George Mitchell had mandated that all matters that brought into question the integrity of the game be investigated in cooperation with law enforcement and with no interference from Labor.

The schemes we were looking into had been created to beat the system, to rob the poor, uneducated players of their signing bonuses. They involved MLB team personnel, including area scouts, regional scouts, international scout supervisors, assistant GMs, academy administrators and officials, DR office directors, supervisors, international operations VPs, local agents, trainers, doctors, priests, government officials, even parents.

The deeper we looked, the more we began to discover absolute corruption. We interviewed thousands of people ranging from *buscones* to employees of banks in the DR and money exchange locations in Venezuela where scouts would walk off with cash from players' bonus checks, to doctors and nurses who were injecting players with PEDs, to hospitals whose staffers were being paid off to alter birth certificates.

In many cases, all those involved would pay a family to sell their son's identity to another player. That player would move in with his new family, and the scheme would start to get complicated. The neighbors, the priest, the hospital, local government officials were all paid off, so that when an honest investigator came by they would all lie. Unless, of course, that honest investigator was also paid off.

We discovered many variations on these schemes and made headway in dismantling them, at least in the beginning. We fired several team employees, worked with law enforcement agencies internationally and in the United States, and initiated criminal investigations that sent some to jail. We worked with the Anaheim Angels, whose general manager, Tony Reagins, fired the team's international scouting director and dismantled its entire international team during that period. It took the Angels more than a year to put a scouting team back together; they basically sat out the 2009 season without drafting international players.

As time went on and Labor and MLB's international operations got more and more involved, we lost our power to pursue such cases, despite the fact that we were uncovering all kinds of corruption, including MLB players who had lied about their age and/or identity. That created problems with the Players Association and therefore problems with Labor, not to mention some bad press for MLB. Soon we were being told not to look at players who had already sneaked through the system and instead to focus on players who had yet to sign.

The outcomes of our own investigations were decided initially by the DOI supervisors, George Hanna and Dan Mullin, but that also changed with time. Labor pressed to form a committee of its own lawyers and members of the international operations team. That committee would then decide if the investigations were worth pursuing, what the final findings were, and if there would be a suspension.

The committee meetings were a joke, with all sorts of uninformed people adding their two cents' worth. Many investigations were tabled as "undetermined" or labeled as "red flags." All kinds of crap that I would hope Mitchell would've never agreed to became the norm.

One of the last schemes we uncovered before we were basically neutralized involved team scouts in Venezuela. After we had brought to light the fact that scouts were just flat-out stealing money from players' signing bonuses, they started to get trickier with their schemes.

At first a scout would just browbeat a player and his family for money by giving the kid's *buscón* a small piece of the kickback, just to keep him on the team, so to speak. But after we had many of those scouts fired, they began to change their modus operandi and would use *buscones* to negotiate for them with other *buscones* across Latin America and the Caribbean. *Buscón* is Spanish for "finder"—essentially a street agent who operates throughout the baseball business in the Dominican Republic, Venezuela, and other Latin American countries. The men refer to themselves as trainers for young prospects; they latch on to baseball prodigies as young as twelve or fourteen with the hope of grooming the next Latin superstar. They train the prospect and give him equipment, food, even lodging. When it comes time for the prospect to sign with a team, the *buscón* cashes in on the kid's bonus.

In one of the first bonus-skimming investigations we conducted, we received information from prospects Kelvin De Leon and Elio De La Rosa and their family members alleging that Yankees international scouting supervisor Carlos Rios and the team's DR scout supervisor, Ramon Valdivia, had stolen $135,000 in signing bonus money from the players, who had been signed in 2007. As in most of the cases, it was impossible to get the *buscón* who had worked with the players to testify against Rios and Valdivia, and without that testimony we had no firsthand proof that they had actually taken the money. After a lengthy investigation, we gave the Yankees the information we had gathered and the club decided to fire both of them.

Rios and Valdivia then filed lawsuits against the Yankees in the DR court system, which is notorious for corrupt litigation, and won. The Yankees were obligated to pay the remainder of Rios's contract, which ran through 2012. The team had previously settled with Valdivia.

From then on when we came across similar cases, we recommended that teams not fire the culprits but instead release them, pay them what they were owed, and move on.[1]

Once scouts began to use *buscones* to negotiate with other *buscones*, any investigation into wrongdoing would never lead back to the scout; it would stop at the *buscón*, who served as protection for the scout.

Regardless of how convoluted and difficult the schemes became, the bottom line was that we believed the scouts and the *buscones* were scamming players and their families out of huge percentages of the players' signing bonuses, sometimes leaving a player and his family with as little as 25 percent of the bonus. The families we visited were happy to get whatever they could. After all, many lived in one- or two-room cinder-block huts with tin roofs, mud floors, and no running water. You would see a player's mother walking barefoot with a broomstick slung over her shoulders holding buckets of water to take to the house.

I took my findings about various schemes involving *buscones* and scouts to Mullin, who by then had had to hand everything over to Labor and International Ops. Much to our chagrin, MLB decided to bring our investigation to light at the next OPS meeting. The only action taken was that the teams were told that this type of activity would be frowned upon in the future and that they would be punished if they continued—a mere slap on the wrist for what continues to be a massive problem for MLB, one that arose again in 2017 and resulted in a lifetime ban for one of baseball's rising stars, former Braves general manager John Coppolella, and a one-year suspension for longtime executive Gordon Blakeley, a Braves special assistant.

Manfred issued a lengthy statement detailing MLB's findings during the investigation, but basically the Braves were charged with major infractions in the international free-agent market, most notably circumventing signing rules by signing players to bonuses lower than what the club had agreed to pay. "As a result of the 2015–16 circumvention, the Braves were able to sign nine high-value players during the 2016–17 signing period who would have been unavailable to them had the club accurately accounted for its signings during the 2015–16 signing period," he said in a statement announcing the Braves' punishment.[2]

He added that the investigation had also determined that the Braves had agreed to sign six players to inflated signing bonuses pursuant to an agreement with prospect Robert Puason's agent in exchange for a commitment that Puason would sign with the team in the 2019–20 signing period. The Braves offered another prospect extra compensation in order to remedy those violations. In other words, they were reserving a star player for the future. Regarding the six prospects' inflated compensation, it's industrywide knowledge that those six players were not worth what the Braves were paying, an automatic red flag for a *buscón* who has an up-and-coming star player like Puason.

These types of MLB rule violations occur every year, and not all teams get punished. I question whether the investigators looked into the possibility that the scouts involved had received a kickback from Puason's *buscón*, a practice we saw often when we were conducting our investigations. The agents and *buscones* I still speak to say it hasn't slowed down.

For their sins, Manfred said the Braves would also forfeit rights to thirteen international prospects, would be prohibited from signing any international player for more than $10,000 during the 2019–20 signing period, and would be restricted from signing players in the next two signing periods for contracts with bonuses greater than $300,000.

In my opinion, of course, all that could have been avoided had we been allowed to follow Mitchell's instructions and pursue our investigations with no interference from Labor and the others who weren't particularly interested in reform.

The information we gathered on MLB teams that were cheating and cutting corners on signing players in violation of MLB rules was extensive, the abuses were rampant, and we reported many to MLB. Some were handled by the Labor Relations Department; others weren't handled at all.

I thought many of the violations we uncovered were nothing short of shocking. We went to the developmental academies sponsored by MLB's teams and gave presentations to the players to try to show them that we were there to stop the unethical behavior infesting their game. We were told by many players that they had complained for years to those in charge before our arrival about bonus kickbacks, stolen tax returns, even PED injections being forced upon them. Nothing was ever done.

In November 2008, I had received a call from two Venezuelan players who claimed that a woman by the name of Virginia Pacheco had filled out their US tax returns and that they had been waiting for their refund money for several years. They were the first of dozens and dozens of Venezuelan and Dominican players who would contact me and tell me that for years they had complained to no avail to the MLB DR office about Pacheco taking their refunds. Pacheco had been childhood friends with Rafael Perez and Ronaldo Peralta, the two men who had run the MLB Dominican office prior to Alderson taking the post in 2010, and had been given the job, along with Arlina Espaillat, of handling players' tax returns and refunds.

Before 2007, international players would pay taxes from their signing bonuses to the IRS, but if a player did not travel to the United States during the year he received his bonus and his tax return showed that he had stayed in his country of origin, the IRS would refund the taxes that had been taken out. In 2007, before the formation of the DOI, the MLB DR office had come to an agreement with the IRS that international players' signing bonuses would not be taxed unless and until the players traveled to the United States.

I contacted Pacheco, who told me that she had been preparing tax returns for MLB players in the Dominican Republic and Venezuela since 2001, nearly four thousand in that time span. Through the many interviews we conducted, we found out that she had stolen part or in some cases all of the players' tax refunds by using several different schemes.

At first, Pacheco blamed the missing money on delays caused

by the IRS, but after several interviews, she admitted that she had cashed and kept the refunds of four Venezuelan players, along with those of nine players who were still with major league teams and playing in the United States. She told us she had gotten a call a couple of years before from an IRS investigator who told her he suspected she was assisting players with tax evasion, but she said she had gotten the agency to back off by taking some advice from an IRS supervisor she had befriended in Puerto Rico. She declined to say what that advice was.

Pacheco realized that she had given us information that might cause her another problem with the IRS and asked if she could cooperate with us. She told us that there were scouts and *buscones* who were tampering with players' bonuses, that players were victims of loan sharking and age fraud, and that one player who was then in the pros was using a completely fictional name. She detailed corruption that had gone on at the highest levels of the Dominican Republic's MLB office for years.

We investigated all the allegations and were able to prove only some of them, since many went back years. All of our investigations and findings were documented and reported back to 245 Park Avenue.

Pacheco had asked us to come to her with any questions we had about her before we went to authorities. We told her we would give her a chance to explain herself after we finished the investigation and before we went to the authorities. We then turned our findings over to IRS agent Harlan Daar, who used the evidence to build a case against Pacheco that would then be presented to a US Attorney's Office for prosecution.

Dan Halem insisted on taking the case to a college friend of his by the name of Andrew Levi, who was at the time an assistant US attorney in Miami. Levi would end up declining to prosecute the case, citing a host of problems with it, including the relatively small amount of money involved compared to what the Miami office generally dealt with, the length of time that had passed since the alleged crimes had occurred, and potential problems with getting players to cooperate. Both Agent Daar and AUSA Levi said it would be tough to get approval to prosecute the case since the amount would be the lowest ever prosecuted by the IRS in the Southern District of Florida.

Never mind that Pacheco had abused the trust of young ballplayers for years and that many of the players had reported her actions to the MLB DR office, to no avail. The Pacheco case was the beginning of an insurmountable number of issues we would deal with in the Dominican Republic and Venezuela, many of which were simply shelved by MLB. We tried our best to correct those problems. Unfortunately, our bosses weren't always interested.

What fascinates me about the so-called revamped DOI of today is that when we were there, we were swamped with work, often carrying out twenty, thirty, forty investigations at any given time. Not a day went by that we didn't solve five cases and have ten more added to our plate. When MLB terminated us, they got rid of the two top guys, Dan Mullin and George Hanna, along with the two senior investigators, Tom Reilly and myself, and Nancy Zamudio, the lead assistant, and replaced us with one assistant US attorney with no field investigative experience. Dan, George, Tom, and I had more than one hundred years of combined investigative experience, and they covered that with one former prosecutor, Bryan Seeley, who was hired in September 2014. In a somewhat amusing side note, *USA Today* Sports published a "100 Most Powerful People in MLB" list in April 2017 that listed Seeley as number 17, albeit with his first name misspelled. In a less-than-amusing reference, at least to me, Seeley was credited in the *USA Today* story as follows: "In 2014, [Seeley] led the investigative unit that exposed the Biogenesis doping scandal— one of the most extensive drug investigations in sports history—

that resulted in 14 player suspensions."[3] Biogenesis, of course, had long been resolved by the time Seeley came aboard.

While we were still in operation, we sought out corruption, developed informants, worked with law enforcement agencies at home and abroad, and received constant vital information that we acted upon.

I am told that the DOI now primarily reacts to problems as they are about to become public and does little or no proactive investigating. Sure, it investigated the Braves and suspended some high-ranking officials, and I'm sure it will suspend or fire many of the international team members, but do you think for one second that scouts are no longer stealing money from players or conspiring to change a player's age?

I recently spoke to an agent who has been in the business for years, and he told me that the corruption in the Caribbean and Latin and South America is worse than ever.

Beyond the corruption issues, one of the biggest problems we encountered during our trips to Venezuela was and still is the kidnapping epidemic. Players of any renown, and their families and associates, become targets of kidnappers.

Joel Rengifo, one of the most respected and well-connected law enforcement officials in Venezuela, became an RSA for baseball in that country before Mullin hired him full-time upon my recommendation and MLB's approval. Rengifo had established an antikidnapping unit in the country and became well known in MLB circles when he directed the rescue of the mother of former pitcher Ugueth Urbina—a harrowing operation that led him and his unit into the deep jungles of southern Venezuela and culminated with a gunfight between Rengifo's group and the kidnappers.

Late in 2011, I got a call from Joel saying he had been tipped off to the kidnapping of Washington Nationals catcher Wilson Ramos.

Joel had contacts throughout the country, and while he was watching a baseball game in Caracas on the night of November 9, he got word that Ramos had been abducted in his hometown of Valencia, west of Caracas, the country's capital and Joel's base. Joel immediately mobilized, and a frenetic seventy-two hours followed, during which I was working the phones in the United States as the point person between Joel—who was providing me with updates every couple hours—and all of Ramos's circle. That included calling the Nationals and GM Mike Rizzo, as well as Ramos's agent, Fernando Cuza, and of course relaying information to George and Dan. George wanted me to get onto a plane to Venezuela immediately, and I had to talk him off the ledge several times.

"By the time I get on a plane, fly there, and get acclimated, the case will be over," I kept saying. "We have the right guy leading the investigation."

Ramos was ultimately rescued two days later in a remote mountainous region south of Valencia, where he was being held in a dirty barn. The kidnappers made a dumb mistake, using the same cell phones they had used in a separate kidnapping, right before Ramos's abduction. Joel and other authorities were able to trace the phones and found Ramos. There were several arrests of the Colombian and Venezuelan gang members behind the ordeal.

Ramos, who was not physically harmed, was thankful to be alive. The police and the kidnappers had exchanged fire in the remote mountainous area where he was being held, and the final moments had been hair-raising.[4]

Our work in that country went a long way toward mitigating the dangers players from Venezuela face. Unfortunately, the country's political instability has only deteriorated, which hasn't improved matters at all.

CHAPTER 9

THE EARLY SHOCKS OF BIOGENESIS

There was a reason that the phrase "Manny being Manny" was permanently attached to Manny Ramirez.

By the time he signed with the Red Sox as a free agent in the winter of 2000, my second year as a team RSA, he was already a feared slugger who had helped propel the Indians to two World Series appearances (1995 and '97). When he came to Beantown, Manny brought his big bat—and a whole lot of odd behavior. He was a strange duck, to say the least, but somehow we got along, and Manny respected me. The entire time he was in Boston—including in 2004, when Manny, Ortiz, Pedro, and the rest of the wild bunch of Red Sox players won the club's first World Series title since 1918—there was always a mixture of aloofness, great talent, and eccentric behavior coming from the Dominican-born Washington Heights high school legend.[1]

Manny was so absentminded that he would shuffle out of Fenway Park after a game and forget that he had left his six-year-old son in the clubhouse. He would often leave tens of thousands of dollars in cash and checks in his locker or lose track of his diamond earrings. Once he crouched in the infield dirt looking for an earring during a rehab game. Another time he left in the middle of a game at

Fenway to relieve himself inside the stadium's famed left-field wall, the Green Monster.

I'll never forget one exchange between us early in Manny's first year in Boston. The Red Sox were in New York to play the Yankees for the first time that season. It was at the old Yankee Stadium; the visiting clubhouse was packed with media—no shock there—and you literally could not make your way from one end of the locker room to the other. But one Sox player, Manny, was biding his time in the bathroom, where he could conveniently avoid reporters. I went in to use the bathroom, and Manny stopped me to talk. We had been introduced but hadn't had any conversations of length.

"Dominguez, I would give the Red Sox back every penny if they would just let me go back to Cleveland," he told me in Spanish. "Too much press. Too much pressure. I just want to play baseball. I want no part of this madness with all these media people. I just want to be left alone."

Later during his Sox tenure, Manny asked me to help him with the security system in his apartment atop the Ritz-Carlton in Boston, and he would frequently approach me with issues he had on and off the field.

Eventually he wore out his welcome in Boston, and in 2008 he got shipped to the Dodgers to play for Joe Torre, who had managed the Yankees during the heyday of the drama between the Red Sox and Yanks, with Manny smack in the middle of the action. But in 2009, he was in the spotlight for the wrong reason: suspended by baseball for doping. It was the Dominican slugger's first time being punished for PEDs. Manny got hit with a fifty-game ban, which came as a result of what a *Daily News* report said was "documentary evidence" of his use of a female fertility drug—hCG, or human chorionic gonadotropin. Male athletes cycling off steroids are known to use hCG to bolster testosterone production.

I felt as if I had established a decent relationship with Manny in Boston and that I should be the DOI member to interview him in the wake of the positive test. Manny trusted me, and I knew I could get him to confide in me and perhaps reveal some valuable information, such as where he was getting his drugs or who was his supplier. The BALCO doping scandal had taken place in the early part of my RSA days and pre-DOI, and had involved no real baseball investigation, so this was an opportunity to dig into the performance-enhancing drug issue.

George Hanna was assigning cases for DOI, but when I told him of my interest in taking on the Ramirez case, I was immediately stonewalled. George said DOI was forbidden to interview forty-man-roster players unless we made a request in writing and submitted it to the Labor Relations Department. Labor would then contact the player, his agent, and the Players Association before deciding if we could proceed. It was a blatant 180-degree turn from what I believed the Mitchell Report had recommended. I understood that because of the collective bargaining agreement between MLB and the Players Association we had to ask permission to interview roster players but I also believed we should be advised of when a player tested positive and apprised of what the player's defense was. "Unless there are compelling individual circumstances to the contrary, the Department of Investigations, once established, should promptly seek to interview any player about whom allegations are received of performance enhancing substance violations and insist upon full cooperation," Mitchell wrote.[2] The DOI was just over a year old, and already our independence was under attack. Mullin and Hanna agreed with me and understood my frustration, but Manfred and Dan Halem were standing firm.

That was the first of many times I questioned my decision to leave the Boston PD for the DOI. It seemed as though the DOI was headed toward handling investigations the same way I had seen MLB security operate before the DOI—not very effectively. I thought back to the executive's warning: you're not wanted. I repeatedly kept after George to let me interview Manny in 2009, after his suspension was announced. I was told the same thing each time: Labor says no.

Years later Mullin explained to me that Halem had told him that Manny and his agent, the powerful Scott Boras, were ready to present a defense during his appeal that would include Manny's saying he had used his uncle's shaving cream, which he claimed contained testosterone. In 2014, a *Newsday* report outlined a similar claim: According to two sources, Anthony Bosch told federal agents during the Biogenesis investigation that Boras had arranged a meeting with him after Ramirez's positive test. Bosch said Boras came up with the alibi that Manny had used an "elderly uncle's testosterone cream" because Manny thought it was aftershave.

After the *Newsday* story, Boras issued a statement that said, in part, that he had never met Anthony Bosch and that he had never conducted any meetings with Bosch.[3]

The MLB Players Association had told Manfred and the Labor boys that Boras had even conducted a test on the alleged uncle's shaving cream and that it had come back positive for testosterone. Labor knew that Manny's testosterone level was at least three times as high as the reported shaving cream levels and shared that information with the Players Association, which withdrew Manny's appeal.

Anthony Bosch's father's name surfaced in several media reports as being linked to Manny right after Manny's suspension came down. Dr. Pedro Bosch, a Cuban-born physician who practiced in the Miami area, was reportedly treating Manny. The Biogenesis scandal wouldn't explode until four years later, in 2013, but I still think that had I been able to talk with Manny in 2009, we might have gotten to Anthony Bosch, the more infamous of the two Bosch men, a whole lot sooner. But in 2009, we had minimal evidence and information to go on, and Pedro Bosch denied having Manny as a patient, much less prescribing him drugs of any kind, as had been reported by ESPN. Pedro Bosch also denied being the subject of a DEA probe that also included his son and called the allegations by ESPN slanderous. "I consider the allegations of ESPN outrageous and slanderous, and issue this statement to correct the misrepresentations made by ESPN," he said. "First, Manny Ramirez is not, nor has he ever been my patient. I have never prescribed drugs of any kind whatsoever to Mr. Ramirez. Second, in my thirty-three years of practicing medicine in Coral Gables, Florida, I have never prescribed hCG, not to Mr. Manny Ramirez nor to anyone else."[4]

The problem with Pedro Bosch's denials was that the MLB Public Relations Department had issued a statement confirming that we were cooperating with the DEA regarding Dr. Bosch. Granted, it was an administrative review of the doctor—we didn't have enough for it to open a full-blown investigation. A federal agency like the DEA picks and chooses which cases it will pursue, and if the information any field office receives doesn't meet its criteria for opening an investigation, it ain't going to happen.

As the Biogenesis case unwound years later, Anthony Bosch would admit under oath that he had indeed given performance-enhancing drugs to Ramirez in 2009, but all we had then for Pedro and his son was scant evidence, a lot of rumors and media reports. Again, had I been given the opportunity to talk with Manny then, I like to think it would have been a different story. It's tough to investigate when you are refused access to the evidence.

Three years later, we would run into another frustrating case, this one involving the questionable administration by medical and training staffs of the pain reliever Toradol, a powerful nonsteroidal anti-inflammatory drug that had become wildly popular among professional football and baseball players trying to stay on the field by masking pain. Toradol comes with a black box warning from the FDA. Pharmaceutical companies are required to include a bold black box warning about the possibility of serious side effects on the packaging of a product.

In the spring of 2012, we got word through former Red Sox medical director Dr. Thomas Gill that trainer and physical therapist Mike Reinold was regularly injecting players with Toradol. Although Toradol was not a banned substance under the MLB drug agreement, Reinold might well have run afoul of state law because only doctors can administer injections in Massachusetts.

We launched an investigation into the Red Sox' medical practices on April 2 at the request of Dr. Gary Green, MLB's medical director, who had received the complaint from Dr. Gill. We discovered that the team had given Reinold final decision-making authority for player medical matters.

We found out that Toradol had become widely abused in baseball and that Reinold was indeed injecting the Red Sox pitchers with the drug prior to every start and had been for several years. Through our investigations we determined that it was common for teams and players to take advantage of vague rules and standards—until they got caught or were seriously challenged, when they would say they hadn't known they were doing anything wrong.

Dr. Gill, the team's medical director until 2011, told us that he had witnessed Reinold injecting a pitcher in the equipment area closet and that he had not prescribed the injection. Former Red Sox head physical therapist Scott Waugh told us he had seen Reinold inject the Red Sox starters in the equipment closet using the equipment trunk as a table. Reinold would inject the players with a 25-gauge needle before every start.

Gill admitted to having occasionally injected some starting pitchers with Toradol but said he had never injected a relief pitcher because the injections should be given only once every five to seven days. He said he thought he might have objected to injecting pitchers before every start and would have at least explained the risks and benefits associated with that level of usage.

I reported what we had found to MLB and noted that Gill had stepped down after the 2011 season—he had been told that he wouldn't be retained—and that Waugh and strength and conditioning coach Dave Page had been fired, too. I also noted that I was unsure about why Gill hadn't reported the incidents while he was still with the team.

We interviewed Reinold in June. Accompanied by his attorney, Daniel Cloherty, Reinold claimed that in 2011 he had injected players with Toradol under the direction of Dr. Gill. His attorney pointed out that under Massachusetts Law 243 CMR 2.07 SGI, a doctor can delegate another trained individual to administer an injection. Reinold claimed that Dr. Gill, his nurse, Sheryl Hassett, and former Red Sox athletic trainer Paul Lessard had shown him how to administer an injection. Reinold told us there was no longer a Red Sox medical director and that he had always answered to the team doctor on clinical matters and to the front office on other matters. He said that he had never injected anyone in a bathroom or an equipment room.

I then interviewed Dr. Gill and Sheryl Hassett, both of whom denied ever having trained Reinold on how to administer an injection. Gill said that he had never given permission to or instructed Reinold to inject anyone. Hassett showed me documents detailing a plan that she and Gill had proposed concerning medical matters. The plan included forms that would be sent to team doctors in the cities to which the Red Sox would be traveling, asking them to administer any medication that needed to be given to players. They also suggested that a safe be installed to store medication at Fenway Park. Gill and Hassett said they were told that the Red Sox did not need to make any changes.

On July 2, 2012, Dr. Gary Green interviewed Paul Lessard, who had been replaced by Reinold, and wrote to me that there were real discrepancies between Gill's and Reinold's versions of whether Dr. Gill had authorized the Toradol injections and that it would take a great deal of effort to sort out what had actually happened. He agreed to leave it up to the DOI and Dan Halem how to proceed, adding that he would be happy to participate in whatever was decided.

I recommended turning over our information to law enforcement but was told by Jonathan Coyles, MLB's vice president of Drug, Health, and Safety Programs, that Halem had said, "No, we'll handle it internally. Don't go any further." The result of our investigation was an MLB directive prohibiting trainers from administering the drug. Manfred issued a statement at the end of our investigation, saying, "At the conclusion of an investigation and against the backdrop of the new industry directive, we reached a set of specific understandings with the Red Sox about how they would operate going forward."

That was the end of that, although I thought we should have taken the matter to the Massachusetts Board of Allied Health Professionals if Reinold had violated a law or put the players' health in jeopardy. The board had previously disciplined multiple trainers for injecting patients, regardless of the drug administered, and official action would have sent a clear message to all other trainers. I also wanted to alert the DEA, which would have started an industrywide federal investigation. Without a formal complaint, though, no investigation would be launched by the board.

The next year the Toradol issue made news when Yahoo! Sports reported that three players, including starting pitcher Curt Schilling, had told reporter Jeff Passan that Reinold had regularly injected players with Toradol. According to the story, Schilling said he had received an injection before "almost every single game" for the last decade of his career. He said Reinold had never directly injected him, but he and two other players told Passan that the trainer had injected other teammates in a secluded area of the clubhouse.[5]

Closer Jonathan Papelbon, who was with the team from 2005 to 2011, also told reporters that he and numerous other Red Sox players had regularly been injected with Toradol, while Clay Buchholz acknowledged that the drug might have contributed to the esophagitis that had sidelined him for twenty games in 2012. Buchholz was hospitalized in intensive care and lost three or four pints of blood while dealing with the condition, which is a known side effect of the pain reliever. Papelbon said that when he was administered a physical by the Phillies before signing as a free agent after the 2011 season, doctors asked him if he had used Toradol. When he answered yes, he was told that he would have to stop.[6]

"They told me, 'We don't do that here.' That kind of surprised me," Papelbon said. "I haven't had a single Toradol shot since."[7]

In 2014, more than 1,300 former pro football players filed a class action lawsuit against the NFL in which they said that the league's medical staffs had routinely violated federal and state laws in plying them with powerful narcotics to mask the pain of injuries on game days. The suit, which was eventually dismissed on a technicality, described players lining up for Toradol shots before games. It also spurred the DEA to get involved, something I thought should have happened as a result of our investigation.[8]

Nevertheless, in November 2014, federal agents conducted surprise game-day inspections of NFL team medical staffs, including in New York, where the San Francisco 49ers were playing the Giants. The inspections entailed bag searches and the questioning of team doctors and, according to the *Washington Post*, were based on the suspicion that NFL teams might have been dispensing drugs illegally to keep players on the field in violation of the Controlled Substances Act.

After reading the *Washington Post* article, I reached out to and met with Robert Polimeno, one of the DEA agents in charge of the Toradol investigation. I told Polimeno about the Reinold case and said I believed that most MLB teams were abusing Toradol and I suspected that other trainers were administering the drug to players. I gave Polimeno a copy of my report but never heard back from him.

Nothing much seems to have come of the DEA's investigation into the NFL's drug practices, but I feel certain that with the contacts and relationships our DOI team had in the DEA, it would have acted on our findings and opened a Toradol investigation in baseball.

The Red Sox fired Mike Reinold after the 2012 season, but according to his website, he is the cofounder and president of Champion Physical Therapy and Performance, a training facility outside Boston. He is also a consultant for the Chicago Cubs. His boss is former Red Sox GM Theo Epstein.

CHAPTER 10

DOUBLE CROSS

The dead end with Toradol was just one of many frustrating experiences we encountered in our journey through Major League Baseball. The strange case of Melky Cabrera was another.

Cabrera was once thought to be a talented Yankees prospect who would wear pinstripes for years to come. After making his debut with the team in 2005, Cabrera made a highlight-reel catch of a Manny Ramirez would-be home run in 2006 and then won a World Series ring in 2009, when the Yankees upended the Phillies.

But there were reports of too much nightlife in Gotham, and in late 2009 the Yankees dealt Cabrera, a switch-hitting Dominican, to Atlanta, where his career went into a tailspin. After playing for Kansas City for a season, he was traded to San Francisco, and it was as a Giant that he had a career rebirth. Or so everyone thought.

Melky claimed in an interview with the New York *Daily News* prior to that year's All-Star Game that the two keys to changing his career had been training with a former Venezuelan bodybuilder named Cesar Paublini and moving closer to Alex Rodriguez's Miami home so that he could work out with A-Rod during the off-season.

"I didn't necessarily encourage Melky [to move to Miami]. He felt it was going to be better for his career to get in an environment that was conducive to him training six days a week," Rodriguez told the *Daily News* that summer. "He wanted to get into a nutritional program and do all the right things to elevate his career. I think he's done that."[1]

But amid the attention being lavished on Cabrera, one American League executive said that the Dominican outfielder was "playing way above his skis" that season with the Giants, an all-too-prescient observation.

Little did the baseball world know that Cabrera was about to go down in flames behind the most bizarre "dog-ate-my-homework" alibi to come along since Manny Ramirez's testosterone-laced shaving cream. Cabrera tested positive for synthetic testosterone that summer of 2012—he was the MVP of the All-Star Game in Kansas City—but in an attempt to beat the fifty-game doping suspension, he and Juan Carlos Nunez, an associate who worked for Cabrera's agents, Seth and Sam Levinson, bought an existing website and added a nonexistent product to the site. Nunez, described by the Levinson brothers in the *Daily News* as a "paid consultant," had purchased the website for $10,000. Cabrera would try to blame his positive drug test on the product—a topical cream—but the scheme quickly went sideways.

The spiked "cream" was supposedly being sold in an open-air market in a Dominican town near Santo Domingo, so I went down to the Dominican Republic with DOI member Nelson Tejada to see if the product existed. In the United States all steroids are illegal to possess, distribute, or manufacture, and you can possess them only if you have a legitimate medical condition and a prescription from a medical professional. It's not illegal to buy steroids in the Dominican Republic, however, and we ended up buying the cream at multiple locations.

Neil Boland, who had started at MLB as an IT guy hired by Mullin and had later ascended to become one of Manfred's right-hand men, became heavily involved in the Melky case, uncovering a link between an Argentinian webmaster and Nunez. As far as I understood, he had somehow tracked down the Argentinian, which had led to a New Jersey IT specialist named Hamlet Batista. After the report about Melky's doctored website was published in August 2012, Boland and a group that included Tejada, Tom Reilly, and MLB Labor Relations Department attorney Steven Gonzalez went to New Jersey to interview Batista. When it became clear that Batista was uncomfortable in the presence of Gonzalez and Boland, Reilly asked them to leave the interview, and he and Tejada continued gathering information from Batista. It turned out that Batista had purchased the Argentinian's IP address on behalf of Nunez, the Levinson Brothers' "paid consultant."

No sooner had Reilly gotten Batista to admit that Nunez was behind the scheme and asked permission to interview Nunez than Gonzalez shut down the process, saying he had to check with his boss, Dan Halem. Gonzalez came back to say "Leave Nunez alone for now." Over the next month Reilly made at least a dozen requests to interview Nunez but was told not to pursue that lead anymore. "No" was the standard response from Gonzalez.

In hindsight, we believed it was a case of MLB wanting to control the situation—it was becoming apparent that Manfred and MLB were escalating their interference—and cutting us out of the picture did just that. Apparently someone other than a DOI member interviewed Nunez. The "associate" would end up taking the fall for the Levinsons, who were investigated by both MLB and the Players Association but found guilty only of not properly supervising Nunez. The agents, who had close ties to the union, were "censured" but escaped decertification, a much more serious punishment. Nunez, at least at the time, took responsibility for creating the website and was banned by MLB from the clubhouses and facilities of all thirty teams.[2]

By February 2018, Nunez had reversed course and blamed the Levinsons for everything that had gone on. Nunez filed a bombshell lawsuit in the New York Supreme Court accusing Seth and Sam Levinson and their agency—Athletes' Careers Enhanced and Secured, Inc. (ACES)—of cheating their "associate" out of millions of dollars in commissions, violating criminal law and MLB and Players Association rules, making under-the-table payments to players and their families to keep clients in the ACES fold, helping players obtain and use performance-enhancing drugs to get bigger contracts, and engaging in an elaborate cover-up to hide their alleged crimes and misdemeanors.[3]

The lawsuit laid out a slew of detailed claims against the Levinsons, including that the bogus website scam, among other misdeeds, had indeed been coordinated by the brothers and that Nunez had basically been forced to do their bidding in order to keep his job. The suit described ACES as "a rogue agency that reaped millions of dollars in fees by cheating the game of baseball."

According to the suit, Sam Levinson had directed Nunez to introduce arbitration-eligible players, free agents, and prospects to Anthony Bosch so they could work with him and "perform better." All told, Nunez said, he took at least ten ACES clients to Bosch. One of the more intriguing claims in the suit detailed the convoluted scheme in which Sam Levinson allegedly directed Nunez to cover up Cabrera's positive test.

"We will get crushed if he's suspended," Levinson told Nunez, according to the suit. "This can't be."

Nunez said he told Levinson that he had discussed the test results with Bosch, who had recommended that Cabrera say he had taken a pill called Extenze, which had caused the positive test. Problem was, in a meeting with the Players Association, Cabrera was told that the levels of synthetic testosterone he had tested positive for wouldn't have been caused by Extenze. The union reps then asked Cabrera if he had taken a homeopathic remedy, and he responded that he had taken a substance akin to a "Dominican Bengay." He agreed that he would provide them with a sample. Cabrera allegedly then gave Nunez a jar of something called Friccilicont and told him to take it to Bosch, who would "know what to do, he'll put the stuff in it."

According to the lawsuit, Levinson approved the plan, and after a threat to Bosch, Nunez says, he picked up the testosterone-spiked cream at Biogenesis and paid Bosch $5,000. After a series of machinations involving Bosch, the cream, product labels, and shipments back and forth from the Dominican Republic to the United States that would rival the plot of a John Le Carré novel, the lawsuit says Hamlet Batista suggested affixing labels with the name "Crema Santiaguera" on the jars of cream to be presented to the Players Association and MLB. In the meantime, Nunez claims, the Levinsons were "intimately involved" in the construction of the phony website, reviewing and directing changes from an office computer at ACES.

Finally, Nunez alleges, he got a call from Seth Levinson telling him, "It's all over." According to the lawsuit, Levinson had received a call from Michael Weiner, the head of the Players Association, telling him the union had spoken to Hamlet Batista, and had "gotten to the bottom of [the scheme]."

The Levinsons denied it all in a harshly worded statement in which they called the lawsuit a "shakedown" and described Nunez as a convicted felon who had spent time in federal prison. They went on to say their agency had been thoroughly investigated by the MLBPA and that they had been exonerated. They vowed to take the fight to Nunez for any meritless and defamatory claims.

Interestingly, before we were marginalized by MLB, we learned a lot about what had transpired during the Cabrera escapade. We didn't know at the time that Bosch had spiked the cream with testosterone, although we were told he later admitted having done so to MLB; what we did know was that the entire episode left Manfred and Selig more determined than ever to get the Levinsons.

Unrelated to the Levinsons, but around the same time the Cabrera case was playing out, DOI investigators went to Port St. Lucie, Florida, to interview a player by the name of Danny Muno. Muno was then with the New York Mets and had tested positive in April of that year for the anabolic steroid drostanolone.

Muno was advised that a second drug test conducted on June 18, 2012, also returned a positive result and that he was subject to a 100-game suspension. Muno was well aware of the probable test result—he had admitted to investigators following the first positive that he would test positive again because the day after he was first tested, he and a teammate had again injected themselves with PEDs.

Muno was further advised that he was being given an opportunity to cooperate to help mitigate the potential 100-game suspension by providing his knowledge of PED use or possession by other players or team personnel. He agreed to cooperate with the DOI and provide all the information he had on the subject.

He described his use of steroids, saying that he and the teammate had injected themselves in the buttocks with testosterone in April in his room at the Brooklyn Holiday Inn. Muno said he had obtained the steroids from a bodybuilder friend who lived in California whom he'd met in college through a Fresno State teammate who had also become a minor-league player. He described receiving shipments at various minor-league stops, including Brooklyn.

He told of adding HGH to his regimen through another dealer operating out of Las Vegas, who advised him on how to stack drostanolone, testosterone, and HGH, which he said he injected into the folds of his stomach. He told of receiving instructions from the dealer to wire $800 to a JPMorgan Chase account belonging to the dealer's father. He also named other players he believed were using PEDs.[4]

The DOI handed over all of Muno's information concerning the dealer to MLB and to the DEA in Las Vegas and to agents in Sacramento. We learned that he had also begun to cooperate with the government.

Muno provided us with the names of players and dealers, but the next thing we knew, Muno had stopped cooperating and Dan Halem was issuing what was becoming a familiar order: Stand down. Stop talking to the DEA. Case closed.

One of the biggest tools we had in the battle against the PED scourge was the fact that we would be the first allowed to approach players in person to either tell them they had flunked a test or interview them about it. That gave us a big advantage in gaining valuable information from the players and even cooperation, as was the case with Muno. At first, the commissioner's office honored that approach, especially as we investigated minor-league positive tests such as Muno's, but slowly we began to realize that MLB was telling the team, the Players Association, the player, and his agent about a failed test before it informed us. As the years went on, we were left to find out about players' suspensions from the media or our sources.

In the Muno case, we suspected that other forces were at work. MLB had chosen to suspend Muno for only fifty games, saying that it had determined that his second positive test had most likely come from his original use of PEDs, an explanation that made no sense in the face of Muno himself telling DOI investigators that he had indeed consumed steroids the day after his first test was conducted.

What could have resulted in arrests, seizures, and intelligence relating to players and their steroid distributors was dead on arrival.

If we needed more proof that our so-called independence was under attack, we found it in a case involving Melky Cabrera's trainer. Cesar Paublini's name had surfaced in the Cabrera case, but we didn't necessarily believe that Paublini was the source of the PEDs Cabrera had tested positive for, and Paublini had escaped the scandal mostly unscathed. We set up a meeting with him.

He was cagey at first, didn't want to talk, and the meeting came about only after Reilly and I had made multiple attempts to speak to him on the phone or in person. We had left business cards at his Florida home and the gym where he trained. We had spoken to his wife. But he had no interest in having anything to do with us, which was not a shock, since Cabrera had gone from All-Star Game stud to drug pariah in a matter of weeks, and, as his trainer, Paublini's name had been made public.

The first time we met with Paublini was in Florida after the Cabrera case had unfolded in the summer of 2012. We met at the Marriott Stanton in Miami Beach, which would prove to be a regular meeting place as we cultivated Paublini as a source. He spoke only Spanish, so I was usually the one doing the talking when we met. It helped that we were staying at the hotel, too.

In that first meeting, I told him that we knew, and that we also knew that he knew, that there were people saying he was the one who had provided PEDs to Melky. "We just want to discuss it with you," we told him. "We don't think it was you. We want to clear your name."

He brought along a man who he said was his lawyer, but having dealt with a few over the years, the man didn't strike me as one. Another "associate" was along for the ride, too, a guy I called "Blinky."

We sat in the hotel lobby and talked. It was a feeling-out process, as we explained to him who we were and what we were trying to accomplish. He was cocky, a five-foot-five pillar of muscle with jet black hair and brown eyes. "I'm here. What do you want?" he asked. "What are you looking for?" But I could tell he was nervous deep down.

The first meeting with Paublini was brief. Reilly, the pasty Irish kid and former NYPD detective, kept silent as Paublini and I engaged in small talk. It was strictly a confidential meeting, meant to build trust and secure what we hoped—and I sensed—would become an invaluable source.

We would meet with Paublini maybe a dozen times over the course of a few months in the fall and winter of 2012. The hotel lobby where we met was a half-story up from the Art Deco entrance, two palm trees bookending the stone steps beneath the black-lettered STANTON sign blaring overhead. When we met Paublini for what turned out to be the final time, he was waiting near the Stanton's pristine turquoise pool, a humid breeze thick on the patio. He was sitting on a tan-and-white cushioned couch, one of several pieces of furniture splayed across the open courtyard.

As usual, Paublini was with his sidekick Blinky, a scrawny thirty-something Venezuelan with jet black hair who looked as though he would blow away in a stiff wind, so nicknamed for his incessant blinking during any conversation. The more the talk veered toward a subject that made Paublini and Blinky uncomfortable, the more Blinky's left eye would flicker up and down, like a hummingbird's wings. Blinky was particularly out of sorts as we sat down for this meeting, his left eye fluttering before the conversation even began. I watched Paublini carefully. Something wasn't right. There was something different about his eyes. He was giving us a vacant, uneasy stare, thirty miles long.

Shit.

Up to that point, Paublini had been becoming what I thought was a valuable source, one we had been cultivating for months. In a tedious process that fostered Paublini's trust, we had peeled back the layers of his background—he was a well-known trainer in Miami, a former bodybuilder who still had the build of a free safety. Photographs of Paublini posted on Facebook showed him posing with Cabrera and MLB player Nelson Cruz at an indoor training center, Paublini's pectoral muscles bulging from beneath a red-and-white T-shirt.[5]

Almost every photo of Paublini on the Facebook account showed him dressed in workout clothes, always smiling, his goatee stretched wide, whether with his arm around actress Cameron Diaz's waist or his fists resting on the shoulders of a girl who appeared to be no more than ten years old but who flaunted a chiseled six-pack that would be the envy of any gym rat.

Paublini was no different from any source I had cultivated as a detective on the Boston police force. He began to open up, but Blinky was more often the contact who reached out to us. We learned that Blinky's motives were more focused on long-term goals centered around opening training centers with Paublini back in Venezuela, where he thought Paublini could capitalize on his name recognition. He had already made a name for himself training ballplayers such as Cabrera and Cruz and movie stars such as Diaz, but he was concerned that Paublini's connection to PED use might cause Paublini's marketability to plummet. Blinky clearly had an eye on both their futures.

Blinky would often call behind Paublini's back, which at first seemed overly cautious to us on his part, but we soon realized that he was merely eager to clear Paublini's name. Blinky had the names of PED suppliers, and he told us what Paublini knew or didn't know about various names on our radar. We were accumulating valuable intel, and we were reporting it all back to New York—where the information was shared among Manfred, Halem, and John McHale, an MLB vice president who was put in charge of the DOI after Bob DuPuy was ousted. Manfred wanted McHale as a buffer between us and him. There was no doubt that McHale did whatever Manfred told him to do.

It was the thinnest of threads tying together a select few people who knew what the DOI had uncovered about Paublini. But that was all it took to torpedo the best chance we had of finding out valuable information on Tony Bosch months before a Miami newsweekly dropped the hammer.

Paublini began proving himself to be a valuable asset. He had his come-to-Jesus moment when he revealed to us that San Diego catcher Yasmani Grandal, a Cuban from Havana, had tested positive for elevated levels of testosterone. Turned out that Paublini was friendly with the father of a high school player he had trained, and the father knew Grandal's agent, Mike Maulini. After Grandal was busted, Maulini contacted the father to tell him that he did not think Paublini had been implicated in the Grandal positive test.

After Paublini dropped that bit of news about Grandal's positive test on us, I immediately phoned Mullin.

"You aware that Grandal, the Padres' catcher, got popped for a positive test?" I asked.

"What? You're shitting me," said Mullin.

"Nope," I replied.

Mullin hung up and immediately called Labor. Sure enough, Halem confirmed that Grandal had indeed been busted. It was another example of Manfred and the rest of his department running interference on the DOI, keeping us in the dark, controlling every aspect—or at least trying to—of our investigative work. The bad news? They knew that Grandal had tested positive but had failed to tell us, another example of their disregarding Senator Mitchell's edict that we be apprised of all information concerning PED use and allowed to participate in interviews with the individuals involved. I had found the arrangement between Labor and DOI requiring Labor to coordinate with the player, his agent, and the Players Association before allowing us to interview forty-man-roster players to be not only against Mitchell's recommendations but illogical and had said as much to my bosses from the beginning. Now Labor was excluding us altogether. The good news? Paublini was providing us with reliable information. Slowly but surely he was spilling his secrets.

Turned out that Paublini had learned from the agent, Maulini, that Alex Rodriguez's cousin, the infamous Yuri Sucart, had made contact with one of Maulini's comrades and a fellow ACES agent based in the Dominican Republic: good ol' cousin Yuri was the drug mule whom A-Rod had ratted out during the 2009 press conference at which the Yankees third baseman had copped to steroid use for the first time, insisting that he had juiced only while playing for Texas from 2001 to 2003. Maulini said Yuri had told his colleague that a US doctor was supplying players with PEDs to make them stronger. And that the drugs the doctor was supplying were undetectable— which in the era of PEDs in baseball was like telling a kid he had free rein in the candy store. I was pretty sure that the "doctor" was Tony Bosch, the Biogenesis founder.

As we cultivated Paublini as a source, he gave us insight into Bosch's world, telling me that he knew that a suitcase of drugs had been sent to Grandal's girlfriend's father's home—and that the drugs had come from Bosch.

Paublini went on to describe in detail what Maulini had found when he and the girlfriend's parents had gone through Grandal's luggage, which the player had sent ahead to the home. There were plastic bags that contained needles, syringes, vials, pills, and bottles of cream with images of the moon and the sun on the labels. The covers of bottles clicked toward the moon or the sun (left and right), releasing a specific amount of cream as they clicked to either side. Specific instructions on how to consume the substances were also found in the bag.

When we met with Paublini and Blinky for the final meeting at the Marriott Stanton, DEA agent Jeannette Moran accompanied us under the guise that she was one of our investigators. The meeting was critical because Paublini had already indicated that he had some important information to convey, so it was serendipitous that Moran was able to come along as well.

We had been dumping plenty of evidence from our investigation into the DEA's lap, but as was the case since Manfred had begun to insinuate himself into DOI business, we would soon be told to cease talking with the DEA. Delay, delay, delay was how we saw it. Followed by control, control, control.

After we exchanged hellos with Paublini and Blinky, I soon realized there was a more immediate hurdle. Speaking in Spanish, I introduced Moran, and then we sat. That's when I got the thirty-yard stare. I asked Paublini what was wrong. It didn't ease my mind that Blinky was already in full, turbocharged blink mode. That left eye was flicking, flicking, flicking.

"*Apuñalado en la espalda*," Paublini said. "You stabbed me in the back."

My heart started pounding, and I caught a glimpse of Moran. She was puzzled and confused—she definitely had the "What the fuck is going on?" face going big time—making for an awkward silence.

We soon found out what was going on.

"You told Maulini, the union, and baseball about Grandal and the package of PEDs he received at his girlfriend's parents' house," Paublini said in rapid-fire Spanish. He unloaded on me, and Blinky only added to the sinking feeling in my stomach by batting that left eye.

"Why would you do that?" Paublini asked.

After Paublini gave me the death stare, the detective in me kicked in and I went into full-blown damage control, the result of years of experience dealing with a source who turns or a confidential arrangement that goes south in a hurry.

"It wasn't DOI, I can promise you that," I said. Moran and Dan were still sitting there with puzzled looks, although Dan's face was starting to turn crimson. He said nothing but reached for his cell phone and motioned that he was going to make a call away from our meeting area.

"Baseball has the story, it happened today," said Paublini, his goatee no longer stretched in a smile as in all of our previous meetings. "I can never trust you again."

And just like that, he and Blinky were gone, swiftly disappearing into the Miami night. No recourse. Nothing. A source burned forever, months of work down the shitter. I explained to Jeannette what had happened and what Paublini had said.

"Did DOI do that?" she asked.

"Nope, but I have a feeling I know who did," I said.

Only three people other than Grandal and his girlfriend and her parents (and they weren't going to tell on themselves) had known about the suitcase full of drugs: Paublini, Grandal's agent, Maulini, and one person Maulini called "a trusted friend." But during a prearbitration hearing for Grandal, during which the player had a chance, with his lawyer, to come up with an excuse as to why he tested positive, Halem just came right out and told Grandal, "If you are even thinking of putting up a challenge, we have a source that told us X, Y, and Z." Maulini, who was present at the hearing, called Paublini and said, "You have to be the guy who told, because it wasn't me. I'm the agent. And it wasn't the other guy." Paublini was understandably upset. He thought we had double-crossed him and that Maulini and Grandal would spread the word about his so-called betrayal to other players and agents.

Mullin returned from his phone call, his face looking like a raspberry. He started doing what I called "the face rake"—when he got upset he would run his right hand from his forehead to his chin in rapid-fire, machine-gun fashion. The madder El Guapo got, the more that right hand raked his face. He was fuming like a madman now, and when he told us about his conversation with Halem, I nearly blew my top as well.

"Halem told the union, Grandal, and Maulini about the package of drugs. I asked him why the fuck he did that, and he had this bullshit response that if Grandal was considering contesting his positive test, MLB had the goods on him," Mullin told us. "I asked him why baseball would ruin one of our sources. All he said was 'I don't know if you know this, but we're in the business of suspending players. Too bad.'"

Too bad. That was it. I looked at the table in front of us, littered with glasses. There was laughter from a nearby group. Everyone else at the hotel was oblivious to the crater Paublini had created with his abrupt exit.

Too bad.

Years later, Moran, who had seen firsthand how MLB had undermined us, would describe the incident as "the beginning of a lot of frustrating moments in the case for me."

"Eddie and Dan and Tom, those were the guys," she said. "They were down here, they were looking for information, digging up sources, they were on the ground. They were in Miami, it seemed like, for months, more than they were home. We were gaining momentum in our case. It seemed as if things were going pretty smoothly."

She said that Paublini's help would have been an important step toward making the connection between Bosch and Biogenesis and the rest of the steroid networks permeating Florida. "That was just the beginning of a lot of really weird things. There were a lot of those moments, I guess you could say," she concluded.[6]

I'm not sure if identifying Bosch as Grandal's PED supplier would have changed the course of the Biogenesis investigation, but protecting Paublini would have given us a solid, long-term source. We'll never know what else Paublini knew or where he would have taken us. Tony Bosch wasn't the only one dealing steroids.

As Halem said, too bad.

CHAPTER 11

"TELL THE DEA I WANT THIS DONE F—ING NOW!"

The DEA agents we first met in the Biogenesis investigation weren't exactly your type A sports fans. Tom Reilly and I went to the DEA's Weston, Florida, offices about thirty-five miles northwest of Miami in the summer of 2012 to lay out what we had uncovered on Anthony Bosch, his father, Pedro, and the antiaging clinic on South Dixie Highway in Coral Gables. We got a few blank stares when we started to mention the possible connection between professional baseball players and Bosch. But despite the sports information gap, we clicked with our DEA counterparts right away, and their interest in launching a case seemed apparent from the outset.

Moran described it this way. "They [the DOI] were professionals. They were investigators. They brought us a pile of info. It was a little daunting at first because there were a couple females on the [DEA] investigative team—we're baseball fans—but we were not privy to a lot of the lingo, and everything that came along with it. It was a huge learning curve for everyone. But they were fabulous from the beginning to the end."[1]

Kevin Stanfill, the DEA assistant special agent in charge of the Biogenesis federal case, recalled how adept Reilly and I had been in our presentation of the evidence. "We went into the meeting with Eddie and Tom—I had never seen anybody work iPads. They were pulling up reports, and started telling us about baseball players, who they were getting their dope from—whether it was Bosch—and how they got it. You could tell that they had spent, at the very least, months and months, and they knew it like the back of their hand," he said. "They're talking about the dates the players did this and that, supposed meetings. We were thinking, 'This is not some rent-a-cop type thing. These guys are the real deal.' My job was to make sure that the DEA train was on the DEA track and the MLB train was on the other track. You have some sensitive lines—grand jury, Title 3, when to start intercepting people's phones. Right from the get-go, the DOI guys wooed the agents. These guys really had it going on."[2]

There was one thing missing: a way into Bosch's world. Following those initial meetings with us, the agents set up a room where they started to document the names and key characters related to Biogenesis. The room, known in law enforcement circles as the "wire room" once the wiretaps were approved and in place, would evolve into a teeming center of activity with agents listening in on headphones and keeping track of the names emerging from the perps' conversations, walls covered with sticky notes and papers. The list of names on a whiteboard set up in the room would grow and grow, including those in Alex Rodriguez's inner circle, such as Jorge "Ugi" Velazquez, Yuri Sucart, and Carlos Acevedo, along with peripheral characters, including a guy whose sole purpose, the DEA found out, was to supply needles to Acevedo. The public would first learn about most of those names months later, when MLB filed a lawsuit against Tony Bosch and his associates on March 22, 2013, in Florida state court.

But first the DEA needed an informant. We had given the agents a ton of information—reports, names, locations—but it wasn't until we brought in a credible source who could infiltrate Bosch's circle that the DEA crew was officially sold on launching its own probe. The informant, whom I'll call "Frankie," had for years worked with Reilly in numerous high-profile drug and homicide cases on which Reilly had teamed with the DEA task force. Frankie treated this job—as he did all his other undercover assignments—like a pro. Because he trusted Reilly, he had no qualms about cooperating with the DEA in Florida after we flew him down to Weston to meet the agents.

"Everybody was comfortable, very professional. They don't make me feel nervous," Frankie said later. "I was in the hotel with Dominguez, and he speaks Spanish. He explained to me what he wants to do."[3]

Frankie was a man of the streets, unafraid of just about anything, an attribute that would come in handy as we proceeded. Kevin Stanfill, the veteran DEA agent, described Frankie as the "domino that started everything" and recalled that during his thirty-year career in law enforcement he had never seen cooperation from another agency or individual like what he saw with us, where the DEA agents could hit the ground running with the information we brought them. "No one has ever given us a case like that, where you got everything," he said.[4]

Frankie knew Alex Rodriguez and his cousin Yuri Sucart from their early years in Washington Heights, where A-Rod was born and lived during his childhood before his family moved to the Dominican Republic and finally Miami. Years later, Frankie watched as A-Rod casually named Sucart as his drug mule when he confessed during a 2009 Tampa press conference to having used steroids during the three years he played for the Texas Rangers, from 2001 to 2003.

"Business," Frankie said when I asked him why Rodriguez would have thrown his cousin under the bus in such a public setting. "My brother, listen . . . business. He work for me, he's my cousin, but I'm the guy with the money. If I'm gonna take a hit, he takes it for me. Yuri got a little selfish. That's the problem. When A-Rod say that to the media [in 2009], you think that caught [Yuri] by surprise? Nah. It's about business. Somebody's got to go down—the little feet has to go down. It's business, it's life."

It's like what the NFL's Cris Carter told a bunch of young players at the 2014 NFL rookie symposium, while onstage with Hall of Fame defensive star Warren Sapp: "If you gonna have a crew, one of them fools got to know he going to jail. We'll get him out. If you gonna have a crew, make sure you know who gonna be the fall guy. I know none of y'all gonna never drink, [get] laid. I know none of y'all never gonna use no drugs. All y'all gonna go to Bible study. I realize that. But still get you a fall guy."[5]

Carter would apologize profusely for his comments. "Seeing that video has made me realize how wrong I was," Carter wrote in a series of tweets. "I was brought there to educate young people and instead I gave them very bad advice. Every person should take responsibility for his own actions. I'm sorry and I truly regret what I said that day."

Only one year after Rodriguez's Tampa press conference, Cousin Yuri was back in the business of procuring drugs for Rodriguez, and when Frankie went undercover for the DEA in 2012, the first person he called was his old pal Yuri. At first Frankie went alone to buy drugs from him, always a dangerous proposition since you're dealing with shady people and you're carrying money. Even though the agents were always nearby, surveilling from a parked car, it was dicey. Eventually Frankie was joined by a female DEA undercover agent, who ended up making at least five buys from Sucart, both with Frankie and by herself. Frankie never knew what was actually in the boxes he bought from Yuri—he would put in his order, but once the transaction was made, he would hand the evidence over to the DEA. More often than not, what he was buying was either tes-tosterone or HGH.

"It was for the betterment of players," Frankie said. "They become strong and successful."

Wearing a wire, Frankie would meet twice with Carlos Acevedo, Anthony Bosch's business partner who had his own small clinic, to buy drugs that Acevedo said he had gotten from Cuba. "The first time I met Acevedo, I was by myself," Frankie said. "I went the sec-ond time to his little office, like a clinic. The DEA undercover agent, all the time she listened from outside."

Once the undercover drug buys were completed and the DEA had enough to start wiretaps, Frankie's work in south Florida became less direct. This was a textbook undercover operation: get the informant to introduce an undercover agent, and then get the informant out of the way. "We kept in touch with him," Moran said, "and he looked at transcripts of his recorded conversations with Yuri, but once he introduced our undercover agent [to Sucart and Acevedo], we went with the agent."[6]

The world would soon know about Anthony Bosch and his infa-mous notebooks when the calendar turned to 2013, but in the final months of 2012, after we had introduced Frankie to the DEA, Tom Reilly and I stumbled across a trove of information at the clinic run by Acevedo, after he had parted ways with Bosch. Acevedo and Ugi Velazquez had set up a new shop in a rented room in a Miami office building, only to abandon ship once the house of cards began to fall. The building manager happened to be there the day we came by to check out one of the numerous addresses we had compiled in our investigation. He said Acevedo and Ugi had left a month or two before, but much to our delight, they had left some things behind. We told the manager who we were, and he said, "They left a while ago, and as a matter of fact, they left a bunch of shit."

"Oh really? Do you mind if we look?"

"Go ahead. I was ready to throw it out."

"Don't worry," we told him, "we'll throw it out for you."

We got a lot of information out of that trash. In the rush to leave, they had left behind all kinds of stuff. There were used needles, receipts for payments, ledgers, names of clients, brochures that led us to other places where Ugi and Acevedo were peddling their PEDs—like at doctors' offices all over Miami. The stuff had been left in boxes, garbage cans, plastic bags, and on the floor—everywhere. When we went in, Tommy and I were looking at each other with shit-eating grins. We called the DEA, and its agents came in and took all of it. We read through most of it before they arrived, and even though there weren't any obviously explosive documents with names of players on them, there was still valuable information. There's no question that that information helped the DEA's case—though, of course, the informant, Frankie, was the real key to the investigation.

"I remember thinking, 'The case is made. Thanks, DOI,'" said Stanfill.

Everything seemed to be rolling along smoothly with the DEA and our own investigation, even though the interference from MLB had been steadily increasing, including the debacle with my source, Paublini. The DEA had presented the Biogenesis case to US attorney Wifredo Ferrer in Miami, and his office had assigned the highly regarded assistant US attorney Pat Sullivan to lead the investigation.

But trouble would soon begin to brew in New York. Manfred would even hire the law firm Proskauer Rose to investigate how MLB, including the DOI, was handling MLB's foreign practices policies. The "investigation" was started after an anonymous letter was sent to MLB in which claims were made about the DOI investigators that were outrageous, untrue, and ultimately discredited.

We were all brought in for interviews and questioned about silly things: lunch expenses for fellow investigators, access to tickets for law enforcement members who were working security at games, things like that. Nothing came of the investigation, which lasted a few months and cost MLB a ton of money, or we would have been fired right then and there. The whole thing was especially galling to me since from the moment I was put in charge of international age/ID investigations in 2010, I had asked that we hire lawyers from all the countries we dealt with to advise us on how to proceed in compliance with the nation's laws. My requests were ignored.

MLB president Bob DuPuy—the original point person the DOI was supposed to report to—was long gone by 2012, and Manfred's game plan to get rid of us was starting to take shape. The investigation had given Manfred the opening he needed to dig deep into DOI, to try to find something, anything, that could open the door for him to gut the unit altogether.

Needless to say, I saw that this was turning into a witch hunt. The mood in the unit was not good. We couldn't believe that Manfred was drawing the line in the sand based on bullshit in a suspect letter. I had been begging Dan Mullin and George Hanna to let Senator Mitchell know how MLB was circumventing his recommendations. During an MLB Christmas party, MLB spokesman Patrick Courtney had approached Hanna and told him that he should separate himself from Mullin because Manfred didn't like the fact that Mullin wasn't cooperating with Manfred, Labor, and Selig.

It came my time to be interrogated by Sigal Mandelker, an attorney from Proskauer Rose who specialized in foreign corruption practices, and as I was preparing to meet with her, I found it strange that Manfred was waiting for me outside the room. Manfred looked at me and said, "Eddie, do the right thing." I stopped, looked at him straight in the eyes, and said, "Rob, I always do the right thing." I got the message: Manfred wanted me to sink, and he wanted Dan and George and the DOI to go down with me. I smiled as I stepped into the room. What I was thinking was, Rob Manfred doesn't have a clue as to who I am.

The interview lasted for a few hours. Mandelker, who later joined the Trump administration as undersecretary of the treasury, got caught up in asking me about buying lunches for law enforcement officials. I told her that over the years while I had been a cop, and after I had left the Boston PD, not only had I bought lunches for officials, assistant district attorneys, and federal prosecutors, but those people had returned the favor and bought lunches for me, too.

Among the complaints the letter outlined, there were assertions about other investigators we had worked with, including a ridiculous claim that Joel Rengifo, the Venezuelan law enforcement official who had been my supervisor on the age/ID investigations in that country and was one of the most respected officers I had ever known, was unfit to work as an MLB investigator. We had flown Joel in from Venezuela to be interviewed, but he was kept in a room at MLB offices for hours and wasn't given lunch. I called and spoke to Mandelker about Joel and told her that as she was a former prosecutor, certainly she was familiar with the rules of interviewing prisoners: you should break at some point to allow them to eat, maybe even allow them to go to the bathroom. Mandelker didn't like my flip remarks.

After it was over, we all went back to Dan's apartment and climbed up to his rooftop with a few beers. Joel and his wife and daughter were there, along with George, Dan, Tom, and a couple of other guys from the squad. It was a beautiful night, and it seemed you could almost touch the Empire State Building. Joel's wife was concerned about the investigation, but I told her not to worry. MLB's information had come from an unreliable source, and we had done nothing wrong. Sure enough, the investigation went nowhere. After all that, MLB mandated that we no longer provide tickets or buy lunches for law enforcement officials.

Penny Payne-Korte, another highly respected DEA agent, had been singled out in the anonymous letter, too. She was an experienced investigator who had worked on the 2008–09 prosecution of California steroid dealer Dr. Ramon Scruggs, helping send Scruggs to prison for three years after he pleaded guilty to illegally distributing anabolic steroids, smuggling human growth hormone into the country, and laundering money. Scruggs had been investigated for providing steroids to two baseball players and admitted to knowing that the substances would be used for performance enhancement.[7]

Payne-Korte, whose role as a diversion agent included investigating individuals suspected of having violated the Controlled Substances Act, would also be dogged by Alex Rodriguez's camp during the Biogenesis investigation, even though she wasn't involved in the federal case or baseball's investigation of the antiaging clinic and Bosch.

According to Payne-Korte, A-Rod's "investigators" had called her ex-husband of twenty years in 2013 with allegations that she was hanging out with people who were involved in criminal activity, presumably the DOI. The calls to her ex came in the wake of the *Miami New Times* report that detonated the Biogenesis bombshell. The explosive article, published on January 29, 2013, five months after we took the Biogenesis case to the DEA, featured a cover illustration of a swarm of syringes hurtling toward the reader, and it detailed Bosch's extensive files.

"I wasn't involved with Biogenesis at all, so when the calls came to my ex-husband, I called Dan Mullin and asked him what this was about," Payne-Korte said years later. "He was like, 'Have you seen the news headlines?' That's when I looked into what was being reported and realized the scope of the whole thing."[8]

Most damning in the *Miami New Times* story was the list of major- and minor-league players who were reported to have procured performance-enhancing drugs from Bosch, including the biggest name in the sport: Alex Rodriguez. Bosch had a code name for the Yankee third baseman: "El Cacique," a nickname for a pre-Columbian Caribbean chief, according to the *New Times*. The information in the report in large part came from Bosch's notebooks, which had been shared with the newspaper by a disgruntled employee, later identified as Porter Fischer.

The report had a domino effect on the DOI. Manfred's plans to dismantle the DOI were escalating, even though we had been working closely with the DEA and had progressed to the point where a wiretap on Bosch and his associates, including Carlos Acevedo, was imminent. But the headlines and the media attention were getting to Selig and Manfred. The pressure on us from Manfred to nail Rodriguez and finish the probe began the moment the story broke and grew by the day.

Halem and Manfred pressed us to use Halem's college buddy, former Miami prosecutor Andrew Levi, on some of our cases. Levi had been with the US Attorney's Office, but Mullin and I were not big fans of his and resisted bringing him into the Biogenesis investigation. Moreover, the DEA didn't want lawyers from the private sector involved in a federal case. Once the *New Times* article came out, however, Halem and Manfred, desperate to move the case along, brought Levi into the investigation behind our backs. Word of Levi's involvement came back to us, and we were told that Levi hadn't been warmly greeted by Sullivan.

Nonetheless, Manfred ordered us to lean on the DEA to expedite its investigation. I believe Manfred knew, or at least should have known, that once evidence is turned over to a federal agency, it is up to that agency to carry out the investigation, a process that could take months or even years. Ideally, when you open a federal investigation, your goal is to take down the head supplier/distributor, and if the investigation leads to someone bigger than your original target, you follow the bouncing ball for as long as you can. In the end, you indict all the suppliers and distributors. Manfred and Selig were impatient, however, and went behind our backs. Private investigators were hired, unbeknown to us. Players named in the *New Times* report were being interviewed by Labor lawyers, not us. In addition, we were excluded from internal conversations and told to stop sharing information with the DEA. Most of the time Dan and George would tell us that Manfred, Halem, and McHale had brought the two of them into meetings where the DOI members' jobs were threatened if we didn't stop talking to the DEA.

One of the twelve players the *New Times* sent letters to asking why their names were in Bosch's notebooks was a journeyman outfielder named Felix Pie, who was then with the Pittsburgh Pirates. The day after the article came out, Pie agreed to cooperate with MLB in exchange for Dan Halem's promise of no punishment. Baseball was hoping to find out any information about Biogenesis and Anthony Bosch from Pie, and since Pie had agreed to cooperate, it was possible that he could provide the names of players who were clients of Bosch.

Pat Houlihan, the MLB Labor lawyer, flew down to Miami to interview Pie, an interview we felt should have been handled by DOI only. Halem and Labor had asked that I be present for the Pie interview, but in a somewhat degrading capacity—translating the Spanish-speaking Pie (who is Dominican) for Houlihan and Steve Gonzalez, the Labor lawyer who would participate in the interview by phone from New York. When DOI first started, Gonzalez's office was in the same area as the DOI's offices. I first met him then, and Gonzalez, who wore glasses, seemed like an easygoing guy who never strayed too far from the paperwork on his desk.

Now here I was, years later, being asked to translate Spanish while Labor lawyers did the DOI work. That didn't sit well with Mullin, who was already irritated by the fact that Labor had lied to us about an interview it had conducted with another player named Cesar Carrillo, who was a non-forty-man-roster player in the Detroit Tigers' farm system and whose name had shown up in Bosch's notebooks as well. MLB had been aware of the *New Times* letters that had been sent for some time, but no one had shared that information with us. The day before the *New Times* story broke, MLB finally gave us some of the players' names that appeared in the story. That day I was in Miami, where I had been for most of the previous six months, and when I saw Carrillo's name on the list, I asked Mullin to ask Labor to let us interview him. Normally, we would not have been required to ask permission to speak to a non-forty-man-roster player, but because of the chaos surrounding the *New Times* story, I felt we should let Labor know we planned to interview Carrillo.

Regardless, the answer to Mullin's request was that Carrillo was on a plane back to Detroit so that he could be drug tested. It was all a lie. After the Carrillo episode, Labor would later choose which non-forty-man-roster players we interviewed, handcuffing the DOI even more.

I was to pick up Houlihan and Mullin prior to the Pie interview— they were at separate hotels—and when I arrived at Houlihan's hotel first, I asked him when he had arrived in Miami.

"Did you just get in?" I asked.

"No, I came in last night," he said and then dropped a bombshell: he said he had interviewed Carrillo at his hotel. So much for the MLB alibi that Carrillo couldn't be interviewed by the DOI in

Miami because he was already on a plane to Detroit. When Mullin learned about Houlihan interviewing Carrillo the morning of the Pie interview, El Guapo got on the phone to New York and proceeded to curse out Halem and everyone else within hearing distance.

"You mean to tell me that you want Eddie Dominguez, a detective with twenty-nine years' experience and who's interviewed hundreds of drug dealers, acting as a translator?" Mullin yelled at Halem, blasting them about Carrillo, too.

I drove Mullin and Houlihan to the office of Pie's attorney on the outskirts of Miami, and it was a very quiet trip. Mullin didn't budge from the passenger seat when Houlihan and I got out of the car.

"You coming?" I asked Mullin.

"Nope, I'm staying here," said Mullin, still seething. "Okay, I guess you'll need the keys. Here you go," I said. I thought to myself, It's ninety degrees outside, so you might want to turn on the AC at some point.

I ended up asking some of the questions during the Pie interview. Pie told us that he had not spoken to anyone other than his attorneys about the *New Times* story and his cooperation with MLB. He said that in May or June of the previous year, 2012 (when he had played for Atlanta's Triple-A affiliate Gwinnett Braves), he had been contacted by Nunez, the Levinson brothers' "consultant" who had been behind the phony website scam that had led to Melky Cabrera's 2012 doping ban.

Nunez, according to Pie, had offered to supply Pie with undetectable PEDs and told him that Melky Cabrera had already been using the same substances. Pie said Nunez had told him the PEDs had come from "someone in Miami." Pie said he had confirmed through the ACES agency, run by the Levinson brothers, that Nunez worked for the Levinsons. Pie said that Nunez had called him back a few days later and told him the cost of the substances would be

$1,500 a month. Pie said he had agreed to the purchase and said he would send the money through Western Union via one of the clubhouse attendants. Within a week, Pie said, a package had arrived at his apartment in Lawrenceville, Georgia, and inside the box were seven sealed plastic bags, each containing different substances with instructions on how and when to use them. Pie said the box had contained three syringes containing a clear substance that he was to inject into his midsection once a week for the first three weeks; numerous syringes containing a clear substance that he was to inject into his buttocks; a white plastic bottle containing a white, odorless cream that he was to rub on his shoulders daily; a white plastic bottle containing an odorless cream that he was to apply to any area where he experienced pain; a bottle containing ½-inch oblong white pills that Pie was to take once a day every day; and a bottle containing clear tablets—"smaller than a raisin," he said—that he was to put under his tongue prior to games.

The tablets were what Anthony Bosch would refer to as "troches." Pie told us that he had been told by Nunez that Pie's shipments had been marked "El Gato" because that was his nickname to differentiate him from other players—"El Gato" is Spanish for "cat." Pie said he had quit taking the substances for about ten days because he felt ill. He had then quit using any of them after he learned that Melky Cabrera had tested positive. Pie said he had dumped all of what he had left from the shipment into a dumpster at his apartment building complex and had never received a second shipment.

Despite the order not to share the information with the DEA, I emailed my detailed report on Pie to DEA assistant special agent Kevin Stanfill, an act of defiance that I was told greatly upset Manfred. I believed that it was our duty to report all the information we had gathered on this case to the DEA. After all, we were the ones who had brought the case to them, and Manfred had originally given us the green light to do so. I never again participated in an interview of a targeted individual with Labor. I believe that Manfred found out that we were still communicating with the DEA through our emails and text messages.

Felix Pie escaped punishment, and MLB managed to keep his name pretty much out of the media, although he was included in the book *Blood Sport*, co-written by the *New Times* reporter who had broken the Biogenesis story. As for Cesar Carrillo, he received a 100-game suspension shortly after the interview with MLB, reportedly because his name was listed in Bosch's notebooks and for denying that he knew Bosch. Carrillo would later say that he and his agent had never been given an explanation by baseball for why he was suspended. As of early 2018, he was playing baseball in Mexico.

Alex Rodriguez became the top target of baseball, followed closely by the Levinsons. Everyone else was a distant third on the MLB radar, including Milwaukee Brewers outfielder Ryan Braun, whose name also appeared in Bosch's notebooks. MLB had been at odds with Braun since late 2011, when he had tested positive for exogenous testosterone but successfully fought a fifty-game suspension. In his appeal, Braun focused on a chain-of-custody issue with regard to the MLB collector who had handled his urine sample, and independent arbitrator Shyam Das ruled in Braun's favor, overturning his suspension. MLB, and Manfred specifically, were furious with Das's ruling when it came down in February 2012, and Manfred ended up firing Das. The neutral, third-party arbitrator serves both MLB and the Players Association—a collectively bargained arrangement—and either side can terminate the arbitrator for any reason or no reason at all. The only requirement is that either side send written notice that the arbitrator is terminated.[9]

But a year later, in 2013, Braun was in the rearview mirror, although in my eyes what he had done was despicable—basically ruining the life of the man who had collected his urine sample. Braun told lies and was no different from A-Rod. He ended up cooperating with MLB and accepting a sixty-five-game suspension later in the summer of 2013, the second longest suspension of a player disciplined in the Biogenesis case behind Rodriguez's 162 games (reduced from the original punishment of 211 games). In my opinion Braun's sentence, compared to A-Rod's, was ridiculous.

By the time Braun's name was linked to Biogenesis in a Yahoo! Sports report in early February, Selig and Manfred were threatening us to the point of termination unless we got the DEA to refocus its investigation. At one point early in 2013, Mullin was called to John McHale's office at 245 Park Avenue. When Mullin arrived, McHale handed him a document and asked him to sign it. It was a legal form that, if signed, would stop the DOI members from cooperating further with the DEA. In other words, we were either on MLB's team or off it. It would be a few months before Bosch would sign a deal to cooperate with baseball, but in hindsight, the document Mullin was presented with was an early sign of baseball's interference in the government's investigation: MLB wanted to make sure that Bosch wasn't going to get arrested before it could forge its own pact with him.

Mullin told McHale he would not sign the document. He then went to Manfred and explained to him once again that if MLB could sit tight, be patient, and allow the DEA to wrap up its case on Biogenesis and hand up indictments, the players involved would be listed in the indictments and baseball could discipline them accordingly. Mullin had arranged a deal with the DEA, which had no interest in busting users, to go after the drug traffickers and leave the punishment of the players to baseball. That agreement, according to the DEA, had been discussed with Pat Sullivan, the prosecutor in charge of the investigation. Both Selig and Manfred had agreed to the arrangement. In the weeks leading up to the *New Times* article, the DEA investigators had identified at least seventeen players who were involved with the Biogenesis drug-dealing organization.

Manfred's response: "Al from Milwaukee [Selig] doesn't give a fuck about seventeen players. He wants fucking Alex Rodriguez."[10]

There was another conference call with "Al from Milwaukee" and Manfred on February 6. As we phoned in from wherever we were at the time, we knew the call was not going to be one of those "Attaboy!" calls. It was understood that Dan and George would answer any questions on behalf of the DOI, unless the rest of us were asked a direct question. We had discussed the atmosphere at 245 Park Avenue ad nauseam, because George stayed mostly in New York, guarding the fort, and would call us on a daily basis with a "the sky is falling" speech. He sounded almost suicidal at times, which was both sad and disturbing. To be quite honest, the real theater hadn't even started yet, but I was already sick of the bullshit—power-hungry lawyers thinking that because they worked for MLB, they could manipulate a federal investigation. At the time, I thought that MLB should just fire me and get it over with, because I was not going to go back on my word with the DEA. It was the DEA's investigation now—not "Al from Milwaukee's," not Manfred's, not MLB's. Tom Reilly and I pulled over to the side of the road, called in, and muted the call once we checked in. It was both sad and comical.

Selig proceeded to threaten us with our jobs if we didn't get results. He left the call but not before he made it clear that Labor and Dan Halem would be running the investigation. Manfred jumped back onto the call and wasted no time threatening us again. He wanted to manipulate the DEA so that it would be working for MLB. Manfred actually said, "Tell the DEA I want this done fucking now!"

We told him, "That's not how it works, Rob. They're going up on a wire. It takes a while."

"Well, how long can that take?" Manfred wanted to know.

We told him, "First they've got to get probable cause, then an affidavit. The affidavit goes to the US Attorney's Office in Florida. They read it, send it to the US attorney in DC, which sends it back and says, 'Do this, fix that.' Then send it back to the lawyers in Florida and the lawyers in Florida send it back to the DEA. It goes on and on."

"Well, we're Major League fucking Baseball" was Manfred's response. "We need this now!"

We could only say, "Okay, we'll tell them that you need this now."

Reilly and I shook our heads. Manfred wanted the DEA to forget about the wiretap and the drug traffickers. He wanted those ledgers, emails, and text messages and historical information on the Levinsons. And of course, A-Rod was A-number one.

The DEA soon found out that it didn't have a friend in MLB's Labor Relations Department when baseball filed a lawsuit against Anthony Bosch and several of his associates, including Carlos Acevedo, the intended targets of the DEA's wiretap investigation. Those targets had not been named in the media. The lawsuit itself was based on the theory that Bosch had intentionally and unjustifiably interfered with contracts between MLB and its players by providing them with banned substances, a theory widely derided in legal circles. The suit's true purpose was to force Bosch, who by then was basically broke, to cooperate and help nail Rodriguez, which eventually he did.

To say the DEA was baffled by MLB's actions is putting it mildly. "We looked at that. Of course we're down here and Bosch is on the news all the time. He was kind of thumbing his nose at MLB. 'Hey, I haven't done anything,'" Kevin Stanfill, the DEA agent in charge of the Biogenesis investigation, said. "We're like, 'Why are you doing that? We've got this. Let us do our job. We're going to get Bosch.' At the end of the day, we knew that Bosch was going to be answering to us. It was an inconvenience, but we knew that it wouldn't stop us from getting what we needed."[11]

In the meantime, Manfred told Mullin and Hanna, "You better control your people, or I'm firing the whole bunch of you. And tell Dominguez and Reilly to stop making fun of the Labor guys."

We laughed at that, too, but Mullin was becoming increasingly upset and Hanna was getting physically ill as the pressure mounted. Hanna, a mountain of a man who in his younger days could bench-press 600 pounds, was now a shell of his former self. The constant pressure from 245 Park Avenue had made him a psychological and physical mess. He said he was seeing ghosts, and he would call us just to say that Halem had nodded hello to him in the elevator. Hanna thought a gesture like that meant that the DOI was back in Manfred's good graces. An hour later his phone would ring and the yelling from Manfred or Halem would start all over again. It was so bad that his wife told us he hardly slept at night and was grinding his teeth so badly that they were gradually whittling away.

Reilly and I simply shook our heads in disbelief. All along, I kept saying, "They can't do this. They can't interfere with a federal investigation."

Despite all of this, the DEA continued its case and we secretly attempted to keep it informed, even though by that time I was more than wary of Neil Boland, the computer tech who had steadily moved tighter into Manfred's orbit and was at his side constantly during the Biogenesis investigation. I had no idea what Boland might do or how he was doing it, I didn't want him anywhere near my investigations. There was a case involving a Venezuelan player who had reached out to me about threatening emails he had received. Boland got involved in the case, and he had somehow gotten into the computer of the suspect who was threatening the player. That just didn't seem right.

After the *New Times* story landed, we began to follow the leads sent to us by Halem. But those leads were a direct result of player interviews conducted by MLB's lawyers and, it appeared, Boland. We didn't know to what extremes Boland would go to please Manfred, but we suspected he was hacking and that he was answering directly to Manfred instead of to his immediate supervisor, Michael Morris. I had no idea who Boland was targeting in cyberspace on any given day.

We discovered the identity of the *New Times* source—the former Biogenesis employee and Bosch associate Porter Fischer—after weeks of knocking on doors and leaving business cards at an address we had for him. We canvassed the Miami area in early February, trying to track down anyone who might have worked for Bosch or had some link to Biogenesis. But between Labor telling us to "stand down" when we got close to a potential source, visiting dozens of addresses, getting yelled at, having doors slammed in our faces, and conducting surveillance outside random buildings, we ran into a lot of dead ends in the weeks following the *New Times* report.

On February 25, we finally made contact with Fischer outside the SW 113th Street address where he lived in a room above the one-bay garage on the same property as his mother's house. Reilly and his partner Eddie Maldonado, a former NYPD lieutenant and an addition to the DOI, had been surveilling him from a car parked down the street from the house and rapped on his door around 6 p.m. Fischer answered, they told him the nature of their business, and Fischer agreed to talk.

Fischer was a sad, pathetic character who looked like a steroid poster boy. It didn't take long to realize he had some issues.

For roughly an hour and a half, the nervous, paranoid Fischer bared his soul, or at least parts of it. He had been a client of Bosch's for more than a year but said he had had a falling-out with Bosch after Bosch had stiffed him to the tune of $3,600. Fischer had used money from an insurance settlement to invest in Biogenesis. He said that Bosch had given him a marketing job at Biogenesis in exchange for the investment, but by the summer of 2012 the company was imploding, and when Bosch shut down Biogenesis in December and basically went underground, Fischer was left chasing his lost investment.

No money. No job.

A few years later, Bosch would describe that turbulent summer of 2012 as the beginning of the end of his Biogenesis experiment.

"People at the end started testing positive," he said. "Shit was already coming down. . . . After Melky pissed dirty, I was done after that. It was—I was dismantling the [business]—it was not worth it. I was out. I wanted out of the whole thing. . . . Manny Ramirez [testing positive] was on me. Ryan Braun was on me. And Melky's was on me. . . . I could give you a million excuses, but that was the deal. . . . I wanted out of the whole thing."

Bosch said he had kept Biogenesis open for the next six months mainly to collect the money he was owed by sports agents. "They owed me. The agencies, the agents owed me money. This is who I got paid by," he said.[12]

I didn't really buy his explanation for why Biogenesis had closed down. I thought the business had fallen apart because of Bosch's own extensive drug use and for another important reason: Porter Fischer had his notebooks.

Fischer, it turned out, had made a pivotal move amid the Biogenesis shutdown. Bosch had left a big footprint in his wake: notebooks, spreadsheets, and other documents that detailed his extensive client list, dosages of various PEDs, and a timeline of who was taking what and when. That was a big mistake, one from which Bosch probably could have escaped unscathed had he simply paid Fischer the $3,600 he owed him. Instead, Fischer had gotten his hands on a chunk of the contents of the boxes, including Bosch's notebooks, and also copied handwritten notes from Bosch's calendar.

But Fischer made his own missteps, too, starting with placing his trust in Peter Carbone, the owner of a Boca Raton tanning salon. Fischer had been Carbone's first client, and when Carbone learned that Fischer had gotten hold of the Biogenesis trove, he reached out to Fischer with an offer: he would pay Fischer $4,000—the $3,600 plus $400 "for your time and effort," he said—in exchange for the evidence Fischer had. During Fischer's interview with Reilly and Maldonado, he told them that he had given all of the Biogenesis evidence to Carbone for safekeeping. But Carbone told me and Maldonado later that when he had showed up at Fischer's house to complete the deal, Fischer had jumped out of the bushes waving two guns. Carbone had made the exchange anyway and gotten the notebooks, which he had later copied at a Kinko's. He had also transferred the information onto a hard drive and a zip drive.

Another figure who factored into the scenario was Jose "Pepe" Gomez, a longtime business associate in A-Rod's real estate company, Newport Property Ventures. Gomez, who would later cooperate with the government, was cited in court documents as having paid Fischer $4,000 for the documents on behalf of Rodriguez, but I always felt that Gomez's $4,000 payment and Carbone's $4,000 payment were one and the same.[13]

Fischer told the DOI that Carbone had later claimed to have sold the Biogenesis material to "someone in Alex Rodriguez's camp"; Carbone would tell us that he might have sold Rodriguez the books via A-Rod's associate Ugi Velazquez.

Fischer countered that he had also made copies of the Biogenesis documents and had shown a portion of them to the *Miami New Times*, which turned out to be true. Fischer said he had reached out to both the *New Times* and an ESPN reporter, but only the *New Times* returned his call. Fischer also said that three days before the *New Times* story broke, Carbone sent him a threatening text message warning that if he mentioned the drug dealer who had supplied Bosch, he would "end up dead in a canal."

Throughout Reilly's and Maldonado's interviews with Fischer between February 25 and March 11, 2013, he was all over the map—extremely nervous, agitated, and angry at Bosch. One moment he was talking about Rodriguez making $250 million a year, the next he was blurting out that Dominicans or Cubans were going to wax him because A-Rod wasn't going to get into the Hall of Fame. He said that Rodriguez was paying off everyone but the government was doing nothing about Bosch. He also said that Ricky Martinez, another former Biogenesis business partner, had told him that Bosch had flown to Detroit during the playoffs to collect money from Rodriguez for treatments. He said Bosch arrived in Detroit with loaded syringes, prescriptions, and letters from a doctor. According to Fischer, Bosch had flown all over the country meeting players.

Fischer continued to talk with the DOI, and on March 12, Mullin and Reilly arranged to meet him at a beach on the Deering Estate, a historical property on Biscayne Bay. Mullin was going to discuss a cash payment in exchange for the Biogenesis documents: $12,000 up front and a $4,000-per-month fee to act as an MLB consultant for one year. I stayed nearby in the car, although I did get out once to glance into Fischer's truck. The truck had a box inside on the passenger seat, but I couldn't tell if it was the same evidence he had taken from Biogenesis. The rest of the truck was full of trash—it looked as if Fischer unloaded his garbage into his truck on a regular basis.

The day after Mullin's offer, March 13, Fischer called Reilly and went ballistic, screaming into the phone that he was insulted by MLB's proposal, that his safety was not worth "that bullshit offer." Reilly calmly responded that Fischer should make a counteroffer, but Fischer wasn't having any of that. "Bullshit, I want $10 million!" he screamed into the phone. Reilly told him he was crazy, and Fischer only got more angry.

"It is as crazy as the offer made to me yesterday," Fischer said. "That is my final number." He texted Reilly that same day, demanding that he be compensated for his time. Reilly told him that MLB would get the Biogenesis information with or without Fischer's help and that unless he wanted to come back with a counteroffer, Reilly and MLB weren't going to be "held hostage" by him.

"Then our business and contact is concluded," Fischer texted. "Thank you for your time."

Five days later, Maldonado and I interviewed Carbone at a Barnes & Noble near his Boca tanning salon. Carbone showed up looking and sounding like a Mafia wannabe straight out of central casting. He wore a hooded sweatshirt with cutoff sleeves, his tattoos on full display. Like Fischer's, Carbone's gym-rat physique looked as if it were chemically enhanced.

Among the convoluted web of Biogenesis characters we interviewed, Carbone and a guy who called himself "Just Bobby" were two of the most bizarre individuals in the bunch. They were right up there with Blinky, Cesar Paublini's associate. Carbone not only told us about his connection to Fischer but also said he knew another man who had copies of the Biogenesis files whom we could contact. Carbone said the guy's name was Bobby and that he was a fifty-four-year-old male, blue eyes, heavyset, and would be looking for six figures. Carbone said Bobby was who we should deal with going forward. He said Bobby would be calling us.

Sure enough, twenty-four hours later, Mullin received a call from a man who introduced himself as Bobby. Mullin asked him for his last name.

"Just Bobby," he said. We got a kick out of that one.

Bobby told Mullin that he had the same documents as Fischer, that he wanted to get rid of them, and that many people were interested in taking them off his hands. Mullin made arrangements to meet with Just Bobby the next day at the parking lot of the Cosmos Diner in Pompano Beach, a greasy spoon on East Atlantic Boulevard near I-95. With Reilly and Maldonado conducting surveillance, Mullin met Just Bobby—a thug who had done time and whose real name was Gary Jones—and Bobby gave Mullin the flash drive so that he could view the documents on his computer. It was all right there, the same notebook pages from Bosch's records, the same documents Fischer had shown Reilly and Maldonado when they had interviewed him at the garage apartment. Mullin scrolled through the players' names, what Bosch was supplying them with, and the monies each player owed Bosch. Mullin was convinced that the files on Just Bobby's flash drive were real, and he conveyed that information to Manfred. Labor was already running the show and champing at the bit because the Fischer deal had fallen through, and Manfred gave the green light to make the buy. Later we would hear the theory that Mullin had somehow convinced Manfred to buy the documents, which was ludicrous.

On Wednesday, March 20, Mullin, Reilly, Maldonado, and I set out for the same Cosmos Diner in Pompano Beach. The faded yellow paint on the building was made a bit less dreary by the bright blue roof and the blood-red lettering that said DINER above the entrance. Mullin had received authorization from Manfred to purchase the documents from Just Bobby for $100,000. Mullin was to meet with him inside Cosmos, while Reilly and Maldonado did countersurveillance outside. Me? I was the lucky one who would get to sit inside near Mullin and witness the transaction. I would enter the restaurant first and try to determine who Bobby was when he arrived and note if he was with anyone or if I sensed this was going to be a robbery and not an exchange. Mind you, we were unarmed and not accompanied by law enforcement.

One of the enduring questions surrounding the documents was how exactly Porter Fischer had gotten his hands on Tony Bosch's notebooks and ledgers and whether MLB had knowingly paid what would end up totaling $125,000 for what it knew were stolen documents. The story Fischer would tell people—and the one Manfred would repeat throughout the investigation and even during his testimony in the arbitration hearing that followed Rodriguez's appeal of Selig's historic suspension of him later that summer—was that Biogenesis business partner Ricky Martinez had asked Fischer to dispose of Bosch's trash as the clinic was closing down. I never believed that story for one second. It made no sense, and Martinez would later deny the account to Mullin and me. But Fischer's story would give both Manfred and Fischer cover for having procured the documents.

While Mullin and I sat in the car in the parking lot before heading into the Cosmos Diner, I asked him one last time if he was certain we should do the transaction this way.

"Is Manfred ordering this?" I asked. "The documents are stolen, you do realize that? And you do know that someday they're going to try to pin this on you?"

I told him we should contact the DEA and have its agents back us up; we would go in with the money and get the thumb drives, then DEA agents could arrest the guy after we completed the deal.

"The DEA could take the documents and build their case," I said.

The way I looked at it, the alternative to the way baseball handled Bosch and the documents would have been to allow the DEA to proceed with its case, which I was certain would have ended up with Bosch sitting across a table in the US Attorney's Office in an orange jumpsuit, looking for a deal for less jail time. Again, that was what Senator Mitchell had recommended and what I had signed up for. I also believe the DEA would have shared what it had with us. The agency never wanted to indict players—it was after distributors—and Bosch was selling to high school kids, which was a big reason it went after him. Our goal was to suspend players who were using PEDs.

Mullin agreed that involving the DEA would be the right way to do it, but Manfred didn't want it done that way. The problem was, Manfred and Selig couldn't afford to wait; Selig needed to scrub his image before he retired and Manfred needed to cement his run at Selig's job.

We later found out that Labor Relations Department lawyer Steve Gonzalez had reached out to Fischer the same day to see, one last time, if Fischer would accept a deal with MLB. The offer was up to around $100,000, plus the additional stipulation that Fischer would be paid as a consultant to baseball for a year, as long as he cooperated. The way I looked at it, that arrangement looked a whole lot better than meeting in secret in a Florida diner and handing over a hundred grand in a paper bag. But that day Fischer was still looking for seven figures and turned down the offer.

I entered the diner first and immediately spotted a heavyset guy I assumed was Just Bobby. I had never met him or seen him but had been given a description. The guy sitting in a booth had slicked-back salt-and-pepper hair, and was middle-aged with a sizable gut. He wore a blue golf shirt, khaki shorts, and sandals. I sat diagonally across from him and was already mentally cursing myself for not having arrived earlier. Just Bobby had arranged to meet Mullin at noon, but he must have arrived about forty-five minutes earlier, because I walked in and took my seat about 11:30. I knew then that this wasn't his first rodeo.

The diner was of Just Bobby's choosing, a huge no-no in my former line of work in the undercover world. When the person you're meeting chooses the place and you're bringing the cash, it usually means you're going to get robbed. I had told Mullin never to let the bad guy pick the location. When you choose the place, you can have people in there ahead of you or you might know the people in the restaurant, who can serve as lookouts. All the characters we were dealing with were con artists and thieves. Who's to say Just Bobby wouldn't be waiting with some muscle and just take the $100K?

Mullin had picked up the money earlier that morning at a Miami bank, and I was to videotape what I could with an iPad. Once I was sitting across from Just Bobby, I used my cell phone to snap a photo of him, which I texted to Mullin and the other two. They confirmed that it was our guy.

Mullin then came in and went over to shake hands with Bobby. Unfortunately for me, Mullin moved Bobby to the farthest booth at the opposite end of the diner, which meant that now all I could see was the back of Bobby's head and Mullin, who was sitting directly in front of him. I put my iPad on top of the windowsill next to my booth for surveillance, and while the waitress was in the kitchen I took a short video from the new angle.

The two men sat across from each other in one of the diner's blue fake-leather booths, and Mullin pushed a yellowish envelope across the table. Inside were $100 bills in bands of $1,000, which, in turn, were in bands of $10,000 for a total of $100,000 in cash, which Mullin had carried into the diner in the paper bag.

Mullin and Bobby talked for about a half hour, after which Mullin walked out with the four thumb drives that contained Bosch's handwritten notes and Bobby walked out with a bag full of cash.

Years later, respected voices involved in the Biogenesis case opined on MLB's decision to carry through with the document buy.

"Professionally I was offended. To engage in that kind of conduct, to get down in the gutter, is not fitting of any lawyer. I did not think baseball conducted themselves in an honorable way," Pittsburgh sports attorney Jay Reisinger said in 2017. Reisinger represented several of the players who ended up getting suspended by MLB in the Biogenesis case. "Someone higher than Dan Mullin would have had to give the green light [to purchase the documents], but the case had become a runaway freight train."[14]

Pat Sullivan, the assistant US attorney who prosecuted Bosch and the other individuals in the federal case, also recalled his reaction to MLB's strategy for obtaining the Biogenesis documents. "I was surprised about it, that they paid people who turned over documents. That is not the way law enforcement conducts itself. I'm not sure what applies to private investigators with a private organization, but it's certainly not textbook law enforcement," said Sullivan, who retired in 2017 after a four-decade career as a high-profile prosecutor whose cases included taking on former Panamanian dictator Manuel Noriega.[15]

I texted Reilly and Maldonado, and they followed Mullin out of the lot. I stayed behind to make sure there was no countersurveillance and left ten minutes later.

Mullin spoke with Just Bobby again on both April 13 and 14 with regard to a second batch of Biogenesis documents. Just Bobby told Mullin he was in talks with Rodriguez's camp to sell it documents, too, and that A-Rod was willing to pay him upward of $100,000, but he would have to deliver them in person. Just Bobby feared for his safety. During their conversation on April 14, he asked Mullin what MLB's best offer was, and that's when I got word that Manfred had authorized MLB to offer another $25,000. Just Bobby accepted the offer, and for the second MLB buy, in mid-April, we met him at an Office Depot in Boca Raton where Mullin made the exchange and we gained photos and ledgers that Fischer had somehow procured. We believed the information had come from Carbone.

Just Bobby was dressed similarly to the first meeting and was in the same black Cadillac he had driven to the diner. I stayed outside, and when they left the building a few minutes later, Mullin had the documents he wanted and Bobby had his twenty-five grand. Mullin described dealing with Just Bobby, who had done three years in prison for forgery and who we suspected was a true, old-fashioned con man and proud of it, as a pleasure compared to Porter Fischer.

CHAPTER 12

HACKER

Mullin and I had been with Manfred and Halem in Miami only days before the document buy at the Cosmos Diner. MLB executives were there for the World Baseball Classic—the international baseball tournament that had been Bob DuPuy's pet project when he was still MLB president. The tournament was under way, and Marlins Park played host to the semifinals held between March 12 and March 16. Manfred and Halem called for a meeting at the InterContinental Miami hotel to share information about what we were all working on regarding Biogenesis. Once we entered the conference room, we got a jarring surprise: Neil Boland, the MLB IT guy who had risen through the ranks, was stationed in front of two computers and was about to address us. We had known Boland was a big part of Labor's investigation, but for Mullin, the head of the DOI, and me to see him in this setting, conversing with Manfred and Halem about such a sensitive subject, was surreal. Manfred spoke briefly, then handed the conversation over to Boland, who told us only what they wanted us to hear, which wasn't much. Mullin gave them an update on what we were working on, leaving out only that we were still quietly talking to the DEA.

After the meeting ended, Mullin and I just looked at each other. Nothing needed to be said. We had all discussed Boland's role in Biogenesis ad nauseam. We simply couldn't figure out why Manfred was aligning himself with him. MLB had hired Boland to work in the IT department, but Mullin knew that DOI needed technical help and had brought him in to be our chief tech geek. Once he began working special assignments for Manfred, however, we quickly discovered just how adept he was with a keyboard. He was a prototypical computer guy—unassuming looks, a scraggly beard, bland clothes. If Boland walked across Park Avenue outside MLB's offices during a typical busy lunch hour in Midtown, he would blend right into the Manhattan maw.

A fringe character in the Biogenesis case had put Boland into the spotlight when he had named Boland as a defendant in a lawsuit filed in 2016 in New York Supreme Court. Neiman Nix, a journeyman minor-league pitcher who had been drafted by the Reds in the late 1990s, had started his own sports performance complex and baseball academy in Florida called DNA Sports Lab. During baseball's Biogenesis probe, Nix claimed that MLB's investigation into him had damaged his business and reputation.

"An innocent man has been stripped of his livelihood and his business destroyed. It is time we all knew what happened with Biogenesis," Nix's attorney, Vincent White, said during a press con-ference in White's cramped Manhattan office in July 2016.

Nix sat to the left of White during the meeting with reporters, his hulking size dwarfing that of his counsel. The lawsuit outlined how between February and April 2013, MLB investigators, some of whom had falsely represented themselves as FBI and DEA agents, had contacted many of Nix's clients and his colleagues and, as they inquired about Nix, had accused him of "selling illegal substances to MLB players."

Nix had filed suit against MLB in February 2014 in Miami-Dade

County, but it had been dismissed without prejudice. He claimed that approximately a day before he had filed that suit, MLB "began hacking/attacking DNA Sports Lab's social media accounts, severely disrupting Nix's ability to do business."

In Nix's 2016 lawsuit, he named Neil Boland as Manfred's "right-hand man" and said that Boland had been "pulled out of DOI" by Manfred and instructed to report directly to Manfred after Manfred learned of Boland's "expertise as a computer analyst and his ability to skillfully hack computers and accounts through various means and exploits."

Baseball responded to Nix's lawsuit with a lengthy statement, calling the legal action "frivolous," and the New York Supreme Court finally dismissed it in June of 2018, saying Nix had already dismissed two suits stemming from the same incident in Florida and New York. My assumption is that Nix and his attorney hoped they would be able to depose others who had knowledge of Boland's methods.

By March 2013, Boland certainly was in a position of power, and he was dispatched to Miami later that spring to conduct an interview with Lazaro "Lazer" Collazo, a former University of Miami baseball coach. Think about that—an IT guy sent to interview a potential witness in a major investigation initiated by baseball, an investigation that the DOI was uniquely qualified to handle. It was the type of case for which our unit had specifically been created when Mitchell had made his recommendations. Yet here was a computer specialist questioning Collazo.

Years later, Collazo, who is Cuban American, would recall how Boland and Labor lawyer Pat Houlihan appeared at his suburban Miami home "around 10" on the night of April 4 to pepper him with questions about Alex Rodriguez and Biogenesis.[1]

"They asked me about Alex, about Tony Bosch," Collazo said. "They wanted more, and what I mean by wanting more, they kept saying, We feel you know a lot more than what you're saying. You know more. We're going to take this to the newspaper."

Collazo said he feared for his family. "They said if you don't give us more, we're going to embarrass your family on their visas," he said. "Not only was my wife there, but Daniella, my youngest child, was about nine or ten and she heard all this. She got pretty emotional. She heard about jail, because they mentioned jail. You know, they were trying to scare me."

Collazo, who happened to have had jury duty the next day, said that MLB "kept calling me, calling me. We had to break for jury duty, so I called them back. They were getting after me. 'We know that you have more information on Alex. We know you've met with Alex. We know, we know, we know.' Threats, that's the right word to use."[2]

Collazo would be subpoenaed as a witness in the lawsuit MLB would file against Bosch and his cohorts two days after Mullin handed a paper bag containing $100,000 to Gary "Just Bobby" Jones in the Cosmos Diner. He would eventually become a defendant in the federal Biogenesis case out of US attorney Wifredo Ferrer's Miami office. Collazo was charged with one count of conspiracy to distribute testosterone, although he ended up cutting a deal for a misdemeanor and was sentenced to probation. It's safe to say that Collazo's inclusion in the indictment had little or nothing to do with Boland and Houlihan's investigation.

Eventually Collazo hammered back at Rodriguez, suing him in Florida state court in June 2015, accusing A-Rod and two other defendants of violating Florida privacy laws when Rodriguez's camp purchased the Biogenesis documents—which included private medical records—and shared them with third parties. As of December 2017, that case was still open.[3]

"Based on the evidence that we saw in the Biogenesis case, there were many people that should have been charged with serious crimes other than what the defendants were charged with," Miami attorney Frank Quintero Jr., who represented Collazo in the federal criminal case as well as in Collazo's lawsuit against Rodriguez, would say years later, although he wouldn't identify specific names. "Witness tampering, obstruction, bribing witnesses—they were all given a pass."[4]

Collazo would later describe Rodriguez as a "fucking liar." "He—he lies. He has the people to be able, I guess, money, or I don't know what it is. But look at Alex, Texas, Yankees, Biogenesis. Nothing's happened to him. Nothing at all."

Collazo said his career had been ruined because of his inclusion in the feds' case. "All this ruined—all this bullcrap for Biogenesis ruined my career," he said. "I cannot get a professional job because steroids, Biogenesis, it's always going to be there. I can't get a college job because of all of that. Now all those national championship rings, all those [College] World Series things, and my name, Lazer Collazo, which is one of the top names in college baseball, are ruined."[5]

The media and other critics had a field day accusing the DOI of using intimidation tactics during the course of our Biogenesis investigation, but the Boland/Houlihan visit to Collazo was one blatant example of what was really happening: Manfred had created a shadow group consisting of Boland and the lawyers from Labor, plus former Miami law enforcement officers and outside investigators, to take over the investigation. They were operating wholly independently of the DOI. The former law enforcement types were apparently knocking on doors and flashing badges at people, something we were blamed for, as if flashing an old NYPD or Boston PD badge in Miami and yelling "Let us in!" would ever fly.

The DEA group supervisor on the Biogenesis case, Jeannette Moran, would later say she had never seen interference like that. "I've had a twenty-five-year career," she said. "That was the first."[6]

MLB sued Bosch and his associates in Florida state court, accusing Bosch and the five other defendants of "intentional and unjustified tortious interference" with contracts between players and MLB, a lawsuit we read about in the newspaper. We were shocked, to say the least. Then we got the "What the hell is going on?" call from the DEA. We had no explanation. In baseball's view it was a legal strategy designed to get Bosch to flip and cooperate with its investigation, but the DEA had a different take on the validity of MLB's legal theory.

"At the time [Bosch] didn't have a pot to piss in anyway," Kevin Stanfill, the DEA agent, would say. "His main thing for cooperating with MLB was money, attorneys, trying to get somebody to say he was a decent guy."[7]

Against that chaotic backdrop of lawsuits, shadow investigators, and secret document buys, there was also what I considered to be a mini–land mine involving Mullin. The details of an intimate relationship between Mullin and a woman with ties to Biogenesis wouldn't become public until the fall of 2013, when Alex Rodriguez ratcheted up his legal blitz and filed lawsuits against baseball and a Yankee team doctor. A-Rod's lawsuit against MLB included the claim about Mullin, but once the media reports appeared with details about Mullin's brief relationship with the woman, Loraine Delgadillo—who had been ruled out as a witness—I wondered who had leaked the information to reporters.

Delgadillo was described by the Florida Department of Health as the director of patient services for Biogenesis, but when I learned about her through the media accounts and after talking with Mullin, it turned out that she had worked primarily for Pedro Bosch, Tony's father, at Biokem, the predecessor to Biogenesis, years before the Biogenesis mess had unfolded. Mullin's reason for contacting Delgadillo in the first place was to see if she had any insight or leads that might prove valuable. Mullin, divorced for years, had met with her several times and had on one occasion presented her with numerous photos of players—a poor man's police lineup—to see if she recognized any faces or remembered seeing any professional athletes being treated by either Pedro or Tony Bosch. Delgadillo had claimed not to have recognized any of the faces, and she had added no new information to advance the case. Mullin didn't consider her a witness and vetted her status, or lack thereof, through Pat Houlihan in the legal department, who concurred.

None of those details emerged in the media accounts.

According to a *New York Times* report published later in 2013, the meetings between Mullin and Delgadillo took place in February, and the report said Mullin had sent her a bouquet of flowers on Valentine's Day with a note of thanks for her cooperation. In return, Delgadillo had called Mullin to thank him, and the *Times* report said Mullin had subsequently invited Delgadillo to dinner. They had met three times after Valentine's Day 2013, and Mullin had spent at least one night at her home, the *Times* report said, citing an affidavit Delgadillo had signed and had given to A-Rod's camp as they rolled out his legal assault. The affidavit would become part of the lawsuit Rodriguez filed against baseball, and his legal team would make allegations that Mullin's relationship with Delgadillo had been inappropriate and unethical since she was a potential witness. The *Times* report pointed out that Delgadillo had accepted $100,000 from Rodriguez's representatives in exchange for the note Mullin had written her, along with Mullin's business card and access to Delgadillo's text messages. When an independent arbitrator, Fredric Horowitz, later ruled on whether to uphold A-Rod's historic 211-game Biogenesis doping suspension—handed down by Selig in August 2013—Horowitz would cite Mullin's relationship with Delgadillo as insignificant to the overall baseball probe into Biogenesis.[8]

"Also unfounded are the charges of improper conduct by MLB investigators during the investigation," Horowitz wrote in his decision dated January 11, 2014, in which he also upheld A-Rod's punishment but reduced the ban from 211 to 162 games. "Regarding the indiscreet sexual liaison by one MLB investigator with a former Biogenesis employee, that liaison did not yield any information relevant to the investigation or the suspension herein."

I had no direct contact with Delgadillo, and February 2013 was a nonstop slog for the DOI in our pursuit to make progress on any front in the case. I thought Mullin's relationship was a meaningless encounter that had been blown out of proportion, especially since Delgadillo had seemed to provide no concrete information that helped our case and was tied to an earlier chapter in the Bosch family saga, before Biogenesis had blown up. I had certainly heard of worse behavior within MLB circles.

CHAPTER 13

JUSTICE

Alex Rodriguez always drew a crowd, and in the rollicking early days of the Biogenesis hysteria it was no surprise that a mob of reporters surrounded him on opening day at Yankee Stadium—April 1, 2013—even though he wasn't in the lineup and wouldn't be on the big-league roster for more than four months because he was rehabbing from hip surgery. He skipped the pregame introductions that day—his choice, a team spokesman said—when the Yankees played the rival Red Sox.

"I'll tell you what, when I get introduced I want to be on the field and not look back," Rodriguez told reporters. He was coming off his second hip surgery in four years, but his health issues were being dwarfed by the Biogenesis blowback. He talked to reporters on April 1 only for about five minutes and didn't divulge much about the scandal enveloping him. A-Rod said he stood by an earlier statement released by his handlers, a dull paragraph issued in the immediate aftermath of the *New Times* report that said Rodriguez had never been treated by Anthony Bosch.

"The news report about a purported relationship between Alex Rodriguez and Anthony Bosch are not true," said the statement released by Sitrick and Company. "Alex Rodriguez was not

Mr. Bosch's patient, he was never treated by him and he was never advised by him. The purported documents referenced in the [*New Times*] story—at least as they relate to Alex Rodriguez—are not legitimate."

Never mind that detailed accounts of Rodriguez's extensive drug use would emerge in court documents, in our own investigation in conjunction with the DEA, and even in Horowitz's ruling for Rodriguez's arbitration. According to that document—which became public only because Rodriguez's lawyers included it in the federal lawsuit they filed in January 2014 against MLB, Bud Selig, and the Players Association, challenging the yearlong suspension Horowitz had upheld—Bosch and A-Rod were thick as thieves.

"During the course of their relationship, in addition to providing Rodriguez with infusions, Bosch personally injected Rodriguez with banned substances between four to six times, including injecting him with testosterone," Horowitz wrote. "In 2011, Bosch met Rodriguez at least four or five times in New York or Miami to draw blood and infuse him intravenously with substances that always included testosterone and hGH [human growth hormone]."[1]

Horowitz even described secret meetings in a Miami Starbucks bathroom, in an Atlanta hotel room where Rodriguez instructed Bosch to use the hotel service elevator, and during Bosch's trip to Detroit for the 2012 baseball playoffs, where he had supplied A-Rod with "hGH and peptides."

Of course, the A-Rod lies were later revealed in spectacular fashion, despite his constant denials in 2013 of PED use. Once Bosch agreed to cooperate with baseball, Rodriguez's house of cards collapsed.

On June 3, 2013, Bosch made that fateful decision in exchange for having his name removed from MLB's lawsuit and for having his legal fees and expenses, security, and public relations fees paid for by

MLB. According to an analysis of the records, Bosch received perhaps something more.

Jay Reisinger, the Pittsburgh-based lawyer who represented several players suspended in the Biogenesis case, said in 2017 that he believed Bosch received some of MLB's money based on the large amount paid to Bosch's lawyers, particularly to the firm of one of the lead attorneys. "I strongly believe some of that money made its way to Bosch," Reisinger said.[2]

Pat Sullivan said that he had never been part of a case in which the government's primary target agreed to cooperate with a private entity's parallel investigation.

"It was new to me," said Sullivan. "MLB got our target, Bosch, to cooperate with baseball. That was certainly new and different."

Bosch said that it was no easy decision for him to agree to help baseball, mainly because he had always lived by his own rules. "It was very hard. I was out of options. I was never going to cooperate. But, you know, once you put me up against a wall, I mean, there was nowhere I could turn."[3]

Rick Burnham was assigned to serve as Bosch's bodyguard on his frequent trips to New York and reported Bosch's activities to Mullin and Hanna. They were quite spectacular. There were fancy dinners at posh restaurants. Top-shelf booze. After-hours bars frequented by cops. Reports of cocaine use. Strip clubs.

The tab was impressive.

According to a July 10, 2014, letter by Charles Scheeler of George Mitchell's DLA Piper law firm (the same firm Mitchell worked for when he wrote the Mitchell Report) sent to assistant US attorney Sharad Motiani in the Miami US Attorney's office, the legal fees and PR costs MLB paid on behalf of Bosch alone totaled almost $4 million. Of that amount, $1,253,653 went to the law firms of Samuel J. Rabin Jr. and Susy Ribero-Ayala—Bosch's lead attorney—and to Ribero-Ayala's husband's firm, Ribero-Ayala Law. The figures were included in the letter, which was attached to an affidavit in a defense motion in the federal case against Lazer Collazo. The Bosch expenses were as follows:

Security: $1,456,175

Legal fees and expenses: $766,849

Legal fees and expenses: $574,764

Legal fees and expenses: $486,804

Public relations firm retained by Bosch's counsel: $349,683

Legal fees and expenses: $285,474

Several experts, including Reisinger, believed Ribero-Ayala's legal fees were extremely high. In addition, MLB paid several third parties, including the $125,000 to Gary "Just Bobby" Jones; $5,000 to Porter Fischer (he described it as a down payment); $3,762 to Biogenesis employee Kristina Hernandez; $5,000 to Xavier Romero and $2,500 to his attorney; and $3,169 to one of Ricardo Martinez's attorneys and $25,000 to another.

What the letter did not list was a purported $19,000 hotel expense for Bosch's stay at the Biltmore in Coral Gables. The Biltmore tab was one of several expense items detailed in a 2015 *Miami Herald* story, which cited federal court records filed in the Biogenesis case. The report said that the MLB money was used by Bosch for personal expenses that included the Biltmore stay, strip joint junkets, personal loans, leases on ritzy condo properties in Miami and Fisher Island, overdue child support payments, and counseling for Bosch's cocaine addiction.

And that didn't count the cost of putting up the DOI in Florida for months—always three of us, sometimes six—much less Bosch's hotel and extracurricular activities costs.

While things would only intensify for Rodriguez following that Bronx cameo on opening day, the DOI basically disappeared from the Biogenesis landscape. We had received orders from above that we were not to start any new investigations nor even to continue with ones we were already conducting, including the wellness clinics we had pinpointed in Florida and Arizona as drug sources for players. Those issues were forever put on the back burner. I continued to do the age/ID/residency investigations, and we continued to chase leads sent to us by Halem and Boland, but as far as I was concerned, we were chasing ghosts.

At one point I was asked to babysit Bosch in New York because Burnham needed a day off. I bailed on that assignment. No way was I looking after someone I viewed as nothing more than a drug dealer. I told George Hanna it wasn't happening and that I didn't care if I was fired for refusing an order.

A-Rod's legal team, meanwhile, was going through its own version of musical chairs throughout the first half of 2013. Reports had Reisinger and Florida power attorney Roy Black acting as his counsel early on, but Desiree Perez, an influential figure inside hip-hop mogul Jay-Z's empire, which by 2013 included the nascent sports agency called Roc Nation Sports, would soon become a major force dictating Rodriguez's scorched-earth legal strategy. Perez, a former cocaine distributor in the 1990s, had been a drug mole for the DEA and had then gone on the lam, later serving nine months in prison, soon took the reins on A-Rod's case and drove it over a cliff. One of her early moves was to advise Rodriguez to turn down a deal that would have resulted in a much lighter fifty-game suspension. According to an ESPN report, MLB had negotiated a deal with Rodriguez that would have put Rodriguez back on the field in late 2013, had he accepted it. But once Perez got involved, that deal was incinerated. (As it turned out, Rodriguez ended up playing for the Yankees the last two months of the 2013 season after appealing his ban.)[4]

In a lengthy profile of Perez in the *Daily News* in May 2014, details emerged of how she had urged Rodriguez in 2013 to fight MLB, even though Bosch would agree to cooperate with baseball and help MLB compile more than enough evidence of Rodriguez's doping history with Biogenesis. Perez had no legal background and no experience with arbitration or collective bargaining, yet she was calling the shots for Rodriguez.[5]

Reisinger and Black, the attorneys on Rodriguez's legal team, were supplanted later in 2013 by a sizable group of expensive barristers, including Joe Tacopina, the brash and oft-quoted New York tabloid staple. When he wasn't surrounding himself with a questionable inner circle, Rodriguez was putting his foot into his mouth. He used his Twitter account to go public in late June to claim that he had been cleared by Dr. Bryan Kelly of the Hospital for Special Surgery to play baseball again, a statement that led Yankee general manager Brian Cashman to tell ESPN that Rodriguez "should just shut the fuck up. That's it."[6]

Rodriguez was interviewed by Mullin, Manfred, and Halem on July 12 in Tampa while he was in the midst of his rehab assignment, but after that group meeting, he didn't bother to show up at Steinbrenner Field at the Yankees' spring training complex to participate in a Single-A Tampa Yankees game scheduled for later that night.

Why Manfred and Halem took Mullin along to the interview was puzzling even to Dan, and I can only imagine the awkwardness he must have felt in that meeting. The best explanation we could come up with was that at that point MLB was trying to get info from Rodriguez on Toronto physician Anthony Galea, the scandal-ridden doctor caught up in a federal investigation three years earlier, and Dan, Victor Burgos, and I had investigated Galea previously. Galea had treated A-Rod, Tiger Woods, Carlos Beltran, José Reyes, and numerous other athletes despite not having a license to practice medicine in the United States. Eventually he pleaded guilty to bringing misbranded drugs across the border to treat pro athletes, but he avoided jail time and in December 2011 was sentenced to one year of supervised release. Galea claimed to have treated A-Rod only with anti-inflammatory medication following Rodriguez's first hip surgery. Galea's Canadian medical license was eventually suspended for nine months in December 2017, when a Canadian medical regulatory body's discipline committee punished him for what it deemed "an act of professional misconduct."[7]

A few days after the meeting, MLB Players Association executive director Michael Weiner, speaking at an association charity event on Long Island but already confined to a wheelchair due to his battle with brain cancer, painted a dark picture of the Rodriguez situation in an interview with the *Daily News*, even though Weiner didn't mention Rodriguez by name.

"I can tell you, if we have a case where there really is overwhelming evidence that a player committed a violation of the program, our fight is going to be that they make a deal," said Weiner. "We're not interested in having players with overwhelming evidence that they violated the [drug] program out there. Most of the players aren't interested in that. We'd like to have a clean program."[8]

Three days before Bud Selig dropped the hammer on Rodriguez and twelve other major and minor league players—Ryan Braun had already accepted his suspension and was cooperating with MLB—suspending them based on their ties to Biogenesis, A-Rod was in Trenton, New Jersey, in what would be the last of his rehab assignments. He walloped a home run against Reading, but after the game it was clear that he felt even his own team was against him, not to mention the commissioner's office, and tried to switch the focus away from his PED use toward his massive contract.

"I think it's pretty self-explanatory. I think that's the pink elephant in the room," said Rodriguez. "I think we all agree that we want to get rid of PEDs; that's a must. All the players, we feel that way. But when all this stuff is going on in the background, and people are finding creative ways to cancel your contract, that's concerning for me, concerning for present and I think it should be concerning for future players, as well. There is a process. I'm excited about the way I feel tonight and I'm going to keep fighting."[9]

Rodriguez fought, all right, and when the August 5 MLB announcements about the suspensions came out, he was the only player of the fourteen disciplined who appealed. Selig hit A-Rod with a 211-game ban, while the other players got fifty-game suspensions. Ryan Braun had agreed to sit out sixty-five games in late July.

"Rodriguez's discipline under the Joint Drug Prevention and Treatment Program is based on his use and possession of numerous forms of prohibited performance-enhancing substances, including Testosterone and Human Growth Hormone, over the course of multiple years," the MLB announcement said. "Rodriguez's discipline under the Base Agreement is for attempting to cover up his violations of the Program by engaging in a course of conduct intended to obstruct and frustrate the Office of Commissioner's investigation."[10]

It was kind of the same way Labor was obstructing and frustrating everything we had done along the way.

Rodriguez's appeal of the 211-game ban allowed him to take the field against the White Sox in Chicago on August 5, the same day baseball announced the player suspensions. A-Rod blooped a single in his season debut and handled several chances at third but wasn't a savior as the Yankees got clobbered 8–1. "The last seven months have been a nightmare," he said before the game. "Probably the worst time of my life."[11]

Maybe that was true, but a bigger nightmare came in the form of his arbitration hearing, which began on September 30 at MLB's Park Avenue offices. What a shit storm that turned out to be—with Rodriguez arriving to a cheering throng of fans the first day, some of whom held Dominican flags or signs—LEAVE A-ROD ALONE and FAKE JUSTICE—that voiced support for him.

The hearing would play out in a conference room on the twenty-ninth floor of MLB headquarters, where you exit the elevator, make a right, and walk past all the mannequins dressed in major-league uniforms. A photo of Bosch dressed in a tie and jacket walking to the hearing with Rick Burnham to his left became the art for countless media stories during that stretch of time, since no photographers were allowed to document the proceedings inside the MLB offices.

"It was five days—you could make a movie out of those five days," Bosch would say in 2017 of his testimony. "Alex is a very insecure individual. Very insecure. In every aspect."[12]

Alongside Rodriguez was Joe Tacopina, the attorney with the slicked-back hair who had taken the lead in Rodriguez's arbitration and who had barked about A-Rod's mistreatment by MLB in the media from the moment he was retained. Rounding out Rodriguez's legal team were Reed Smith attorneys Jordan Siev and James McCarroll. Rodriguez practically needed Tacopina to block for him to reach the stairs to the 245 Park Avenue entrance, so thick was the crowd near the street.

By the second day, a group billing itself as Hispanics Across America crowded together next to the curb in front of MLB's front entrance, the protesters cordoned off by metal gates. They had grown in strength, and the leader of the pack was a guy named Fernando Mateo, whom I had met early on in the DOI days. Mateo seemed to have his hands in a number of different businesses, including a Latin hotspot called La Marina overlooking the George Washington Bridge and the Hudson River. On the one occasion I interviewed him, I found Mateo to be someone who had a lot of gripes, although I believed his complaints about MLB ignoring PEDs in the Dominican Republic to be justified. In 2005, he orchestrated a demonstration at MLB's offices in which protesters delivered a coffin to league headquarters, symbolic of two Dominican prospects who had died after allegedly injecting themselves with performance-enhancing substances.

Now, on day two of A-Rod's arbitration, Mateo was on the other side of the PED fight, and blabbering away to the media about the unjust treatment of Rodriguez. He also threatened legal action against a security guard for supposedly spilling coffee on him. The A-Rod supporters were taking aim at MLB, holding up signs that read, NO JUSTICE, NO PEACE, FIRE BUD SELIG, TONY BOSCH IS A DRUG DEALER TO MINORS, and IN THE 90S BUD SELIG WAS A STEROID LOVER. They also took a shot at Yankee president Randy Levine with a sign that read, RANDY LEVINE IS THE DEVIL. The posters all seemed to be written in the same handwriting. Then there was the question of whether Rodriguez was paying all of those people to stand outside on the street in support of him. Mateo told the media that donations had helped pay for food for the supporters and for the white T-shirts they would soon wear with SUPPORT A-ROD 13 printed across the front. He didn't really have much of an explanation for the $106,000 full-page ad supporting A-Rod and criticizing MLB placed by Hispanics Across America in the *New York Times*. According to Mateo, the group had received an anonymous $100,000 donation to be used in support of Rodriguez. Clearly the money came in handy. According to the *Daily News*, the group had ended 2011 with just $1 in assets.[13]

The first few days of the arbitration featured Bosch as MLB's star witness, testifying before the three-person panel composed of Rob Manfred, union attorney David Prouty, and Fredric Horowitz, the independent arbitrator and panel chairman. Horowitz, like any independent arbitrator working for baseball and the Players Association, was in a precarious position: he could be fired by either side at any time, as had happened with Shyam Das, his predecessor. The drama outside on the streets with A-Rod's supporters was matched in the huge conference room high above Park Avenue in which A-Rod's attorney, Tacopina, waged a verbal war with Manfred, Bosch, Horowitz, and everyone else not in Rodriguez's camp.

Bosch was under direct questioning on the first day, testifying to how he had come to know Yuri Sucart and later Sucart's famous cousin Alex Rodriguez. Sucart, Bosch testified, had been brought to Bosch by Jorge "Ugi" Velazquez. "I guess for lack of a better term we ran around in the same circles, if you will," he said of Velazquez.

Bosch testified that he had given troches—gellike capsules that could be filled with banned substances such as synthetic testosterone—first to Sucart and later to A-Rod. "[Sucart] told me that he had used one and that it was—it was great, it was unbelievable," he said. Later, during direct examination by MLB attorney Howard Ganz, Bosch was asked if Sucart had ever referenced Rodriguez when Sucart had first started using troches. "[Sucart] said that the cousin—just like that—quote unquote, the cousin—he also used the word 'the man'—loved it, loved—loved the troche, was explosive," he testified.

"And how, just to ask you about the operation of your mind, when Mr. Sucart referred to the cousin, or the man, or/and the man, to whom did you believe he was referring?" asked Ganz.

"I believe he was referring to Alex, Mr. Rodriguez," said Bosch.

Bosch testified in detail about his doping relationship with A-Rod, how he would travel to collect blood samples from A-Rod, and how the concerned Rodriguez wanted constant assurances that he wouldn't test positive by using the drugs Bosch provided, unlike the experience of another client of Bosch's, Manny Ramirez, who had gotten busted in 2009.

"And did you tell Mr. Rodriguez what you had given Ramirez?" Ganz asked.

"Yes," said Bosch.

"And what did you say you had given Ramirez?"

"Well, I—I'm going—I didn't get too detailed in everything, but I told him that it was a protocol that I had arranged for him that consisted of troches, creams—intramuscular injections, subcutaneous injections," said Bosch.

"Those troches and creams include substances that were banned by Major League Baseball?" Ganz asked.

"Yes," said Bosch.

"Testosterone?"

"That was one of the ingredients, yes," said Bosch.

"I think you said that Mr. Rodriguez asked you what you had given Manny Ramirez, correct?" Ganz asked.

"Correct," said Bosch.

"And indeed you had given Manny Ramirez certain substances, correct?"

"Yes."

"And did you proceed to tell Mr. Rodriguez what you had given Ramirez?" asked Ganz.

"Yes, I did," said Bosch.

"And what did you say in that respect?"

"Well, I basically told him that Mr. Ramirez had a certain protocol and it was all—you know, defined by his—by his values, his deficiencies. I spoke about a cream, I spoke about a troche, I spoke about a—subcutaneous injections, intramuscular injections also, and some other supplements," said Bosch.

"Okay. Prior to that time Mr. Ramirez had been suspended for having tested positive for banned substances. Were you aware of that?" Ganz asked.

"Yes," Bosch said.

"And did Mr. Rodriguez ask you anything about that?"

"Yes," said Bosch.

"What did he ask?"

"He asked why he had tested positive," said Bosch.

"And what did you tell him?"

"I told him why he had tested positive and it was due to—an intramuscular injection that he had taken at the wrong time and administered by, I believe, his cousin."

"Did Mr. Rodriguez ask you how he could be assured that if he used whatever you recommended he would not test positive?" asked Ganz. "Was there any discussion about any risk Mr. Rodriguez might encounter from taking substances that you had described?"

"Yes," said Bosch.

"What was that discussion?"

"He asked me several questions on that subject," said Bosch.

"To the best of your recollection, what was the subject?" Ganz asked.

"He asked me the assurance that—or how is it that he wouldn't be able to test positive—you know, what is—what is in the creams—what is in the—in the injections? And he kept asking me the same question over and over again for reassurance purposes," said Bosch. "I basically told [Rodriguez] that Mr. Ramirez had tested positive due to not following instructions or directions. And that if done according—properly, with the right blood values, with the right diagnostic testing and with precise timing on everything, and dos-aging, then it was nearly impossible to get caught."

During the October 1 proceedings, Bosch testified that he had traveled to New York in 2010 to draw blood from Rodriguez at his apartment, but A-Rod had arrived late to their appointment. "Mr. Rodriguez finally arrived. It could have been one a.m., two a.m., three a.m., something to that effect, and I drew his blood and collected his blood properly and then I left," he said. The drugs Bosch had provided for Rodriguez in 2010—"some were prohibited, others weren't," Bosch testified—included, in Bosch's words, "testosterone, IGF-1, growth hormone, GHRP, CJC1295, L-glutathione, cocktails of B complexes."

At numerous times during the hearing, Bosch was asked about the Biogenesis files, and at one point late in the day two proceedings, Tacopina asked Bosch who had stolen his files.

"Porter Fischer stole my files and everything else," Bosch testified. He would later revisit the issue during direct examination by Ganz, reiterating how Fischer had obtained the clinic documents, torpedoing the theory that Biogenesis business partner Ricky Martinez had given them to Fischer.

"Mr. Martinez called me back," Bosch said. "I don't know if it was a phone call or I met him, but eventually he told me that Mr. Fischer had taken the documents and that Mr. Fischer told him that he was not going to give them back until he got paid.

"I addressed that with Mr. Martinez. I said, 'You know, pay this guy. It was your responsibility to make the payments.' Then Mr. Martinez told me there was no money to make the payments, something to that effect."

Later in the proceedings, when Manfred took the stand, both during direct examination and cross-examination, he testified differently, stating that Ricky Martinez, Bosch's former Biogenesis business associate, had "given permission" to Fischer to "take these [Biogenesis] documents" when the clinic was closing.

"Did you know or believe that any of the documents that you purchased from Bobby from Boca—Mr. Jones, Gary Jones—had been stolen?" Manfred was asked.

"No, no, not at that time," Manfred testified. "We understood, as I said, from Mr. Fischer that the CFO of Biogenesis had given him permission to take these documents, so we thought Mr. Fischer had them legitimately. And then, as I said to you previously, because Bobby from Boca, or Gary Jones, knew all sorts of details about our dealings with Mr. Fischer, we assumed we were, they were one and the same, that they were acting in concert, so we assumed that Mr. Jones had them legitimately."[14]

My thought was that Martinez had possibly played ball with Labor. We had interviewed Ricky Martinez and had asked him directly, "Did you give Fischer the files?" The answer had been no. Bosch himself would say later that the person he was most angry with out of the whole cast of characters was Martinez, whom Bosch had known all his life. "You know who I'm fucking bitter with?" he asked. "Little fat fuck Ricky Martinez."[15]

Manfred also testified that once Bosch agreed to cooperate with MLB, an agreement had been established by which Bosch would receive financial help with legal fees and security expenses, in addition to a proffer agreement.

"Did MLB make any direct payments to Mr. Bosch for his cooperation?" Ganz asked Manfred on the stand.

"No, we did not," Manfred said.

"Or for his testimony?"

"No, we did not," said Manfred.

When Tacopina had his turn to cross-examine Manfred, he didn't mince words on the topic of the Biogenesis documents.

"You know they were stolen now, right?" Tacopina asked. "I mean, Mr. Bosch testified. He's your witness."

"Like I said, I don't agree . . . the characterization of how it 'went down' suggests a temporal element that I don't agree with," Manfred replied.

"Before the agreement was executed with Mr. Bosch, did you ask Tony Bosch in that week since you met him, from the time you met him until the time you executed the agreement, did you ask Mr. Bosch about his cocaine use?" Tacopina asked Manfred.

"No, I did not," said Manfred.

"Were you aware of it?" Tacopina asked.

"No."

"So it didn't factor in your decision as to whether to accept his veracity of his statements, correct?" Tacopina asked.

"I didn't know about it at that time. At the time you're asking me I was not aware of it. I didn't become aware of it—as a matter of fact, as I sit here today, all I know is you asked him a question about it and he took the Fifth," said Manfred.

"Okay. So he never admitted to you that during the relevant time period in 2012 and 2013 he was using cocaine, never admitted that to you?" Tacopina said.

"No, he did not," Manfred said.[16]

The "temporal element" notwithstanding, Manfred's answer seemed misleading to me since in report after report we had detailed Bosch's pernicious cocaine habit. Several individuals, including Claudia Cosculluela, Bosch's longtime on-again-off-again girl-friend, had told us about Bosch's great thirst for the white powder. We were told that his once profitable business had taken a nosedive after he had become obsessed with consuming the drug. Manfred and his minions had read everything we had written, and for him to say he didn't know Bosch was a cokehead was laughable. Maybe Manfred was being careful to answer the question exactly the way it was asked.

Anthony Galea, the Canadian doctor who had treated other professional athletes, had said publicly that he had never supplied Rodriguez with anything other than anti-inflammatory medication following A-Rod's 2009 hip surgery. And when Vic Burgos and I interviewed Galea's Canadian attorney, Brian Greenspan, we were told that the growth hormone his assistant, Mary Anne Catalano, had been caught with when she was arrested in 2009 was HGH for Galea's personal use. Greenspan told us that Galea had used anti-inflammatory medication in "cocktails" he had administered, and Reyes and Carlos Beltran told us that Galea had performed platelet-rich plasma (PRP) therapy on them—a legal procedure even though Galea had no US medical license.

When the DOI interviewed A-Rod about Galea, he said he had received PRP therapy as well, but his account of who administered the PRP to him differed from the account given by Dr. Marc Philippon, the surgeon who had performed Rodriguez's hip surgery.

Bosch referenced Galea and Rodriguez almost immediately during day three, October 2, 2013, of his arbitration testimony. With A-Rod sitting in the same room, Ganz, the MLB attorney, asked Bosch, "Did Mr. Rodriguez remain on the program during 2011?"

"Yes, he did," said Bosch, referring to Rodriguez's doping protocol with him.

Bosch then testified to what kind of drug protocol he wrote for A-Rod, confirming that it was developed after Bosch's visit to Rodriguez's apartment "by the Hudson."

"The reason why I know that is because—I have here a note that says order Activagen [sic]," said Bosch.

"A-C-T-I-V-A-G-E-N?" Ganz asked.

"Yes. And I really don't use Activagen. I use IGF-1. The main ingredient in Activagen is IGF-1, but Mr. Rodriguez had told me that Galea would use Activagen on him along with some B complex and L-carnitine, so therefore he asked me for Activagen. I did not order the Activagen, but I had written this down, and this is why I know that this was written by me right after my visit," said Bosch.

Actovegin—the correct spelling—is derived from calf's blood, and it was one of the substances Galea and his assistant Catalano were accused of transporting across the border from Canada into the United States to treat patients, including professional athletes. Actovegin is not on MLB's or the World Anti-Doping Agency's banned substances list, but selling or importing Actovegin is illegal in the United States and the Food and Drug Administration does not approve any use of Actovegin by humans.

Bosch's testimony about A-Rod included revelations of a hyperbaric chamber that Rodriguez told Bosch he had bought and installed in a Greenwich Village apartment in 2012 and a Miami nightclub incident during which Bosch had drawn blood from Rodriguez, only to temporarily lose the vial of blood. Bosch testified that he needed to be available to draw blood from Rodriguez on short notice, and on that occasion A-Rod was at the Liv Nightclub in the Fontainebleau Hotel when Bosch got the call.

"So the blood was drawn in a bathroom, in a stall at a restaurant lounge adjacent to Liv," said Bosch. "I did not put it in any container. I can't go inside a club with a container. I think it would be too obvious. So I stuck the tube in my pocket."

Bosch testified that he had "misplaced" the tube while he was at Liv, "but then I found the tube of blood."

"Where did you find it?" asked Ganz.

"On the floor next to where I was sitting," said Bosch.

"Had you been dancing?" Ganz asked.

"A little bit."

Rodriguez's arbitration was accompanied by the lawsuits he had filed against MLB and Selig and, in a separate complaint, the Yankees' team physician, Chris Ahmad. The first suit, filed in New York Supreme Court on October 4, charged MLB and Selig with engaging in "vigilante justice" to destroy Rodriguez's reputation and career. It said that MLB had engaged in unethical and even criminal behavior against Rodriguez to "gloss over" its past inaction and tacit approval of performance-enhancing drugs in the game. The suit claimed that MLB officials had conducted a "witch hunt" against Rodriguez to secure Bud Selig's legacy as the "savior" of the national pastime.

"They have ignored the procedures set forth in baseball's collectively bargained labor agreement; violated the strict confidentiality imposed by these agreements; paid individuals millions of dollars and made promises of future employment to individuals in order to get them to produce documents and to testify on MLB's behalf; bullied and intimidated those individuals who refused to cooperate with their witch hunt; and singled out plaintiff for an unprecedented 211-game suspension—the longest non-permanent ban in baseball history," Rodriguez's thirty-one-page complaint said.

Internally, the suit itself caused little concern among the MLB execs except for the media attention it attracted and one other unsettling development: as the arbitration hearings were about to start, word got back to 245 Park Avenue that A-Rod's scorched-earth defense now involved tailing several MLB officials. One of them was Rob Manfred, who took no chances with his own safety and immediately arranged for 24/7 security.

We in the DOI all knew what type of person A-Rod was, and that type of action came as no surprise. We weren't too concerned about the threats, either, because in our line of work, threats were a common occurrence. But Manfred and his boys had a different reaction: they put MLB's security department on high alert. Someone would accompany Manfred wherever he went, and other security personnel, including at the 245 Park Avenue building, were put on alert.

Manfred made a trip to Fenway Park during that time, and I was asked to keep an eye on him from a distance, to make sure no one was following him and his security detail. At one point he spotted me and came over to ask if I was all right. I told him yes and asked how he was doing. "I'm okay," he said. "Hopefully this will all be over soon." Nothing ever came of the threats, but they did cause some agita.

My turn to take the stand came toward the end of the arbitration, and although I testified only one day, I will never forget the look on A-Rod's and Tacopina's faces when I was asked about our cooperation with the DEA. Tacopina asked me if any DOI members had gone to law enforcement while we were investigating Biogenesis. I said we had. Tacopina asked which agencies. I spelled it out— D-E-A—and when I glanced over at Rodriguez, he looked as if he had seen a ghost.

Rodriguez made a spectacle out of the second-to-last day of the hearing. He stormed out on November 20 after Horowitz, the arbitrator, ruled that Selig wouldn't have to testify. Rodriguez made a beeline to Mike Francesa's WFAN radio show that afternoon for a lengthy interview and a soft landing spot.

"I've been better," Rodriguez said in the first few moments behind the mic after Francesa asked him how he was doing.

"Well, we had a ruling that the commissioner does not have to come in from Milwaukee. It was very disappointing. I've been there for every pitch. Respecting the process," he said. "Today I just lost my mind. I banged a table, and kicked a briefcase, and slammed out of the room. What we saw today, it was disgusting. The fact that the man from Milwaukee that put this suspension on me, with not one bit of evidence, something I didn't do, and he doesn't have the courage to come look me in the eye and tell me, 'This is why I did 211'?

"I shouldn't serve one inning," the defiant Rodriguez continued, nearly coming to tears. "I love this city. I love being a Yankee."

Rodriguez and Jim McCarroll, the Reed Smith attorney who had accompanied Rodriguez to Francesa's studio, both griped that Selig's decision not to testify sullied the entire process.

"I wasn't there for Natasha," Rodriguez said, referring to the older of his two young daughters and how the arbitration had caused him to miss her ninth birthday in Florida.

To his credit, Francesa did ask Rodriguez point-blank if he had ever used PEDs, and A-Rod repeated over and over that he hadn't doped, although he had already admitted in 2009 to having used banned substances between 2001 and 2003, when he had played for the Rangers.

"So you're guilty in your mind of nothing?" Francesa asked.

"I feel like I should be there opening day [2014]. And that's what I'm working hard for," replied Rodriguez.

"You say you did not do these PEDs that they are accusing you of doing?" Francesa asked.

"You're correct, Mike."[17]

MLB had issued a statement through spokesman Pat Courtney as to why Selig did not have to testify. "In the entire history of the Joint Drug Agreement, the commissioner has not testified in a single case," Courtney said. "Major League Baseball has the burden of proof in this matter. MLB selected Rob Manfred as its witness to explain the penalty imposed in this case. Mr. Rodriguez and the Players' Association have no right to dictate how baseball's case is to proceed any more than baseball has the right to dictate how their case proceeds. Today's antics are an obvious attempt to justify Mr. Rodriguez's continuing refusal to testify under oath."[18]

Before he arrived at Francesa's studio, Rodriguez had issued his own statement that said, in part, "I am disgusted with this abusive process, designed to ensure that the player fails."

I had listened to the interview from my home and, as did most others, viewed the whole thing as a staged performance, lightly disguised as genuine outrage at what had transpired in the arbitration room. Rodriguez knew that he was lying to the public and would soon be knocking on the DEA's door asking for a deal. After my revelation about the DEA being involved and the arbitrator's decision not to force Selig to testify, it was clear that the walls were closing in on him. It was no coincidence that after he left WFAN's studios in Tribeca he spent the rest of the day at his lawyers' Midtown offices, finally emerging close to 10 p.m. "I'm done," he said as he walked away.

I had come to agree with Rodriguez on a couple of matters, though, namely his complaints about the role of the Players Association and its handling of the suspensions of not only Rodriguez but also thirteen other players. I found it odd that the players had gone belly-up without a fight and that the union, one of the most powerful in the country, had gone along. I had had exchanges with a couple of them over the years and, having seen them draw a definite line over small issues, I found it baffling. Those lawyers always fought. They went right after your throat. And in this case they had a defense: there were medical records that had been stolen.

But during the arbitration they were like a lump on a log. If Rodriguez hadn't had his own lawyers there, he would have been defenseless.

All I know for sure is that the union had no use for our unit and was happy to see it dismantled. And that A-Rod would include the

Players Association in another lawsuit he would file in January 2014 naming Selig, MLB, and the union as defendants.

In that suit, Rodriguez accused the Players Association of completely abdicating "its responsibility to Mr. Rodriguez to protect his rights under the agreements between MLB and the MLBPA by: failing to intervene to stop the continuous leaking of prejudicial information concerning Mr. Rodriguez and [the] grievance by MLB and its officials; failing to stop MLB's commencement of a sham lawsuit in Florida solely aimed at obtaining evidence to be used against MLB players like Mr. Rodriguez; and failing to stop the abusive investigative tactics taken by MLB and its investigators to obtain evidence against Mr. Rodriguez."

The suit added that Weiner's statement to the media "falsely declaring Mr. Rodriguez's guilt and stating that he should accept a suspension and resolve the grievance at issue—all, of course, without Mr. Rodriguez's consent and even without consulting him," made matters worse.

Rodriguez claimed that the union had determined early on that it didn't want to take on MLB and that its inaction created a climate in which baseball felt free to "trample on Mr. Rodriguez's (and indeed all players') confidentiality rights." He then referenced what he called a "long planned, carefully orchestrated smear campaign against Mr. Rodriguez on '60 Minutes,'" a segment that aired on January 12, 2014, in which Manfred and Selig laid out the case against Rodriguez and Bosch shared details of his client's doping history.[19]

Rodriguez was vilified for suing his union, including by MLBPA executive director Tony Clark, who had taken over after Weiner's death from brain cancer in November 2013, and A-Rod would drop the suit in February and accept his suspension. Clark called the suit "baseless" and "outrageous" and said Rodriguez's attacks on Weiner were inexcusable.

That might have been true, but I couldn't help but wonder if some of it had merit.

On *60 Minutes*, Bosch talked about the threats he said he had received from A-Rod's camp. After the story of the Biogenesis scandal initially broke, Bosch said, he had had a meeting with some "associates" of Rodriguez during which he was asked to sign an affidavit saying he had never supplied A-Rod with PEDs. Bosch said he had felt "uncomfortable" during the meeting. He said that later he had been told by the associates that he needed to go to Colombia for a while and that he'd be taken care of monetarily (upward of $150,000) while he was there.

"One of [Rodriguez's] associates said, 'Well you should, I think you should leave town. We're gonna get you a plane ticket to Colombia,'" Bosch said on *60 Minutes*. "'We want you to stay there until this blows over. We're gonna pay you,' I forgot what the number was, $25,000 or $20,000 a month. 'Then when you come back, we'll, you know, we'll give you another $150,000.'"

After he had turned down the offer to lie low, Bosch said in the *60 Minutes* interview, his ex-girlfriend had received a text message in Spanish saying Bosch would not live to see the end of the year.

"The individual that was of greatest concern to Mr. Bosch was a known associate of Mr. Rodriguez," Rob Manfred told *60 Minutes* correspondent Scott Pelley.

"Are you saying that Alex Rodriguez and/or his associates were involved in threatening to kill Tony Bosch?" Pelley asked Manfred.

"I don't know what Mr. Rodriguez knew," Manfred replied. "I know that the individual involved has been an associate of Mr. Rodriguez for some time."

When Pelley asked what Rodriguez would have known about threats made by Rodriguez's camp or offers to leave the country,

Bosch seemed certain about his answer. "I used to be in that inner circle," he said. "And nothing happens without Alex approving."

But as close as Rodriguez might have been to his drug dealer, the bond quickly went sour once Rodriguez's name was linked to Bosch's now defunct clinic. Team A-Rod, according to Bosch, had pressured Bosch to sign the affidavit that would protect Rodriguez's doping past, as well as the offer for Bosch to disappear until the matter "blows over." He did neither.

Bosch also revisited the incident in the bathroom stall at the Liv Nightclub when he had drawn blood from Rodriguez.

"People coming in and out of the men's room, I take it. And you're in a stall with Alex Rodriguez drawing his blood?" Pelley asked Bosch on *60 Minutes*.

"Yes. As crazy as that sounds," said Bosch.

"What were you thinking?" asked Pelley.

"I'm not getting paid enough," said Bosch.[20]

CHAPTER 14

"QUEEN FOR A DAY"

Alex Rodriguez's visit with the DEA in Weston, Florida, in late January 2014 bore no resemblance to the defiant, dissembling performance he had given on Mike Francesa's radio show two months earlier. Back then, A-Rod had been in the final stages of his failed attacks against MLB, the Players Association, the Yankees, and Bud Selig, a desperate attempt to have his suspension vacated.

Now, with the possibility that the feds were on his tail, it was much easier for him to find the truth. The humbled A-Rod, accompanied by his attorney, Joe Tacopina, quietly went to the DEA to cut a partial immunity deal—what is referred to in legal circles as a "queen for a day" agreement—and the Yankees' aging and tainted slugger made quite an impression on the federal agents who interviewed him on January 29. Rodriguez's business associate Jose "Pepe" Gomez would also sign a limited immunity agreement.

"I was pretty impressed with A-Rod," said DEA agent Kevin Stanfill. "He gets such a bad reputation. When the time came, A-Rod manned up. He wasn't one of those guys who was a punk, that said, 'I didn't know. I thought it was vitamins.' I remember sitting there saying 'We all make mistakes in life,' and he owned up to it."[1]

Rodriguez had agreed to cooperate in exchange for being granted limited immunity and, provided he told the truth, avoiding prosecution. He seemed to lay on the charm when he met with the feds, and DEA agent Jeannette Moran agreed with Stanfill that despite some of their fears going into the meeting, A-Rod had been frank and up-front. "He was extremely personable," she said. "I think we were all a little surprised. Very forthcoming. The fact that [the interview] wasn't leaked, or nobody knew about it for that long, was pretty amazing in this case. I think we all expected him to come in and not be forthcoming, and he was extremely forthcoming."[2]

Media reports of Rodriguez's immunity deal did not surface until late 2014, after Bosch, Yuri Sucart, Ugi Velazquez, and the others had been indicted on federal charges and after Rodriguez had served his season-long doping suspension.

Stanfill and Moran were also impressed with how different their experience with Rodriguez was compared to their dealings with Ryan Braun, the Milwaukee Brewers' outfielder who had received the second longest ban in the Biogenesis group behind A-Rod.

"Another player who was a pure wimp and ought to have his man card pulled [was] Braun," said Stanfill. "Most of our investigators were female, and they were like, 'C'mon dude, man up a little bit.' A-Rod manned up more than anybody else."[3]

Moran recalled that Braun was one of the first players the DEA interviewed during its probe, and they were duly unimpressed. "When we talked to Ryan, it was before he was getting married. I think we were all collectively disappointed in him," she said. "None of us felt that he was being truthful. I remember thinking at the time, 'This is going to be a long list of interviews that are going to be similar.' It wasn't. He was probably one of the only ones that came in and was not forthcoming."

Rodriguez's interview lasted several hours before he signed off on the proffer agreement. Before he left the building, Moran recalled, there had been an amusing encounter between one of her colleagues—a huge Yankees fan—and the DEA's newest cooperating witness.

"Imagine, we had to try to get [Rodriguez] in and out of our building with minimal people seeing him," she said. "We picked him up, brought him to the building, and when he was ready to leave he was with his lawyer [Tacopina]. They stopped by the men's room, and when they walked in nobody was there. Then right behind them walked our agent wearing a Yankee jersey. I think he's from New York. He walked into the bathroom not having any idea who's in there. No clue. Just happened to be wearing an A-Rod Yankee jersey that day. We see him come out and he's kind of like, 'Did I see what I just saw?' We couldn't have planned that if we had tried. Rodriguez was a good sport about it."[4]

Using the words "A-Rod" and "forthcoming" in the same sentence might seem incongruous, but it's understandable that he ended up falling on his own sword, certainly at that point in the game, down 0–2 and facing his greatest adversary, his own lies. He had lied to the DOI, the media, and, finally, the arbitrator. When I testified at the arbitration hearing that the DOI was cooperating with the DEA, Rodriguez's and Tacopina's eyes bugged out of their heads. Soon after my testimony, they ran down to Miami and bared their souls. Why? Because they were scared. They knew the jig was up, and losing $20 million, $30 million, even $40 million in pay because of the suspension was nothing compared to doing jail time.

A-Rod can be very charming when he has to be, as shown by his current success on television, and I'm sure he turned it on in the DEA's office. I'm glad he treated my friends at the DEA well. But the truth is that he had to.

Rodriguez dropped his lawsuits against MLB, Selig, and the Players Association on February 7, 2014, filing papers in federal court that showed he was waving the white flag. He had conceded and would sit out the 2014 season. Later, in June, he dropped his malpractice suit against Yankee team physician Dr. Chris Ahmad, ending his ill-advised legal strategy.

By the time the Biogenesis case played out, the DOI had been gutted. MLB would try to utilize the car service receipts to show my violation of MLB employee bylaws and tried to get me to sign a confidentiality agreement, but I refused. The other DOI members who were terminated—Mullin, Hanna, Reilly—chose to sign. Mullin was the only one of us to publicly comment after we got fired in April 2014, telling the *New York Times*, "Everything is amicable and good. I have no complaints."[5]

But the DEA agents we had worked with, as well as numerous people inside MLB, were stunned by the news of our terminations.

"I was very sad about that, for many reasons," Jeannette Moran recalled. "The whole point, from what I understood, they explained to us how the DOI was formed after the congressional hearings, why they were there. It seemed like it should be a perfect mix—have them here doing investigations, have the legal side with the commissioner over there doing their thing, and they worked together as they should."[6]

From the start, the DEA had made it clear that its objective was to pursue distributors regardless of whom they were dealing to and that it wasn't particularly interested in prosecuting players. There was the agreement, though, that its agents would share their findings with us as they pertained to players and violations of the collectively bargained drug agreement. The agents on the Biogenesis case, including Moran, had a hard time understanding MLB's reasons for dismissing the concept of independence and dismantling a unit that George Mitchell had strongly advocated for in his report.

"I thought [the DOI members] were doing what they were put there to do, which was to investigate and not go after one specific player," Moran said. "We looked at it like—obviously Alex Rodriguez might have been the most recognizable name—but why go after one player? You have a problem here. There are many names on that list, and not just baseball players. You had teenagers, police officers, other doctors. You had tons of different people on that list. I know MLB can't do anything about that. But rather than just make one person an example, I think they could have done a lot more with it. I think if they had let Eddie and Tom [Reilly] and Dan [Mullin] do their thing, they probably would have gotten even more [players]. With us, our case could have had more information. They [MLB] would have gotten a lot more [from that], too. They could have made some important changes. I can't say that for sure, but that's just my feeling."[7]

I heard later that within MLB our firings were referred to as "a massacre." While we were still employed, Dan, George, and I were approached time and again by other employees and colleagues who needed advice on any number of personal or professional problems. We were the go-to guys, kind of like a pro bono human resources department.

Kevin Stanfill, the former DEA agent who worked the case, said he is still baffled by the fact that Bosch was seemingly taken care of by MLB while the DOI members were kicked to the curb.

"Of course we didn't know firsthand, but we were told [Bosch] had bodyguards, a limo, living high on the hog, living it up in New York," Stanfill said. "And New York is a great town if you're a millionaire. If you're not a millionaire, it's nice to go there for a weekend because after that you run out of money. I found it ironic that he's in Manhattan at a five-star hotel and the guys that put the case on him are out looking for a job. Something is not quite right with this picture. [MLB] really screwed these guys over. The guy that was the scumbag ends up living high on the hog. You would like for the commissioner of baseball to take a look around his table and say, 'We screwed this one up. We didn't take care of our people. We looked like shit on this.' That would be real nice."[8]

Moran said she wondered if the DOI members had been fired because they were too good at what they did and that the possibility that baseball's underbelly would be revealed had generated real fear in the corridors of 245 Park Avenue.

"I hate to think that," she said. "I really don't understand why [MLB] did some of the things that they did, unless it was for something like that. You've come to a federal agency and said, 'Hey, look, we have this info, run with it.' That's what you should let [the DOI] do. You should let them do their investigation, but not all of a sudden in the middle of it, decide. . . .

"I'm not sure what their reasoning was," she added, "that they didn't think we were moving quickly enough or that they didn't want us to go any further than we were going. I don't know. I wasn't privy to all that. Why would you start us on a path, then try to get in the middle of it? Not let us do what we're there to do—investigate. That made no sense."[9]

It was Thursday, May 1, 2014, and I hadn't slept much since I'd gotten the call from MLB the afternoon of April 28, the day MLB had fired me. My lack of sleep wasn't because I missed being in that *Game of Thrones* atmosphere on Park Avenue.

I had wanted out for some time and had expressed my desire to Mullin and Hanna on numerous occasions. At the beginning they had both tried to convince me that things were going to be okay, but I had become more and more convinced that I had been sold a bill of goods. Little did MLB know that once it fired Mullin and Hanna, I would have quit on my own; instead it made up some bogus claims about the car service. I had never been fired from anything. My work ethic and character had never been questioned, and now here were these Labor Relations Department lawyers making ludicrous allegations. I had investigated thousands of cases and testified in the district courts in Suffolk County as well as in Suffolk Superior Court. I had done numerous investigations for the FBI, undercover and otherwise, had testified in federal court, and was a highly respected law enforcement officer. Now MLB and its Labor lawyers were calling my character into question.

I was fifty-seven, had given up the police job I loved to end up with a job I would come to hate, and had taken early retirement to do so. I had left behind substantial money, all because I had been tempted by a mirage.

Donna and I had decided on April 28 that I would not sign the confidentiality agreement, so now I had to figure out what I was going to do and how I was going to do it. I wanted to tell my story and let the world know that the congressional investigation into MLB and the Mitchell Report that had followed were, as far as I was concerned, a lie. Selig and Manfred reminded me of former player Rafael Palmeiro sitting there at the 2005 congressional hearings, waving his finger and saying "Let me start by telling you this: I have never used steroids, period. I don't know how to say it any more clearly than that. Never."

A few months later, Palmeiro tested positive and the whole world knew that he was a liar and that his false declaration of being steroid-free ensured that he had officially flushed his chance to make it into the Hall of Fame down the toilet. But I had decided it was my turn to point a finger at what I had witnessed. To do that, I knew that I needed support, people with the cojones to take on MLB. I needed a lawyer willing to do battle with baseball, and I needed a job. Plenty to worry about.

The angst had kept me up. Donna let it go for three nights, until she finally had to say something. We were in bed and she turned over and said, "I know you haven't slept. I know you are concerned, but this is just a small bump in the road. We have each other, the kids are healthy, and we are healthy." Those words would come into greater focus a few months later.

Our love story is and always has been a complicated, one-of-a-kind journey, one that stretches back to when I worked in the Boston PD Drug Control Unit for two years. The work and its hours had taken their toll on my first marriage. It just didn't work out—plain and simple—and most of the problems that developed in the relationship were my fault. But I also never expected what happened between Donna, my second wife, and me. I met Donna in 1988, while I was estranged from my first wife and in and out of our house. Donna always tells the story that she saw me one day in the open-air plaza outside Suffolk Superior Court at Center Plaza in Boston. She was working as an assistant at the Suffolk County District Attorney's Office in the Homicide Unit. She says that from the moment she saw me across that plaza, she knew I was the one. She immediately went up to her office and told a coworker that she had just seen the man of her dreams. By chance, former homicide assistant district attorney Michael Joyce, who is a friend of mine, was leaving the DA's office and being made a judge. Donna was selling tickets to Joyce's farewell party from the DA's office, and there were flyers posted around the courthouse that listed a number to call to make a purchase. I called the number and asked about buying a ticket, not realizing that Donna was on the other end of the line. And she didn't know the man calling was the person she had just seen in Center Plaza.

The woman on the phone told me that she had the tickets at her desk and that all I needed to do was come up to the ninth floor of the DA's office. When I walked through the door, Donna said, she could barely speak. While I was writing a check, she kept signaling to the other assistant, 'Hey, this is the guy I just saw in the plaza!' She knew one thing for sure: she would be going to Joyce's farewell party.

Our relationship produced the only biological child we share—our daughter, Sunni—but it wasn't until 2008 that Donna and I got back together after almost a two-decade hiatus. We had both tried to make our first marriages work, but we had failed and eventually found our way back to each other.

It was only a week after A-Rod dropped the suit against Ahmad that things went from bad to dire for me personally. I noticed what I thought was blood in my urine, the first indication that something was very wrong.

On Friday, June 27, 2014, we were getting ready to go for our weekly dinner at Mai Place, a Chinese restaurant we visited just about every Friday. When we walk in the door they start mixing our Scorpion Bowl for two. The problem was that things weren't as they had been every Friday for years prior. Earlier that day, I had again noticed what I thought was blood in my urine. I wasn't concerned, as I thought it would just go away, or at least I was hoping it would, so I didn't tell Donna. At Mai Place I didn't eat as I usually do and told Donna I had a stomachache.

Saturday came, and the ache hadn't gone away, my appetite wasn't good, and I started to get concerned. That night Donna noticed I wasn't eating, and I had to tell her. She understandably wasn't happy and told me I would have to go to the Care Central Urgent Care in Stoughton, Massachusetts, near our home, first thing in the morning.

I tried to go by myself, but she would have no part of that. The nurse at the Care Central clinic knew Donna from many visits with the children and took us in right away. The nurse did some blood tests and gave me a checkup. She said my blood level, body temperature, blood pressure, and all other primary tests seemed to be okay. She told us the tests would be back later in the week but said that she had noticed that I was a little jaundiced and it wouldn't be a bad idea to pay my primary care doctor a visit.

We left the Care Central and Donna gave me the *malocchio*— the Italian word for the evil eye.

"You are going to see Fang, right?"

Dr. Leslie Fang is a nephrologist who works out of Massachusetts General Hospital, and I am so lucky that he's my primary care doctor. He is considered one of the best kidney specialists in the country, referred to me about thirty years ago by my friend the former Massachusetts attorney general Francis Xavier Bellotti.

When I arrived at Fang's office the following morning, I ran into Kevin Hayes, a mountain of a man. It was rush hour, and he was standing in the street staring at me with no vehicles beeping at him. It was eerie. I've known Kevin for years, and he's the father of two great kids, Kevin and Jimmy Hayes, who happen to be professional hockey players. Kevin had just battled throat cancer and was making a full recovery. We exchanged pleasantries, but my mind was frozen. I believe in fate, and someone was sending me a message. I had a sinking feeling that I would receive bad news from Fang.

I went into Fang's office and, after several blood tests, went home and told Donna that the doctor thought I was maybe passing a kidney stone but wanted to make sure and had told me to get a scan.

The next day, I received a 6 a.m. phone call from Fang's assistant asking me to come in as soon as possible, and to bring someone with me.

"I have bad news and good news," Fang told Donna and me while he typed away at his keyboard. Not asking which I wanted to hear first, he came right out with the bad news: "You have pancreatic cancer."

I felt as though I wasn't there. Like I was a fly on the wall looking at Donna, who was gasping for air, and at Dr. Fang banging at the keys, me with my left hand on my chin, staring straight ahead. I squeezed Donna's hand, which I had been holding since we had entered the room, and tried to give her a comforting look.

As Fang continued to type, he delivered the good news. "I believe we caught it early enough where you will be eligible for the Whipple surgery," he told me. "I'm emailing Dr. Carlos Fernandez-del Castillo, the best pancreatic cancer surgeon in the world. He's a busy doctor, but I'm asking him to put you at the top of the list."

Fang told us that the tumor was located at the top of my pancreas and was blocking my bile duct. What I had thought was blood in my urine was actually bile. If it hadn't been for that, I would have never known I had anything wrong with me until it was too late.

"I'm asking you not to look up this disease on the Internet, but I know that will fall on deaf ears, so I'll tell you it's the deadliest type of cancer. But again, I believe we caught it early enough," Fang said. "Usually by the time it's diagnosed it has metastasized all over your body. I'm sending you for a full body scan, and you'll be hearing from me and Dr. Fernandez."

We walked out of Dr. Fang's office in shock. Donna, who is seldom speechless, was stone-faced and silent. We got into the car, looked at each other, and hugged. She then looked at me and said, "We're going to fight this, and we're going to do whatever it takes."

My thoughts turned to how to tell my family. Without question, the toughest thing I had to do throughout that episode was talk with my family about the news.

We first drove to Quincy, a city just south of Boston where my mother lives by herself in a two-bedroom condo. We rang her bell, and Tata was surprised to see us. We almost never visited her during the day, so she knew right away that something was wrong. When we told her, she started crying and hugged me, and I hugged her back. We then went and told Sunni, who was understandably very upset by the news.

Telling my brother and the boys was not easy either. I hurt for each of them every time I repeated the message. There are five guys I consider my closest friends in New York City—Dan Mullin, George Hanna, Tom Reilly, Noel Firth, and Marty Rodriguez—and I had become friends with all of them, other than Mullin, through MLB. For that, I am thankful.

After the calls, I got my ducks in a row: life insurance policies, retirement funds, an appointment to get my will squared away.

Prior to the diagnosis, I had received calls from various individuals I had met during my twenty-nine years on the BPD, and they were offering me jobs. I wasn't ready to jump fully back into the workforce, especially after my last experience, but an old friend I had met in the RSA program, Barry Fox, had given me a call to get my spirits up after being fired.

Barry is a retired Pittsburgh police detective who was a legend in that department and had become an RSA for the Pirates. Once he retired from the department, he also had to leave the RSA program. He had opened his own private investigation firm and told me that I would love that kind of work and should consider starting my own firm. I thought about it and entertained some job offers that would give me a taste of what it was about. I was offered a consultant's job at the Liberty Hotel, which is about ten feet from Mass General, and agreed to meet with the hotel manager, who offered me a job to assess security at the hotel. The job, which lasted just over a week, kept my mind on something other than the cancer.

Three days later, I met with Dr. Fernandez. He has a calming way about him. He's a humble man who I would later learn is referred to by the Mass General medical staff as "God."

He asked me where I was from, and I proceeded to tell him about my background, that I had been born in Cuba and come to the United States when I was a kid. I told him I had been a Boston police officer for twenty-nine years and had worked for the MLB Commissioner's Office for fifteen years in different capacities. Dr. Fernandez showed genuine interest in my story and kept asking questions. I then asked him about his personal life, and he told me he had been born and educated in Mexico. He was married and had nine children. Seven of them were older, and then he and his wife had decided to have two more ten years after the youngest of the first batch was born. We hit it off pretty well.

He proceeded to explain all about pancreatic cancer, my particular tumor, and how he wanted to attack it. The simple fact that he thought he could attack it was great news. He explained that I was eligible for Whipple surgery, a complex and risky procedure in which a surgeon opens up your chest cavity and removes part of the pancreas (the head); it can sometimes also involve removing the small intestine, bile duct, gallbladder, and part of the stomach. Once a tumor is surgically removed, the surgeon then connects the intestine, bile duct, and pancreas so the patient can digest food.

He then said there was an additional option. "I have been doing this for years, and the percentages of survival after the Whipple remain the same, around twenty-five percent," he told us. He added that he was working on a clinical trial headed by Dr. Theodore Hong involving a drug by the name of hydroxychloroquine. It's a drug that was used for malaria years ago, and it has been shown to kill or retard the growth of pancreatic cancer in rodents. Dr. Fernandez said that the one problem was that he would not be able to do the Whipple surgery right away since the study called for certain procedures to be done before he could operate.

He said he could do the surgery as soon as the following week if we chose not to go into the clinical trial. From his perspective, though, he was tired of the same unacceptable results from the Whipple surgery and the clinical trial had shown promise, so he would prefer to go with the trial. I told him I was interested but asked if I had to decide that day. He said I didn't but that I shouldn't wait much longer. The one thing that he said that day that I have lived by for the past three years is this: Don't think too far ahead. Take things one day at a time.

I then spoke with Dr. Hong, a young doctor and Harvard grad. He explained what the trial entailed and told me I would have to go through some proton radiation and when that was done Dr. Fernandez would do the Whipple. Lucky for me, Mass General is one of only twenty-four hospitals in the United States that has a proton radiation machine. The radiation was a pre-Whipple procedure that was part of Dr. Hong's study. There was no choice of having or not having the Whipple after—it was either have the Whipple procedure or die.

Later that week we heard from the Care Central clinic concerning my blood tests. According to them, I was all set. Nothing to worry about.

As usual, the family's Fourth of July holiday party was held at our house and our entire family was there. We had told everyone about what was going on but asked them not to make the day about me. We celebrated the Fourth as best as we could. On Monday, I called the doctors and told them I was all in on the clinical trial. First I needed to get a stent placed in my bile duct so that it could start working properly. According to the doctors, that was a minor procedure that shouldn't cause any problems.

But of course there were problems. The doctor had a hard time attempting to place the stent in the bile duct, which caused irritation and swelling. She said that poking around could cause pancreatitis and that we would need to wait a few days and try again. She asked me to monitor my pain closely and said that if I developed pancreatitis I would know because the pain would be intolerable. We went home and the pain started at around 10 p.m., but I didn't want to scare Donna, so I tried to weather the storm. By 3 a.m., I was doubled over. I couldn't take it anymore, and we went back to Mass General. I was immediately admitted and stayed there for about two weeks. During my stay I developed an *E. coli* infection and was in pretty bad shape. They made a second attempt to put in the stent and were successful. The first stent had been made out of plastic and had to be replaced by a metal stent. The doctors believed that the pancreatitis was caused by the difficulty of attempting to insert the first stent. I started losing weight and at one point was down from about 180 pounds to 145. All the time Dr. Fang kept an eye on me. The radiation had to wait.

My hospital room overlooked the Charles River, which divides Cambridge from Boston. On one side of the Charles, across the street from the hospital, is the old Science Museum swimming pool, with its adjacent softball fields. Back forty years before, I had practiced football on that same field with my high school team, Don Bosco Tech. Plenty of memories crossed my mind. How fast those years had flown by.

Once I started to gain strength after I left the hospital, the radiation treatment began. The doctors gave me proton radiation as opposed to neutron radiation, which is what most people get. The proton radiation machine looks like a spaceship and is several stories high. The first time you see it, you feel as if you're blasting into outer space. First they build a metal mold to pinpoint the tumor from different angles. The radiation goes through needle-sized holes in the mold and directly attacks the tumor. The radiation was going well, but the *E. coli* infection was not completely cleared, and several weeks later, following a radiation treatment, there were complications that would delay the Whipple surgery and alter the plan. One night I started to feel cold and tremble. That night was definitely the weakest I would feel throughout the ordeal. I told Donna I had to get to the hospital, and she practically had to carry me down the stairs to the car. She called my brother on the way to the hospital, and luckily Carlos was able to show up with his wife, Colleen. When we arrived I could not get out of the car, and my brother had to help me into a wheelchair. We had also alerted Dr. Fang, who had called ahead and made sure I didn't have to get into line with the other fifty people waiting in the ER.

The *E. coli* infection had returned, and the doctors started giving me massive doses of antibiotics. They hit me with everything they had. I stayed there for another two weeks. Donna, my mother, my brother, and my kids were constantly at the hospital.

I began to gain strength, and finally, in late August, I was wheeled into the operating room. Donna later told me that only two hours into what should have been an eight-hour surgery, as she waited in the family room, she saw Dr. Fernandez walk in. She was petrified. He told her that he had opened me up but had had to close me again. Donna's first thought was that the cancer had spread. He explained that the pancreas was so swollen from the stents and the infections that if he had tried to do the surgery, I would have died on the operating table. Not many doctors would have closed me back up. His experience and expertise were vital to that decision.

Several days later, we met with Dr. Hong, who said that he had spoken to Dr. Fernandez and that although this wasn't the way the clinical trial was meant to work, he would make some alterations and I was going to stay in the study. They prescribed the strongest doses of chemotherapy they could give me for approximately three months. The purpose of the chemo was to try to stop the cancer from spreading. If it spread, all bets were off. The hope was that after three months the swelling would have gone down and Fernandez could operate again.

The chemotherapy weakened me, but it also made me aware of how lucky I was. As I sat in the chemo room, I saw parents standing over their children as they received the drugs. I'm not sure I could deal with that. I never asked, "Why me?" and seeing these poor kids battling the disease made me more convinced that I was a lucky man.

I would sit for hours as the poison ran through my veins. The doctors would then send me home with a chemo bag that I would carry around for two days. I have to tell you, I can still hear the hissing sound the machine made every several minutes as it poured the poison into my body. It was a constant reminder that I was dealing with a deadly disease. My mind would wander off as I tried to stay busy by working on telling my story, taking the boys to hockey practice, helping Donna as much as I could, and going to the gym to exercise.

I really didn't want to speak to anyone outside my immediate family and did not take many calls that whole second half of 2014. I did text friends every now and then. I just didn't want to bother anyone with my problems—we all have them—and I certainly didn't want any pity.

My FBI and BPD families prayed for me, texted me for updates, and offered to help with anything we needed. I heard from guys in the gym, who told me that BPD commissioner William Evans had started a command meeting by having the staff pray for me. There were prayer meetings during which priests blessed me. My FBI family sent cards and raised money to help me. I called and thanked them for the money but asked them to donate it to the Granara-Skerry Trust, which raises money for pancreatic cancer research, and they did. Not only did they donate the money, but dozens of agents ran in an annual 5K walk/run race sponsored by the trust. I showed up at the first one in 2014 while in the midst of getting chemo and cheered them on. Donna, my family and friends, and I have run in the road race ever since and have helped raise more than $15,000 for the trust, and we hope to continue doing so.

When I began going to Granara-Skerry gatherings, I started meeting a lot of family members of deceased pancreatic cancer patients. I also met a few who had been recently diagnosed and even fewer survivors. I'm sorry to say that not one of the people I met who had recently been diagnosed is still around. RIP.

We were asked to go to Mass General with the Granara-Skerry Trust to meet with the doctors and technicians working on cures for the disease. We joined other families that had raised substantial amounts of money. Unfortunately, I was the only survivor in the group. One of the doctors who spoke said that the reason it is so hard to raise money for this cancer is because all or most of the people afflicted with the disease have died.

The months passed slowly, and the chemo sessions ended. It was time to get another scan. The scan would determine if the cancer had spread. If it had, the Whipple would be out. Good news came, and the surgery was set for January 23, 2015.

Operation day arrived, and again my family was there with me. I saw Dr. Fernandez just before the surgery, and he said, "I told you I would do your surgery." I looked at him and said, "One day at a time, Doc."

Donna sat in the family room, and this time it took more than eight hours before Dr. Fernandez came down. He looked beat up. He told Donna that it had been a tough battle but he was pretty certain he had removed all of the cancer.

This time when I woke up and opened my eyes, Donna had a smile on her face, and I knew we had overcome a huge obstacle.

That day after the surgery, Tom Reilly, Noel Firth, and Marty Rodriguez, the NYPD boys, showed up in my hospital room, all dressed in long black raincoats, looking, as Donna said, like the Secret Service. They came to put a smile on my face. I fell asleep, and they took all our kids out to dinner, during which Noel found out that his brother had died unexpectedly. He returned to New York that night, and Tom and Marty stayed behind. Noel never said a word to me about his brother's death. I think he thought I had enough on my plate. Those guys will never know how much that visit meant to Donna and me.

About a month before the surgery, just before Christmas 2014, as I waited for Dr. Fernandez to decide whether the swelling in my pancreas had gone down enough for him to operate, I had told Sunni that I wanted to buy her mother a ring and ask her to marry me. Sunni was ecstatic. Donna is not an easy person to surprise, and Sunni thought it would be a good idea to include Donna's mother, Fran, in the secret plan. I told Fran that I wanted to marry her daughter and I was buying her a ring.

In a roundabout way, I was asking her permission. Fran thought about it for a minute, then said, in her inimitable way, "Yes, you're kind of slow. She wanted this to happen twenty-five years ago."

I then asked Donna's father, Ronnie, and got his blessing as well.

The ring arrived, and Sunni was so excited. I had wanted to wait until Christmas, but Sunni would have none of that. So on December 23, in the kitchen of our home in Canton, with our daughter as witness, I got down on one knee and proposed.

Sunni was to be Donna's maid of honor. She took the role very seriously. She took Donna to buy her dress and insisted on paying for it. As Donna tried on her dress, the saleswoman helping them started talking to Sunni outside the dressing room. Donna could hear them clearly from the stall. The woman was asking Sunni how she felt about her mother getting remarried, and Sunni said she was thrilled. The woman told her that she couldn't believe Sunni was taking it so well since the woman's own daughter had not reacted favorably when she had decided to remarry. Sunni was taking it all in, and Donna was in the dressing room laughing to herself. Here this woman was having such a tough time with her own daughter, and she was raving about how lucky Donna was to have a daughter who was so supportive of her marriage. Donna pushed aside the dressing room curtain and said, "Don't give her so much credit—I'm marrying her father!" The woman stood there dumbfounded.

We got married on April 17, 2015, three months after my Whipple surgery. It was a small wedding with only our immediate family present. I had asked my son Andrew to give a toast, as he was the oldest, but both of my sons made speeches. Earlier in the day I had given all the kids the option to say a few words. Christopher worked on his speech in his bedroom until minutes before the wedding. He said the day he had found out I was diagnosed with pancreatic cancer he had been worried that I was going to die. He had then thought some more and said, "Wait a minute, not on Donna's watch."

The winter of 2015 was a record breaker. The temperature plummeted, and we were blanketed with snow and ice. Following the surgery, when I was back home recuperating, I realized how much more sensitive I had become to the cold New England winters. I was used to shoveling snow and ice and clearing the gutters, but I had to watch from inside as Donna and the kids shoveled mountains of snow. I couldn't handle any of those chores now.

Two or three months after the surgery, as the spring thaw kicked in and the weather improved, I decided to dive back into work and started my own PI agency, Dominguez Investigations. One of my first cases was providing security for a famous singer whose husband was being treated for cancer at Mass General.

In the fall of 2016, we surprised Dr. Fernandez at the National Pancreas Foundation's annual fund-raising dinner in Boston, during which he was honored for his outstanding work in researching and raising awareness of the disease. He was very happy to see us and introduced us to his family. After Donna and I told Dr. Fernandez's wife how much her husband meant to us, she made an interesting comment: "He's the one guy who people say is the best at what he does, yet nobody wants to ever really meet him," meaning that if you're meeting Dr. Fernandez on a professional basis, your days are probably numbered.

A year later, on Dr. Fernandez's recommendation and on the occasion of its twentieth anniversary, the organization gave me a courage award at the Harvard Club in Boston. I was honored, especially because Dr. Fernandez had recommended me, and I was fortunate to share the honor with my family and friends and the doctors whose support, prayers, and expertise had gotten me that far. But at the same time I felt unworthy: all I had done was stay alive. The real heroes in the audience were the family members, the medical staffs, and all those who work on finding a cure for this devastating disease.

In a weird way the cancer has been a blessing. My relationship with Donna is a complicated one that began in the late 1980s, produced our only biological child, was rekindled in 2008, and finally resulted in marriage. In between, we raised children from previous unions. The cancer played a role in bringing all of us closer. Our daughter finally saw her mother and father get married. I found out that people I thought were just acquaintances were true friends. Donna and I became better Catholics as a result. We certainly learned that health is everything, and I love my wife more than ever.

Every three months when I go in for a scan, I hold my breath. I live one day at a time and consider myself the luckiest man in the world. On one of the three-month visits, Dr. Hong told us I had been to hell and back. He said that while we had been living it we hadn't realized what we were going through, but that the problems that had popped up were like nothing he had ever seen.

So far, my scans have been clean. After each one, I live for another three-month interval. The weight is off for ninety days. I've lived in three-month time chunks since 2015, not that I'm complaining. One day at a time, Doc. One day at a time.

I was at Mass General when I heard about the indictments of Bosch and the others on August 5, 2014, and DEA agent Mark Trouville, the DEA special agent in charge of the Biogenesis case, called to let me know about the impending arrests. The indictments came a year to the day after MLB had issued its suspensions of Rodriguez and the twelve other players (Braun had been disciplined in late July 2013). The indictments actually helped serve as a distraction, even though I was months removed from working for MLB. I followed the developments and kept in touch with the DEA agents, usually through texts.

That fall, MLB announced that Bryan Seeley, a former assistant US attorney in the Washington office, would take over the DOI. I was hardly surprised by MLB's choice: a federal prosecutor whom the Labor Relations Department and Manfred could control.

"The way law enforcement is set up, ultimately a prosecutor determines whether to bring charges," Dan Halem said following Seeley's hire in early September 2014. "We don't have law enforcement power, but our goal is similar—to bring about discipline or sanctions when warranted, figure out which witnesses to use and what evidence can be presented. Much of the job is interacting with actual prosecutors, and it's helpful to have a former prosecutor doing that."[10]

Halem obviously forgot to add that it's the law enforcement agencies—the DEA, the FBI, state and local police departments—that conduct the investigations and take cases to US attorneys.

Seeley came to the job with eight years of prosecutorial experience, mostly dealing with fraud and corruption cases. He didn't appear to have any law enforcement background, and certainly not anywhere close to Mullin's experience and résumé. I heard later from other law enforcement people that Seeley was in over his head.

After Rodriguez served his suspension and months after the indictments of Bosch and A-Rod's cousin Yuri Sucart and the other Biogenesis defendants, a New York *Daily News* report in November 2014 detailed a bizarre anecdote involving Rodriguez. Sucart's wife, Carmen, told the paper that Rodriguez had gone to the Sucart home in 2012 to try to get Yuri to sign a confidentiality agreement. Carmen said that Yuri had refused, which had prompted A-Rod to march outside the couple's home and urinate on the wall by the pool.

"He was arrogant. You know what he did? He peed outside on my wall, next to the pool. He didn't ask for the bathroom. He go outside and he just pee right there. He came over, took his thing out and went right there," Carmen Sucart told the *Daily News* reporter, gesturing at the tan wall. Yuri was bedridden while Carmen participated in the interview, and she described the horrible conditions her husband had endured after his arrest by federal authorities.

"He couldn't stand up," she said, sobbing as she told her story. "Yuri told me, crying, 'Carmen, I couldn't stand up to get water.' They didn't even give water to him. He told me they threw the food under the little door." She told the paper that Yuri had been behind bars for twelve days before he had been transferred to a hospital, and at one point, in the jail cell, guards had found Yuri covered in his own urine and feces, too weak to rise from the prison floor. Yuri was photographed in bed for the story, and during the interview, he had a mountain of pill bottles on a bedside table. Carmen said that A-Rod had lied to federal investigators when court documents in the Biogenesis case alleged that an attorney representing Yuri had sent a shakedown letter to Rodriguez in 2012, demanding $5 million in exchange for Yuri's silence about Rodriguez's relationship with Bosch. "He is the devil. He is evil," she said of Rodriguez.[11]

Rodriguez would enter into a settlement agreement with Sucart in 2013, in which Yuri was paid approximately $900,000. Yuri ended up pleading guilty to one count of conspiracy to distribute HGH in March 2015 in Miami federal court, and his link to the Biogenesis case earned him seven months in federal prison after he was sentenced in June 2015. His attorney, Edward O'Donnell IV, had pleaded with prosecutors for home confinement due to Yuri's myriad health problems, but to no avail.

By the time Yuri had entered his guilty plea in Miami, I had already gone through the Whipple surgery on January 23, 2015, and had watched the Patriots win another Super Bowl in the shadow of what would become Deflategate. Sunni and I watched New England beat Seattle from my bedroom, even though I was still pretty weak and could barely eat much of anything. I would have had to be either in surgery or dead to miss a Patriots Super Bowl.

While Yuri was headed to prison, Rodriguez returned to the Yankees for the 2015 season with great fanfare and a media horde describing his every move during spring training and throughout the season. He was more than serviceable to his club, swatting thirty-three home runs at age thirty-nine (he would turn forty that

July 27). The Yankees made the playoffs, barely, but were ousted in the wild-card game, while the crosstown Mets advanced to the World Series against Kansas City.

I spent that fall working with Al-Jazeera on a doping documentary called *The Dark Side*, which would be released that December.

Curiously, Neil Boland appeared on a panel at a November 2015 event sponsored by the International Centre for Sport Security (ICSS). Many reporters attending were there to try to interview Sunil Gulati, the president of the United States Soccer Federation, since the sport was engulfed in scandal months after federal indictments had been unsealed in Brooklyn federal court. Boland, however, spoke on a separate panel at the Securing Sport 2015 symposium; the panel included moderator Jane Lute, a former Department of Homeland Security deputy secretary; Andy Roth, a partner and chair of Dentons' global privacy and cybersecurity group; Lisa Ellman, a partner and cochair of Global Unmanned Aircraft Systems Practice, Hogan Lovells; and Boland, whose bio in the ICSS program read "Head of Cybersecurity, Major League Baseball."

"Neil Boland is responsible for the leagues [*sic*] cyber defense strategy, operations and incident response capabilities," read the bio. "MLB's cyber group is also responsible for digital investigations and forensics, with a focus on IP theft, digital counterfeiting, and piracy. Boland is a member of the Department of Homeland Security's Science and Technology working group, exploring emerging technologies in the areas such as drone detection and interdiction, cyber countermeasures, and facial recognition."

During Lute's introduction of Boland, she quipped about the recently concluded 2015 World Series, in which the Mets had fallen to the Royals: "And for the New Yorkers in the room, [Boland] is not responsible for the outcome of the World Series, but partially responsible for the fact that it was, from a cybersecurity point of view, a very successful event. We'll talk about that and what goes into it."

The event was held at Manhattan's Harold Pratt House, only a few blocks north of MLB's offices on Park Avenue. Lute asked Boland how MLB was doing business differently from in the past.

"I think we're blessed, at least in Major League Baseball," Boland said at the outset of the discussion. "Our leadership has been very supportive of investing early on in a cybersecurity strategy: Looking at the right technologies, processes, and procedures to better position ourselves."

But Boland seemed to be a bit taken aback when the floor was opened for questions and a *Daily News* reporter asked him how he went about conducting investigations without any traditional law enforcement experience. He gave a rambling response. "We handle traditional information, security and the additional investigations, and forensics aspect of the business," he said. "It does make it a little bit easier at times to both find and contain talent, when you can tell them, 'Today you're going to be defending, tomorrow you're going to be investigating,' and both skill sets help develop the other side of the equation. Yes, we are involved in that. It makes our unit stronger and, I think, much more effective at the end of the day."

"This is really a terrific question, because of the technology challenging the integrity of the game," added Lute. "Now there's advantage in recruiting, advantage in on-field play, there's an advantage in messaging, positioning, smack-talking and reaching audiences that technology is giving. Who should make the rules? We had a conversation on one of the panels earlier, leave the sporting industry to manage its own affairs. Are we all OK with that?"[12]

CHAPTER 15

"THIS TOWN IS A HUSTLER'S TOWN"

For a guy who had served more than a year behind bars, Tony Bosch looked tanned and no worse for wear when he strolled into the Bertoni Gelato Caffe beneath the swank Brickell House condos on Brickell Bay Drive, his white cotton shirt untucked from his jeans. The top two buttons of his shirt were unfastened, and he wore a small necklace, his hair slicked back like Gordon Gekko's in *Wall Street*.

It was early fall of 2017, and I found myself meeting my one-time nemesis for the first time, a man I had never thought I would spend any amount of time with, certainly not in the aftermath of Biogenesis and my departure from MLB. For a long time, I'd had dreams of meeting Bosch, but in my dreams he was wearing an orange jumpsuit and had a nice pair of matching silver wrist and ankle bracelets.

Bosch had already served his prison sentence when he had agreed to meet me and two reporters at a location of his choosing. After the introductions were finished at Bertoni—a split-level café that serves gourmet coffee, Italian gelato, smoothies, and assorted snacks—he suggested we adjourn to a forty-third-floor condo he referred to as an office space, where we could meet with his business associate, Marcus Armstrong, who looked like Rodney Harrison, the retired free safety of the Patriots.

Bosch guided us into the elevator, and when we arrived at the apartment—Suite 4302—we were greeted with an Andy Warhol-type painting of Barack Obama directly opposite the front entrance. The apartment overlooked the Miami South Channel, not far from A-Rod's old house on Star Island, and the minimalist decor included a stocked bar, a dark gray sectional couch, a painting of Martin Luther King Jr., and, of course, a stunning view.

Bosch said he now spends his days with his five children.

"I stopped partying," he said. "I think I have one drink every three weeks, if that. But I no longer do any drugs. And as you know, I love cocaine, and so therefore—and I love women and I love the party lifestyle. So I put a stop to all that. So I've been clean for about, you know, three years almost. Ever since I got—when I got out I went to a halfway house. So I had to do that for a little bit."

He said he belonged to a nonprofit organization that deals with autistic children and had done some work on antidoping and some consulting with supplement companies. He said he planned to reenter the health care business, focusing on helping people take back their health.

He talked about the projects he's involved in—one with ESPN, another with HBO—and said he had appeared in a documentary, and he made it clear that he's open for business.

"I'll help you, too, you know, but there are boundaries I have—and there's obligations," he said. "I am going to look out for me first. Fair enough? And if there's any business opportunity, you know, I would like to make a dollar, too."

Bosch was a long way from the bathroom of a Miami nightclub where he once huddled with Alex Rodriguez and stuck a needle into the slugger to draw blood, far from the high life in Miami and New

York, the August 2014 perp walk around the DEA's Weston field office, and even his fourteen-month stay in prison.

His original sentence had been almost four years, but he'd had powerful people lobbying to get him far less time for his crimes, including former senator George Mitchell, the same man who had recommended establishing the DOI to root out wrongdoing in baseball.

Mitchell's DLA Piper colleague Charlie Scheeler had written a ten-page letter dated January 23, 2014, to US attorney Wifredo Ferrer in Miami, citing the cooperation agreement Bosch had signed in June 2013 and explaining why he felt Bosch should get special consideration. In exchange for his full cooperation, the letter said, MLB would agree to dismiss the lawsuit it had filed against him and inform prosecutors of his cooperation. In other words, it asked for leniency.

The letter had been attached to court documents filed by Frank Quintero Jr., on behalf of Biogenesis defendant Lazer Collazo and had arrived after Ferrer had met with Mitchell, Scheeler, and another DLA Piper attorney, Ignacio Sanchez, in Miami in September 2013. We referred to the letter as the "Dear Willy" letter, since Scheeler invoked Ferrer's nickname in the letter's salutation.

"Bosch's decision to assist MLB carried with it a high degree of personal sacrifice and risk on his part," Scheeler wrote in the letter, referring to the likelihood that the US Attorney's Office would subpoena his "incriminating testimony."

Scheeler credited Bosch with turning over to MLB detailed notes about his sale of testosterone and human growth hormone to Rodriguez and others and with providing text messages from them regarding their use of the drugs. He noted that Bosch had also admitted distributing steroids to high school athletes, which, he said, was of "significance beyond baseball."

"To be clear, this letter makes no attempt to address Bosch's criminal liability for his conduct," the letter said. "Below, however, we describe months of work by Bosch that was critical to MLB's efforts to successfully sanction fourteen MLB players for use of banned substances—thirteen of whom accepted their discipline without challenge. We describe the significance of this cooperation, not only to MLB, but also to important public interests."

Scheeler also cited no fewer than five news reports that demonstrated Rodriguez and his camp's "efforts to impugn Bosch's credibility" both during the arbitration hearing and in public. One such report included in the letter focused on Bosch's cocaine use.

The entire letter infuriated me. The idea that Bosch had opened himself up to prosecution during the arbitration hearing by helping MLB was preposterous. The DEA had had wiretaps going up and had been going to indict Bosch with or without his arbitration testimony. Frankie, the confidential informant we had brought to the DEA, had already led the government to Sucart and Acevedo, whose recorded conversations would lead it directly to Bosch. There is no question he would have been indicted whether he cooperated with MLB or not. The agents had listened on wiretaps and had recorded conversations that included Bosch's voice. They'd made undercover buys and followed up with surveillance. Two months after Bosch reached his agreement with baseball, a grand jury would hear testimony from all the witnesses.

Ferrer himself said that his office's investigation hadn't depended upon Bosch's cooperation with MLB. "We have repeatedly made it very clear that our investigation was going to be independent of Major League Baseball," he told the *Miami Herald* in a January 2015 story.

To me it sounded as though Scheeler and Mitchell were desperate to transform Bosch into the perfect witness, as if somehow God had appeared on Bosch's shoulder one morning and said, "Tony, do the right thing." I also thought MLB was worried that Bosch might start to think that his benefactors hadn't really lived up to their agreement with him and might decide to renege on it himself.

I am not sure if Mitchell knew we had been ordered by MLB not to share information with the DEA while the investigation was ongoing, but I would have liked to believe that had he known, he would have been against it. I wondered, too, how much MLB had paid Mitchell's firm to go to the US Attorney's Office on behalf of a known drug user and peddler.

Mitchell would provide some answers in an interview he agreed to do with a *Daily News* reporter in late 2017, which coincided with the tenth anniversary of the Mitchell Report's release.

"I believe the DOI is now more effective than when it originally was put into place," Mitchell wrote in an email response to numerous questions, including whether or not he felt his original mandate that Labor and DOI be separate had been honored, now that a former federal prosecutor was running the unit. "MLB has adopted a federal law enforcement model—a seasoned former federal prosecutor working with investigators (most of them with law enforcement experience as well) to develop and implement strategies to bring down networks of PED sellers and users where testing is inadequate to gather the evidence needed," said Mitchell. "In this day and age, everyone in a steroids investigation retains a lawyer immediately. MLB would be at a disadvantage if it did not have an experienced lawyer with prosecutorial and investigative skills in its corner."[1]

I would love to ask Mitchell two questions: What does he mean when he says MLB has adopted a federal law enforcement model? I worked ten years on an FBI federal task force and investigated, arrested, and convicted many drug dealers. Not once did a federal prosecutor tell me where to go, who to target, or how to conduct my investigations.

And what exactly did he mean when he said, "In this day and age, everyone in a steroids investigation retains a lawyer immediately. MLB would be at a disadvantage if it did not have an experienced lawyer with prosecutorial and investigative skills in its corner"?

Is he forgetting that you first have to find who you're going to investigate before you worry about whether the person has a lawyer? What investigation has this "experienced lawyer" ever started? What source has he ever cultivated? What dark alley has he ever walked into in Miami, Puerto Rico, the Dominican Republic, never mind Venezuela, looking for a steroid dealer? When has he ever led a unit with three thousand detectives? Has he ever met with drug dealers, mobsters, or murderers outside of the comfort and safety of his air-conditioned office? Right. That's exactly what MLB needed—another lawyer.

Mitchell went on, "I also am confident that the DOI operates without interference from the Labor Department even though it relies on Labor's longstanding relationships with the Players Association in conducting investigations. My colleague, Charlie Scheeler, worked with the Commissioner's office in connection with the aspects of the Biogenesis/Alex Rodriguez matter, and came away from that experience convinced that MLB is committed to the aggressive pursuit of non-drug testing evidence of PED use."

I have news for Senator Mitchell and Charlie Scheeler: As I've made clear in these pages, we certainly were told what to do by both Manfred and Halem on many occasions, including but not limited to Biogenesis, and we weren't even handpicked by them, as Seeley was. What makes Mitchell and Scheeler think a prosecutor who answers directly to Halem is not told what to do by Labor?

It also strains credulity to imagine how a comparison could be made between Seeley and Dan Mullin, who supervised more than three thousand NYPD detectives, had a law degree, and worked as an investigator in the NYPD for more than twenty-five years.

As for Scheeler and Mitchell, they never asked us what was going on, certainly not during the Biogenesis case. As far as I know, they never went to the DEA to ask what was going on, either, about our dealings with that agency before we were told to stop.

And what about Sullivan, the prosecutor? Did either Mitchell or Scheeler talk with him about what we had done?

What was amusing to me was how Manfred responded to reporters' questions about the Cardinals-Astros hacking scandal that came to light in 2015. Eventually Chris Correa, a Cardinals executive, was sentenced to forty-six months in jail for hacking into Houston's player development database and received a lifetime ban from baseball, joining a select list that includes Pete Rose, the infamous 1919 Black Sox players, former Mets pitcher Jenrry Mejía, and former Braves general manager John Coppolella, who was hit with the life sentence in November 2017 after MLB looked into his team's international signing practices.

Manfred, in an about-face from Biogenesis, said MLB would wait for the feds to finish their investigation of the Cardinals-Astros case before he would act. The same man who had ordered us not to cooperate with the DEA's Biogenesis investigation and launched one of his own that, in my eyes, had hindered a government investigation was now saying, in effect, "Let's not interfere with what the feds are doing." Had he taken the same approach with Biogenesis, we would have had information on more than the fourteen players who were suspended for using PEDs. Moreover, I believe Manfred would not have become the next commissioner—not exactly what Rob nor the old man from Milwaukee wanted.

"Because I don't know exactly what the facts are . . . it really doesn't make sense for me to speculate," Manfred said in July 2015. "This is a federal investigation, not a baseball investigation. We've stayed in touch, we've been cooperative, I think we're going to have to rely on what we learn from the federal government."[2]

As for Bosch's relatively short stay in federal prison, thanks in part to Mitchell's endorsement, Bosch described his transition from jail back to civilian life as "difficult."

"When I got out, I went to a halfway house," he said. "I was in home confinement afterwards, and it was very limited. They wouldn't allow me to do a lot of things. The Bureau of Prisons wouldn't let me speak to the media. I couldn't get a job that dealt with the public because they didn't want me to deal with the public.

"Those fourteen months [in jail] gave me the perspective. It definitely gave me humility. I saw it from the other side," he continued. "I saw what I did wrong. I saw where I took my own shortcuts. My intentions were good. My methods were wrong."

In that 2017 meeting, I found Bosch to be exactly what I thought he would be—a fast-talking con artist, friendly enough and just open enough to reinforce some of what I already knew about him. I had hoped that he would divulge more information about his arrangement with Major League Baseball, in particular my suspicion that he had been paid to cooperate. I believe he will someday, but what he said that day was interesting in itself.

He described MLB as having tried to "choke me out. And they were successful. I mean, I could only last so long with, you know, five different individuals or organizations coming after me. Some are Mickey Mouse. And some, like MLB, are extremely powerful. As powerful as the US government."

He said he had been "able to save a little from this whole debacle," which I found odd since he had made it clear that he had cut his deal with MLB because "it got to the point I got suffocated. I don't have the resources MLB has. I'm a working man. Sure, I made a good living but still, I'm a working man. I don't have five hundred million dollars or five billion dollars to protect myself. I ran out of steakhouses. I ran out of resources. I ran out of everything."[3]

I wondered how he could have saved money when he was in jail and had five kids to feed. His ex-wife had claimed in court documents he had failed to pay child support, and Bosch himself had said in a child support filing that he had been so broke when he agreed to cooperate with MLB, he had only $100 to his name.

Whose money did he put away?[4]

Bosch said he didn't have anything bad to say about MLB or Manfred. "I like Manfred a lot," he said. "Yeah, I'm a fan. And no, MLB did not pay me any money. I wish. MLB paid for everything. MLB paid for my lawyers. For security. But contrary to popular opinion, no, MLB did not—and don't get me wrong, I asked for money. I'm not that stupid, you know. You want me to help you? Manfred said, 'I would love to write you a check, but I can't.' The only reason I went back to him was because of my safety. That was it. I can make my own money. Money is easy to make."[5]

I never believed Bosch's claims that he felt his life had been threatened by A-Rod's thugs. First of all, they were wannabe thugs. Second, Bosch's lifestyle was such that if someone wanted to kill him, they would have done so long ago. Unlike Manfred, who hired 24/7 security when he suspected A-Rod's people were following him, Bosch lived in a different world. He was a street hood, and I seriously doubt he was afraid of Ugi Velasquez. Certainly, Bosch had not been afraid of Porter Fischer when he had decided not to repay the money Fischer had lent him—and Fischer had guns and was seemingly unstable. But shortly after the *Miami New Times* story broke, Bosch described the meeting with some "associates" of Rodriguez's during which he had been asked to sign the affidavit saying he had never supplied A-Rod with PEDs. It was at that meeting that Bosch said he had felt "uncomfortable" and that he was then told he needed to go to Colombia for a while. He implied that he had believed if he went to Colombia he would not come back alive.

In his *60 Minutes* appearance with Manfred, Bosch reiterated his fears, and Manfred—not surprisingly—backed him up. It provided good cover for the "security" bills that were growing.

There had been another hit put out on him, too, Bosch told us. "I just found out, to give you an idea, while I was being investigated and I was running for my life, you know there was a hit on me, right?"

The information about the hit, he said, had come courtesy of one of the Biogenesis characters who had ended up in jail on drug charges in 2014 and "was with a guy who was selling off the hit like he was subleasing an apartment. Subleasing the hit to somebody else, and it was an undercover DA [agent]."

Bosch described another scene in a restaurant after he agreed to work with MLB during which he says he was followed to the bathroom by an A-Rod associate and had to call his MLB-paid bodyguard, Bahlraj Badree, for help from inside the toilet.

"So I'm in the bathroom, you know, there's one bathroom and although it's loud outside you could actually hear, because you're in a hollow place, a quiet place, you're hearing what they're saying. You know, 'Motherfucker, he has no—he's nothing without his security team. We're going to fuck him up now when he comes out.' So I take out my phone, I go 'Raj, I need you to get me out of the bathroom.' It was A-Rod's people. So I dispatched my people to A-Rod's people, Pepe Gomez, and boom, you know, peace."

Bosch attributed that incident to Rodriguez's posse of "hoods."

"A-Rod has, like, seven hundred employees," Bosch said. "They all want to be his—'Oh, I'm the guy—I'm the guy who took out Tony' . . . And they're all hoods. That's Alex—you can have all the money in the world, but he's still who he is, you know?"

"Listen," he continued, "the sharks came out to feed, when this whole thing—MLB, Alex Rodriguez—money, money, money. This town is a hustler's town. New York is an angle town. Everybody has an angle to make a fast buck. 'Here is what I am going to do to rip you off.' So that's what was going on."

I looked at it a different way. I believe that by saying he had sent his people to negotiate a truce with A-Rod's people he was proving that he really had no fear of them. I don't believe MLB's claim that it was necessary to pay huge sums for Bosch's security because of threats on his life.

Bosch described reporters who formed relationships with his "ex-chicks" and shadowed him in restaurants. He claimed that law enforcement agents were in on the game, too, sitting next to his table in a restaurant, although I doubt that happened unless Bosch was meeting with an informant or undercover, and I don't believe that was ever the case. "It was a she-DEA and a he-DEA," he said of the couple who dined at a table next to his. "It was fun for a little bit, but then there was no residence I could go to that, you know, dude in the middle of the night trying to break in."

Bosch said MLB is not helping him, "nor do I care to get help. You know, God knows, I needed the help, but I'm not going to sit there and lament over that or beg or do like Porter Fischer does and pray for money, and 'Give me money' and all that bullshit."

Nonetheless, Bosch said, he remains in touch with Manfred. "I text Rob all the time," he said. "'How you doin', buddy?' Swear to God. Let me see if I got his text. I have it.

"'Hey, I'm in New York.'

"'Sure, come by.'

"Nice guy. I don't owe him anything. He doesn't owe me anything."

Bosch talked about his hard-partying lifestyle and blamed it on the players and celebrities he was doing business with. "I started doing drugs or that party lifestyle due to my lifestyle with all these players," he said. "And remember, it wasn't only the athletes, I had a bunch of celebrities."

He described Rodriguez as a "very insecure individual. Very insecure. In every aspect. You know, 'Am I good enough?' You know, 'If I'm going to be with a chick, they're going to have to be blond, you know. Are my eyes blue enough? Am I tall enough? Am I strong enough?' I would go into his house, and in his living room he would have, like, this-size TV, maybe a little smaller, and he would have them in different locations, and every TV had a different game on of his highlights."

He said A-Rod paid him extra to be with him "almost 24/7," no doubt a function of the player's fear of testing positive or somehow getting caught. According to Bosch, most of the players he dealt with had been abusing testosterone for years—in A-Rod's case since high school—and had built up a tolerance to the drug. But Bosch ridiculed MLB's drug program and said he doesn't think there is an effective one in sports, even though several of his clients tested positive.

"They have the better of the worst," he said of MLB's program. "The least of my worries was [players] pissing dirty. The ones that did piss dirty were those that thought I was invincible and that I could fix everything, and they didn't follow protocol."

He singled out Ryan Braun as a particularly reckless user. "Ryan Braun had something called troches—they called it gummy bears—

they're actually lozenges. They had testosterone in them—fifteen percent. I already had these guys juiced, so all they had to do was, this was an activator. A little testosterone. They would drop it in the first inning—it was gone by the fifth inning—and unless you pulled him out of a game and tested him, you would never find out. So you could test him before and test him after and never know."

"And so what happened with Braun was real simple," he said. "The guy took, like, thirty gummy bears. He took one in the third inning, then he took one in the fifth inning, then he took one in the seventh inning, then he took one . . . he was just popping it like it was—candy."

Bosch re-created a conversation with Braun, and I had to smile after hearing the anecdote retold.

"How many did you take?"

"I took five, I took six."

"How much did you take?"

"Okay. I took the whole thing."

Bosch described a testing policy full of holes, including when and where players are tested. "I didn't start working until midnight, and I didn't finish until five a.m. That was my workday with these athletes," he said. "You'd never see me during the day with these guys. We did everything in the middle of the night. . . . Even if you wanted to use liquid testosterone, all right. You're going to get it at twelve o'clock at night, at midnight, and by nine a.m., ten a.m., it's out of your system. And if you microdose it, good luck testing for it.

"Another example—off-season. Like, really? My guys, they were in the middle of the ocean on a boat. What are you going to do? Send a helicopter? Because they're on vacation. Let's say the urine guys, the testing guys, say, 'I'm coming over.' I'm fishing in Bimini. They gave me three days, that was the policy. It's like forty-eight hours. In forty-eight hours we could have changed the world over and over again as far as this is concerned. I mean, we had this shit down pat. Listen to me, this doesn't take brilliance. It just takes, it takes desire, motivation, commitment, and a little bit of, you know, bullshit, a little bit of money."

He was right about that. As long as the game rewards cheaters, not much will change. His statement goes back to what I've said all along: all the testing in the world will not get rid of performance-enhancing drug use.

MLB and the Players Association know that the testing is useless and that they can both cover themselves with the PED-testing security blanket. MLB can say we have the best testing and because of it the players aren't using performance enhancers, which is a lie that was revealed by the Biogenesis case.

As Bosch says, everybody wins. MLB can say it has the best testing, and the union can say its players are clean.

"It's simple math," Bosch said. "Look at the history. Let's see, I'm a number four outfielder earning $1.1 million. I get on the juice, and in my free-agent year, if I make it as a starting outfielder, let me see, that's $4.3 million. I get caught, I lose $500,000. But I made $4 million. Simple math. Look at all the guys that got caught—they got better contracts after, Melky included. How are you going to beat the system if you're rewarding these guys? Now the Hall of Fame? Fuck the Hall of Fame. [Players] don't care about the Hall. [Players] care about the dollar, brother. This is a business. There's no, you know, slapping on the ass. Good game. That's on TV."

He said he had done a lot of work in the Dominican Republic, which was no surprise to anyone familiar with that Wild West landscape, and that he would send an associate to speak with a player. "You wanted to catch everybody, you should have gone in the winter to Boca Chica, that's where everything, where all the work was done," he said. "There was a process. It was like a six-month vetting process that would take place. I would have them pay a deposit to [the associate]; then [the associate] would give me the money. Half of that deposit would go to set up everything, and then I would start in on it. But I would only do the work in the winter. So I would rent a place and the work was done in the off-season, so all the levels I was testing, all the diagnostic tests, all the blood tests, when I would mix peptides and use different acids to make sure they coincide with your pH and your pH was always balanced, so everything was done there."

I was not surprised at all to hear Bosch say he had done most of his work in the off-season, as well as the blood tests and all the other work he mentioned. Over the six years I was assigned to the DOI, I made people like Bosch my most sought-after sources. And I targeted antiaging clinics as the most likely places for athletes to get their PEDs.

As I've said before, in my twenty-three years working narcotics I didn't spend much time investigating performance-enhancing drugs. We had our hands full chasing cocaine and heroin dealers, which present much more danger to the general public. A drug dealer is a drug dealer, though, and in the end the investigations are the same. When I decided to join the DOI, I did my homework and started reading and searching for people who distributed PEDs. Even the Mitchell Report was helpful in pointing me in the right direction.

As Mitchell wrote in his report:

The recommendations below focus on three principal areas: investigations based upon non-testing evidence; player education; and further improvements in the testing program. These recommendations are designed to work in combination with one another to more effectively combat performance enhancing substance violations. It bears emphasis that no testing program, standing alone, is enough. Certain illegal substances are difficult or virtually impossible to detect, and law enforcement investigations of Kirk Radomski and compounding pharmacies and anti-aging clinics show that, even in this era of testing, players can continue to use performance-enhancing substances while avoiding detection. Indeed, one leading expert has argued that "testing only scratches the surface." The ability to vigorously investigate allegations of performance-enhancing substance violations is an essential part of any meaningful drug prevention program.[6]

Along the way I investigated the likes of Anthony Galea and searched for and found PED distributors, some active and some in hiding. They all had the same modus operandi. As Bosch said, it all starts with a blood test; then they find the products that best suit what you're looking to accomplish, followed by a protocol that keeps you one step ahead of the testing. It ends with a large invoice that is paid in cash.

I found one PED dealer who would become a source hiding in Puerto Rico. Prior to the release of the Mitchell Report and before Mitchell's investigation began, that dealer used to supply several players with PEDs. Some of those players were with the Red Sox. Soon after the congressional hearings began, the dealer was told by his clients that he needed to get out of town. This source was the son of a pharmacist in Puerto Rico and learned his craft by reading and traveling to Europe and Asia, where many PED dealers get their latest and best products. This source broke down the process just as Bosch did. He claimed to have been hired by a future Hall of Fame player late in his career and said that after giving the player a blood test, he broke the news to the player that he couldn't help him.

According to the source, he could tell from the player's blood that he had been using PEDs for years and there was nothing he could give him that would help.

I also found a doctor in Puerto Rico whose office was in a strip mall in the middle of nowhere. I went in to ask him some questions and noticed that he had autographed photos of all the well-known Latin players at the time adorning his personal office. I ran into a dead end in the investigation and turned it over to the DEA, which tried to get some undercovers into the doctor's world, but he smelled a rat and didn't bite.

The doctor did tell me that he had treated many of the players who were on his wall and that he used to shut down his office for a month to go to spring training to treat his players.

Just as I still wonder how someone like Alex Rodriguez, with all the financial backing in the world, ended up being injected in a restaurant bathroom by someone like Bosch, I wondered why those players, with all the money they have, would travel to a strip mall in Puerto Rico to get treated by that doctor.

By the time the Biogenesis investigation started, I had targeted several antiaging clinics and had already gone into several of them in an undercover capacity as a trainer to buy PEDs for some younger players I was allegedly training. After a brief conversation, followed by my commitment to pay cash, I had agreements to do business. I was looking forward to taking all those cases to law enforcement when MLB said good-bye.

The bottom line is that you can spend millions and millions of dollars on testing and you'll catch a few stupid or financially strapped younger athletes, but you won't catch the A-Rods of the world.

The couple of hours we spent with Anthony Bosch that October afternoon were surreal. In my dream I had met him for the first time at the US Attorney's Office as I sat on one side of the table with my DEA friends and he sat on the other side in handcuffs with his attorney, Susy Ribero-Ayala, whose one actual conversation with me ended in her screaming "Do not call my client again, DO YOU UNDERSTAND?!" That conversation was followed by a call from Halem with the usual "Dominguez, stand down" order.

That's how I wanted to meet Mr. Bosch, but things don't always turn out the way you want them to.

Biogenesis was the case that I thought would put the frosting on the cake for our unit. The DOI had accomplished so much even with the constant interference from Manfred and Labor, and that was the case that would really have put us on the map. We had other chances to make a huge splash, like the Viciedo human-trafficking case, but baseball didn't want that. They couldn't afford for us to go there.

In my dreams, DOI would have been responsible for taking down Biogenesis without having purchased stolen documents, with no interference from Labor, with information gathered through a textbook investigation conducted by the DEA that would have ended up with more suspensions than MLB handed down. I thought about how Mullin had reminded Manfred about the deal we had with the DEA, that it was up to seventeen players it was going to name and that it estimated the case would be wrapped up by July. There were players on the DEA's radar whose names never emerged on MLB's suspended list.

Who knows who the MLB commissioner would have been if Manfred hadn't been named the "PED sheriff"? If the *Miami New Times* article hadn't come out, if Fischer hadn't stolen Bosch's ledgers, the DOI as it was meant to be would still be policing baseball. Bigger and better than ever.

But that wasn't meant to be, and I found myself listening to Anthony Bosch, taking notes, and thinking that he might as well have been talking about all the scandals that plagued Major League Baseball: the Steroid Era, the Mitchell Report, Biogenesis, trafficking, all of it.

Maybe it took a guy like Bosch to sum up the whole sordid story, the one I had believed would have a happy ending way back in 2008. We could clean up this game.

"Let's educate the athlete to do the right thing. Let's educate somebody like MLB, in order so they could understand what is a performance-enhancing drug and what isn't and what you're doing about it," Bosch said. "Now, having said that, you know, unfortunately, who cares? I don't think anybody gives a shit. I think everything that was done, you know, was for personal gain. That's the bottom line . . . for everybody that was involved."

When Bosch said he didn't think anybody gave a shit, he was talking about those who run Major League Baseball—the commissioner, the lawyers, the businesspeople, the owners of the teams, the union, the agents, even the players—and maybe some of the fans, too. Everybody got what they wanted. "Manfred got his job, the other one left on a high note," Bosch said. "You know, blah, blah, blah."

EPILOGUE

I loved my twenty-nine years as a Boston police officer. I loved the guys I worked with, loved the work, loved the idea that we could make a difference in the communities around the city. I lived for the investigations—the hunt, as I called it—but never the kill. Most of my investigations involved the sale of narcotics, and I couldn't see people going to jail for years for selling drugs.

The shift over to MLB and the Department of Investigations was natural, I thought. When the job offer presented itself, I really believed I would be taking part in something unique, a once-in-a-lifetime opportunity to be part of a groundbreaking team of investigators in a world that had never really been policed.

I headed to New York City thinking we would focus on performance-enhancing drugs, but it didn't take long for us to realize that "integrity of the game" issues ran much deeper than just PEDs. I took the show on the road, spending much of my time in the Dominican Republic, Puerto Rico, Venezuela, even Cuba.

As soon as MLB assigned me to work international age/ID investigations, I had to spend two weeks a month in the Dominican Republic. I stayed in an apartment owned by my colleague Nelson

Tejada and rented by MLB/DOI about a half mile from the MLB office in Santo Domingo. I would get up at 5 a.m. and go for a run before heading to the office. We had a housemaid, Melvi, who took really good care of us. She cooked and cleaned. It was a beautiful apartment except for the crazy rooster across the street whose clock was a bit off.

Being away from my family was not fun, but that's the life for everyone in baseball.

I found and vetted investigators all over the world and leaned heavily on the US embassies and the FBI and DEA agents assigned to those countries. All embassies employ former law enforcement agents to help them conduct visa investigations, and they were a great help in pointing me in the right direction. The Dominican Republic was easy since Nelson had already set up a team of investigators, and I used them when necessary. All told, there were four full-time DOI employees and more than a dozen contract investigators in the Dominican Republic.

The rest of the world was not so easy. We ended up having investigators in Japan, Australia, Spain, the Netherlands, Curaçao, Panama, Brazil, Colombia, Costa Rica, Mexico, Saint Maarten, El Salvador, Honduras, and the second busiest country for signing players internationally behind the Dominican Republic, Venezuela.

In the beginning, I spent a lot of time in Venezuela, where we had close to twenty investigators because of the size of the country and the number of players signed. The best thing I did in my time in DOI was to convince Dan Mullin and George Hanna to hire Joel Rengifo as a full-time employee. It didn't take much convincing since they both knew what Joel was capable of doing following his rescue of MLB relief pitcher Ugueth Urbina's mother after she was kidnapped by FARC (Revolutionary Armed Forces of Colombia) leaders in 2004 and held captive in a remote jungle region for five and a half months.

After hiring the investigators, training them, and getting the lay of the land, I would travel to Venezuela when needed, usually every other month. When emergencies—usually kidnappings—occurred, I would take off for Caracas in a hurry. My trusted friend Joel would pick me up at the Caracas airport, and thank God for that. Joel is the most respected law enforcement official in Venezuela, but that honor comes with enemies.

When you're in law enforcement, you make enemies—and he had. Notorious for taking down kidnappers, he was always armed, and he made life easy for me. We stayed in hotels and took cabs, motorcycles, or rented vehicles when available. Most of the time we stayed in Valencia or Caracas. The trips over mountainside roads were bad enough, but riding on a scooter in Caracas traffic to a meeting at the US Embassy was as close to death as I ever came. Joel would laugh as I hung on to the scooter's Uber driver with my eyes closed and in total prayer mode. Nobody at MLB ever asked for my car service receipts from any of those trips. We experienced kidnappings in Mexico, too, but the kidnappings in Venezuela were second to none.

It wasn't long after joining MLB that I began to think about telling my story. It was less than a year after we had been hired—a Friday night in November 2008—when I received the call from Dan Mullin concerning Dayan Viciedo and heard Rob Manfred's voice on the line. I couldn't believe what I was hearing, yet I could. The anger in Manfred's voice was unmistakable, and the mandate was clear: Stand down. Don't cross the line.

That call prompted me to contact some close friends in command positions in the Boston Police Department: Could I come back? The answer was yes. All I would have to do was say "uncle." When I told

George and Dan that I was ready to leave, they pleaded with me to stay. They believed that Manfred's hissy fit would be a passing thing. I agreed to stay, but my gut told me they were wrong, and I told them so.

I don't consider myself naive, but looking back, I guess I was. Until I got the call from Mullin asking me to join him as an investigator, I would have never taken a full-time job with MLB. I already knew what MLB's security department was all about: Years after accepting the RSA job, Hallinan offered me a full-time MLB security job on two separate occasions and I had respectfully turned down the offers. But with the newly established DOI, I believed we could hold MLB accountable for its actions. I can't say that I bought 100 percent into the idea, but pretty close to it. The government had made such a big deal out of how the game was being disrupted and damaged by performance-enhancing drugs, and MLB was so afraid that Congress would stick its nose into its business, that it had hired former senator George Mitchell to do an investigation that uncovered illegal behavior that had been going on for years.

Mitchell's recommendations were on point, or at least I thought they were: form an independent investigative body composed of highly respected and accomplished law enforcement officials who would work hand in hand with law enforcement and with no interference from Major League Baseball's Labor Relations Department.

At first, with the exception of some whispering from a couple of people who I thought were just naysayers within baseball, it seemed as though it could work. But the whispering got louder and louder until the noise was deafening. There were some in the commissioner's office, including President and COO Bob DuPuy and President and CEO of MLB International Tim Brosnan, who let us do our jobs and never ordered Mullin to hide anything. People like Brosnan were big fans of the DOI, but I got the feeling from the beginning that Rob Manfred was against the idea of an independent

Department of Investigations. And once DuPuy was pushed out in 2010, we were dead men walking.

I can say with complete certainty that I gave the DOI job 100 percent, that I worked my ass off, and that my immediate bosses recognized the effort. I traveled to places where few wanted to go, was assigned more cases than you can imagine, and finished every job I was allowed to.

The momentum had been building, but the Biogenesis investigation was the straw that broke the camel's back for the DOI. Manfred and Halem turned our unit upside down, and the toxic culture caused Hanna to become physically ill. Manfred and Halem were able to divide the unit, and they got rid of those of us who wouldn't lie down for them.

Tony Bosch was right: everyone on the baseball side got what he wanted. Manfred got his commissioner's job (in 2014), Selig got into the Hall of Fame (in 2017), and Dan Halem got promoted to deputy commissioner (in December 2017). Neil Boland ended up with a fancy title, too: vice president of information security and special projects. Imagine that.

You could even say that A-Rod eventually got what he wanted— after serving his record suspension, which looked to be an event that would torpedo his career for good, not only did he come back to play in 2015, he also played in 2016 and then transitioned into glitzy baseball analyst gigs. He has other entertainment ventures, presides over his A-Rod Corporation, and surely enjoyed the comforts of the $20 million he was paid by the Yankees in 2017—the last year of his contract—to make a couple of appearances as a special "adviser" to Hal Steinbrenner after the team released him in August 2016. By 2018, he'd added special adviser to GM Brian Cashman to his résumé. Last time I checked, he was dating J-Lo and had purchased a Park Avenue apartment with her.

And the supposed bad blood between Rodriguez and Manfred? That seemed to be nothing more than a phony back-and-forth. As Bosch says, it's all about the money. During his 2015 World Series assignment for Fox, A-Rod was seen embracing Manfred behind the batting cage at Citi Field before Game 3 between the Mets and Royals, and during All-Star Week in A-Rod's hometown of Miami in 2017, Rodriguez posted a photo of himself and Jennifer Lopez in between Manfred and Manfred's wife, Colleen, everyone with their arms wrapped around one another and the grinning Manfred parked next to J-Lo. One big happy family.

Fortunately, my DOI colleagues were able to bounce back professionally, with Dan and George landing jobs at a global financial services firm and Tom Reilly working as the head of another security company. The two other members of the "three amigos"—Noel Firth and Marty "The Chinch" Rodriguez—are also doing well. Noel remains part owner and manager of Legends, and Marty is now the head of security at one of the many skyscrapers in New York City.

Telling my story took me on an incredible journey and allowed me the opportunity to reconnect with the DEA agents we had worked with so closely during Biogenesis, at least until we were told not to. Meeting with Kevin Stanfill and Mark Trouville in Miami years later and laughing and talking with Jeannette Moran at length, sharing stories about A-Rod, baseball, Biogenesis, and the fallout meant the world to me, even if we had to revisit some painful chapters along the way.

It was great to rekindle an old friendship with the DEA's Joe Rannazzisi. It was even better seeing him on *60 Minutes*, where he detailed how he had singlehandedly taken on major pharmaceutical companies as he battled the opioid scourge rampaging through the country. Standing up for what he believes in is what Joe does best.

I was able to reconnect with sources such as Frankie, the informant we brought to the DEA during Biogenesis, without whom there would have been no investigation and prosecution. Talking with him in a cramped patio next to an indoor batting cage in a hardscrabble inner-city neighborhood was like something out of *The Wire*. Frankie was the same friendly guy, unfazed by any of the danger he encounters on a daily basis.

At one point, the comparison between the Mafia and baseball came up, and Frankie smiled at that one. "You can call it that. We're not Italian, but you can call it that," he said. "My personal opinion—there's too many games, [players] have to use something. You got to perform for the owners of the league and the public. I pay my money to see this guy hit a home run or go three for three. It's a big business."

Frankie, his cell phone constantly buzzing, even offered to meet me down the street for beers after we finished our conversation.

I might have been naive to think the DOI project would work, but I'm not naive enough to think every baseball fan in the country cares if athletes are using performance-enhancing drugs. Most fans don't understand the risks that come with the rewards, not to mention the enormous ability of the drugs to obliterate any possibility of a level playing field. I never thought the cost of doing business as an athlete should be that you have to use drugs to succeed, but to the vast audience out there, I'm not sure it matters. I also realize that big business demands all kinds of questionable behavior from employees and that executives are adept at keeping that behavior quiet.

As for me, with the help of great doctors, nurses, friends, a loving family, my trusted private nurse, Donna, prayer, and the will of God, I remain cancer free. Since I was diagnosed with the disease, I have been contacted on a regular basis by family members and others who have been dealt the same terrible hand. I give them the advice and information available to me, and I pray for them.

I met some great people in baseball, but the truth is I no longer see the game I played on the sandlots of Havana and the green playing fields of Boston, the game I loved and taught my kids to love.

I gave a lot of thought to writing this book. At the end of our lives we say one of two things: I wish I had or I'm glad I did. I'm glad I did.

My hope is that this book reveals the secrets hidden behind the closed doors of that beautiful game, but even more than that, I hope it is a beacon of light through the vast darkness of pancreatic cancer.

ACKNOWLEDGMENTS

I have spent my life keeping my head down, working hard, and moving on to my next chapter. Not once have I ever engaged someone in the media for the purposes of sharing information or promoting any cause. I have been approached by many members of the media over the years, whether as a police officer, an RSA, or a full-time employee of MLB, but I have always respectfully declined to comment, sending them to my superiors for comments.

I wrote this book because what people see and read isn't always what it seems to be. Many of the articles published during the Biogenesis investigation painted the DOI in a bad light, and I wanted the public to know the rest of the story.

To all the hardworking people in MLB whom I befriended over the years and who befriended me, and who for the most part go unnoticed, thank you for your friendship.

To all the members of MLB's RSA program whom I've come to know and respect, I imagine that some of you will agree and some will disagree with what I have detailed in this book concerning the program. Kevin Hallinan did a great job putting the program together and picking nothing but the best law enforcement officers from their respective cities. I disagreed with the way he sometimes treated his people, but that, of course, is in the eye of the beholder. I do know that you guys have a tough job and you do it well. Stay safe.

To my agent, Tim Hays, who took this book project head on and never blinked an eye, thank you. To my writers and partners in this project, Teri Thompson and Christian Red, without your long hours of hard work and dedication, this book would have never happened.

I owe a debt of gratitude to my three steady law enforcement partners who over the years kept me in one piece, beginning with Bob Tully at the Boston Police Department and then John Woudenberg and Jill Heeter at the FBI.

When I was diagnosed with cancer, I couldn't believe the number of people who came to my aid, prayed for me, and kept me upbeat. I'm sure I will miss some names, and I apologize beforehand, but know that you all mean the world to me. A heartfelt thank-you to all my friends who were there for me during my trying times.

A special thank-you to the Granara-Skerry Trust and our dear friend Nancy. The Granara-Skerry family have dedicated their lives to keeping alive the memory of their beloved family member Kathy, who died of pancreatic cancer. Through their fund-raisers they have generated more than $1 million for the Massachusetts General Hospital for pancreatic cancer research. Ever since I was diagnosed, my family has helped this wonderful cause, and we will continue to do so. My thoughts and prayers go out to all the people who have fought this disease and are no longer here. I also pray for all of their family members. My family plans to donate 50 percent of all sales of this book to the Granara-Skerry Trust to further Massachusetts General Hospital's pancreatic cancer research efforts.

To all my Don Bosco High School teammates who sent me emails, text messages, and cards loaded with well-wishes, thank you. A special thanks to Al Libardoni and Peter Masciola, who made special trips to see me when I was sick.

Special thanks to my Southie boys, Sal Paterna and his gang, and Al Petrilli and Fred Kelloway, whose text messages constantly made me laugh. To the Ryan family, who have been dear friends for more than thirty years—Joe, Stevie, and his sons, Steve and Mattie.

To my golfing buddies and dear friends Dan Keeler, Jimmy Maher, Jack Doyle, Bill Laughnane, Dan Maloney, Pat Troy, Paul Tansey, Bill O'Connell, and Kevin McGill, my close friend for more than thirty years, thank you.

To my entire BPD family, which supported and prayed for me, including Commissioner Bill Evans and his command staff and all its officers, thank you for your prayers. To my old drug control unit gang, Gil Griffiths, Joe Driscoll, Skippy O'Connell, Bobby Morris, Steve Brady, and Tim Duggan, my loyal and dear friend, thank you.

A special thanks to retired BPD detective bureau chief Jack Boyle for being a good partner and a great friend, and to BPD chief Dan Linskey for helping me out in my current life as a private investigator.

To my longtime friend BPD detective Fred Waggett, a fellow cancer survivor, health and happiness.

To my BPD undercover buddies, Jay Broderick, Paul Quinn, Felipe and Frank Colon, Scott Mackie, Jimmy Griffin, and Juan Seoane, my unofficially adopted Cuban son, thank you.

A special thanks to my FBI family, which from day one was there to help in any way possible and helped raise money for pancreatic cancer awareness. And to my dear friends and colleagues Jay Fallon, Tim McElroy, Katy Roberts, Tony Dillon, Mike Gibeley, Mike DeLapena, John Elkalubie, and many others who were so kind and thoughtful. A special thanks to Mike McGowan, who has been a close and trusted friend from the day I met him. His book, *Ghost*, will be released in the fall of 2018.

To my doctors at the Massachusetts General Hospital—they saved my life. Dr. Leslie Fang, Dr. Carlos Fernandez-del Castillo, Dr.

Theodore Hong, Dr. Eunice Kwak, Dr. Jill Allen, and all the wonderful nurses at the MGH, I can't thank you enough.

Soon after I had decided to write this book, I was searching for a lawyer to represent me, and my longtime friend Tom Frongillo and his firm, Fish and Richardson, stepped up to the plate. I can't thank Tom enough. I also want to thank his sidekick and partner Caroline Simmons for all the work she's done on my behalf.

When the two NYPD officers working for the Manhattan DA's office showed up in my driveway, I was upset, and Tom Frongillo called upon an old friend to help me out in New York. My many thanks go out to Dan McGillycuddy of the law firm Dwayne Morris for his work with the Manhattan DA's office on my behalf.

To my MLB friends and coworkers who dedicated themselves to their jobs and in turn were summarily dismissed, thank you for your friendship. To Dan Mullin and George Hanna, whom I respect and love. I know we went different ways at the end of our MLB journeys, and I hope that as I understood you had to go your way, I hope you understand that I had to go mine.

Thanks to my three amigos from the NYPD, my roommate and "bunky," Noel Firth; Tom Reilly, my DOI partner during the Biogenesis investigation; and "The Chinch," aka Marty Rodriguez. Some of my best memories from my nineteen years with MLB came with those three guys—with Noel at his bar Legends at 6 West 33rd Street; with Tom from mid-2012 through our last days in MLB as we rode the streets of Miami chasing Anthony Bosch; with The Chinch on that almost magical 2006 trip to Cuba and the phenomenal game against the Cuban team. You will never know how much you guys showing up to the Massachusetts General Hospital the day of my operation meant to us. Love you guys.

Thank you to all my Braintree friends for your thoughts and

prayers. A special thanks to Roy and Marta Goggins, who officiated at our wedding.

A deep and sincere thank-you to my family; without them I would be lost. To my immediate family on my wife's side, who prayed for me and helped in every way needed. To my mother-in-law, Fran, and her husband, Stan, my father-in-law, Ron Holmes, and his partner, Lynn, to Ronnie and Lori, Frank and Kirsten, Rhonda and Kevin, Steven and Lauren, Mark, Ricky, and Scott, thank you.

To the Dominguez side of the family—my cousins George and his wife, Tina, Gus and his wife, Marcy, Marlen, Marina, Sonita, and Maribel—thank you for praying for me.

To Tata, my dear mother, who gave up everything to bring me and my brother from Cuba. To my father, Eduardo, who loved us to death. May he rest in peace. To my grandfather Andres, who played such a huge role in a short period of time, making me who I am.

To my dear brother, Carlos, his wife, Colleen, and her family, who were there for me every step of the way, and to my nephew and godson, Alex "The Great One." Love you all.

To my sons and their significant others, Andrew and Sarah, Chris and his wife, Jenny, and my soon-to-arrive grandson AJ, Mike and Kevin, whose love and support mean so much to me, love you. To my beautiful daughter, Sunni, who is her mother's image in every way, for caring for me and showing me unwavering love. To Sunni's fiancé, Dan, thank you for being there for Sunni and for me.

To the most important person in my life, my friend, my partner, my love, my wife, Donna. I cannot thank you enough for all the wonderful things you have done for me and our families. You are the glue that keeps us together and has kept me alive. Love you.

And last but not least to my God and Savior, Jesus Christ, to whom I owe everything.

NOTES

PROLOGUE

1 Jay Jaffe, "JAWS and the 2015 Hall of Fame Ballot," *Sports Illustrated*, December 7, 2014, https://www.si.com/mlb/2014/12/17/jaws-2015-hall-of-fame-ballot-nomar-garciaparra; Gordon Edes, "Morgan: No Sign of Steroids in His Years Here," February 23, 2005, http://archive.boston.com/sports/baseball/redsox/articles/2005/02/23/morgan_no_sign_of_steroid_users_in_his_years_here/; Boston Herald: 3/4/2004 "Suspicions to Nag Nomar . . . " https://www.nexis.com/search/homesubmitForm.do.

2 From *Daily News* story on Feb. 15, 2005 "They Knew!" http://www.nydailynews.com/archives/sports/fbi-agent-hits-mlb-roids-baseball-knew-canseco-probe-article-1.550654.

3 From the *New York Daily News*, March 13, 2005, http://www.nydailynews.com/archives/sports/hitting-mark-fbi-informants-mcgwire-juiced-article-1.559684

4 Greg Skejskal, "FBI Probe into Illegal Steroids Broke New Ground," Tickle the Wire, January 5, 2010, http://ticklethewire.com/2010/01/05/fbi-probe-into-illegal-steroids-broke-new-ground/.

5 https://archive.nytimes.com/www.nytimes.com/learning/teachers/featured_articles/20050318friday.html?ncid=txtlnkusaolp00000619.

6 George J. Mitchell, *Report to the Commissioner of Baseball of an Independent Investigation into the Illegal Use of Steroids and Other Performance Enhancing Substances by Players in Major League Baseball*, December 13, 2007, http://files.mlb.com/mitchrpt.pdf, 288.

7 Ibid., 289.

CHAPTER 1: THE BEGINNING OF THE END

1 George J. Mitchell, *Report to the Commissioner of Baseball of an Independent Investigation into the Illegal Use of Steroids and Other Performance Enhancing Substances by Players in Major League Baseball*, December 13, 2007, http://files.mlb.com/mitchrpt.pdf, 289.

2 Ibid., 290.

3 Ibid.

4 Authors' phone interview with Kevin Stanfill, August 30, 2017.

5 Ibid.

6 *The Dark Side: Secrets of the Sports Dopers*, Al Jazeera, December 26, 2015, https://www.youtube.com/watch?v=wJRPxmTuxoI.

7 "At the Heart of a Vast Doping Network, an Alias," *New York Times*, March 26, 2018.

CHAPTER 4: THE FBI DRUG TASK FORCE

1 Boston.com. http://archive.boston.com/news/specials/whitey/articles/profile_of_john_morris/. As the head of the FBI's Boston organized crime squad in the late 1970s and early 1980s, John Morris supervised agent John J. Connolly Jr. and oversaw the cultivation of "Whitey" Bulger and Stephen Flemmi as informants. Granted immunity from prosecution in exchange for his testimony during 1998 federal court hearings, Morris confirmed scathing allegations of FBI misconduct, admitting that he had alerted Flemmi and Bulger to an investigation targeting bookmakers in 1988 and had asked a federal prosecutor to keep them out of a 1979 indictment for fixing horse races.

CHAPTER 5: OPERATION BARBERSHOP

1 George J. Mitchell, *Report to the Commissioner of Baseball of an Independent Investigation into the Illegal Use of Steroids and Other Performance Enhancing Substances by Players in Major League Baseball*, December 13, 2007, http://files.mlb.com/mitchrpt.pdf, 288.

2 Stan Grossfeld, "Batboy Finds It Tough to Pick Up His Life," *Boston Globe*, April 27, 2005, http://archive.boston.com/sports/baseball/redsox/articles/2005/04/27/batboy_finds_it_tough_to_pick_up_his_life/.

3 Mitchell, *Report to the Commissioner of Baseball*, 92.

4 T. J. Quinn, Michael O'Keeffe, and Christian Red, "Bag Men: Gonzalez & Trainer Linked to 2001 Steroid Probe," *Daily News* [New York], July 30, 2006, http://www.nydailynews.com/archives/sports/bag-men-gonzalez-trainer-linked-2001-steroid-probe-article-1.578387; also, http://www.nydailynews.com/sports/baseball/yankees/santo-domingo-roads-lead-tainted-trainer-angel-presinal-article-1.389844.

5 Associated Press, "After Wife's Request, Charge Dropped vs. Phils' Myers," October 6, 2006, http://www.espn.com/mlb/news/story?id=2614037.

6 Ken Belson, "Ray Rice Wins Reinstatement to N.F.L. in Arbitration," November 28, 2014, https://www.nytimes.com/2014/11/29/sports/football/ray-rice-suspension-overturned-in-arbitration.html?_r=0;.

7 Kevin Spain, "Before Russia Investigation, Robert Muller Oversaw Probe into NFL's Handling of Ray Rice Case," *USA Today*, May 17, 2017, https://www.usatoday.com/story/sports/nfl/2017/05/17/robert-mueller-ray-rice-russia-investigation/101809590/.

8 US District Court motion filed by Marquez, Also *Boston Globe*, Feb. 25, 2009. https://www.nexis.com/search/homesubmitForm.do.

9 The defendant was charged with nine counts of violating 18 U.S.C. § 911 (false claim of US citizenship).

10 Lisa Redmond, "Big Papi's Former Aide Doesn't Get Charges Dropped," *Lowell Sun*, March 4, 2009, http://www.lowellsun.com/ci_11833104.

CHAPTER 7: PLAYER TRAFFICKING

1 https://sports.abs-cbn.com/baseball/news/2017/02/15/cuban-players-we-paid-thousands-journey-us-baseball-21916.

2 Jay Weaver, "Agent, Trainer Smuggled Cuban Ballplayers into U.S. Now They're Headed to Prison," *Miami Herald*, November 2, 2017, http://www.miamiherald.com/news/local/article182319971.html.

CHAPTER 8: BONUS SKIMMING

1 Jorge Arangure Jr., "Dominican Court Finds for Former Scout," ESPN, January 15, 2010, www.espn.com/mlb/news/story?id=4826863.

2 MLB press release, November 21, 2017, announcing Atlanta Braves' violations of major-league rules.

3 "The 100 Most Powerful People in Baseball," *USA Today*, April 8, 2017, https://www.usatoday.com/story/sports/mlb/2017/04/08/mlb-100-most-powerful-people/100172102/.

4   Associated Press, "Gunfight Preceded Rescue of Ramos," *New York Times*, November 12, 2011, http://www.nytimes.com/2011/11/13/sports/baseball/in-venezuela-gunfight-preceded-rescue-of-ramos.html.

CHAPTER 9: THE EARLY SHOCKS OF BIOGENESIS

1   Teri Thompson, Michael O'Keeffe, and Nathaniel Vinton, "Dodgers Slugger Manny Ramirez Gets 50-Game Suspension from MLB for Using Banned Substance," *Daily News* [New York], May 9, 2009, http://www.nydailynews.com/sports/baseball/dodgers-slugger-manny-ramirez-50-game-suspension-mlb-banned-substance-article-1.409177.

2   George J. Mitchell, *Report to the Commissioner of Baseball of an Independent Investigation into the Illegal Use of Steroids and Other Performance Enhancing Substances by Players in Major League Baseball*, December 13, 2007, http://files.mlb.com/mitchrpt.pdf, 292.

3   Gus Garcia-Roberts, "Anthony Bosch Told Feds That Agent Scott Boras Tried to Cover Up Manny Ramirez's PED Use, Sources Say," *Newsday*, November 14, 2014, https://www.newsday.com/sports/baseball/anthony-bosch-told-feds-that-agent-scott-boras-tried-to-cover-up-manny-ramirez-s-ped-use-sources-say-1.9618541.

4   T. J. Quinn, "Doctor Says He's Never Prescribed hCG," ESPN, July 10, 2009, http://www.espn.com/mlb/news/story?id=4319776.

5   Jeff Passan, "Red Sox's Use of Toradol Could Put Ex-trainer at Odds with State Law, Industry Guidelines," Yahoo! Sports, February 15, 2013, https://sports.yahoo.com/news/red-sox-s-use-of-toradol-could-put-ex-trainer-at-odds-with-state-law--industry-guidelines---060042869.html.

6   Gordon Edes, "Jonathan Papelbon Used Toradol," ESPN, February 11, 2013, http://www.espn.com/espnw/news-commentary/article/8935151/jonathan-papelbon-says-took-toradol-shots-boston-red-sox; David Geier, "Boston Red Sox Pitchers Frequently Received Toradol Injections," Bleacher Report, February 12, 2013, http://bleacherreport.com/articles/1526070-boston-red-sox-pitchers-frequently-received-toradol-injections.

7   Edes, "Jonathan Papelbon Used Toradol."

8   Robert Klemko, "The NFL Can't Outrun a Legacy of Abuse," *Sports Illustrated*, March 28, 2017, https://www.si.com/mmqb/2017/03/28/nfl-toradol-lawsuit-painkillers-nflpa-union-team-doctor-conflict-interest.

CHAPTER 10: DOUBLE CROSS

1   Christian Red, "How Ex-Yankee Melky Cabrera Has Done a Body Good & Turned Around His Career with San Francisco Giants," *Daily News* [New York], July 8, 2012, http://www.nydailynews.com/sports/ baseball/ex-yankee-melky-cabrera-body-good-turned-career-san-francisco-giants-article-1.1109739.

2   Teri Thompson, Bill Madden, Michael O'Keeffe, and Nathaniel Vinton, "MLB Bans Melky Cabrera Associate Juan Nunez, Who Built Bogus Website in Plot to Help Giants All-Star Dodge 50-Game Testosterone Suspension," *Daily News* [New York], August 21, 2012, http://www.nydailynews.com/sports/baseball/mlb-bans-melky-cabrera-associate-juan-nunez-built-bogus-website-plot-giants-all-star-dodge-50-game-testosterone-suspension-article-1.1141120.

3   *Juan Carlos Nunez, Plaintiff, Against Athletes' Careers Enhanced and Secured, Inc., Sam Levinson, and Seth Levinson, Supreme Court of the State of New York Kings County*, February 12, 2018, https://d3d2maoophos6y.cloudfront.net/wp-content/ uploads/2018/02/13105945/document.pdf.

4   News reports on Muno's fifty-game suspension from positive test: https://www.nexis.com/results/enhdocview.do?docLinkInd=true&ers Key=23_T27274874618&format=GNBFI&startDocNo=0&results UrlKey=0_T27274874620&backKey=20_T27274874621&csi= 144566&docNo=1.

5   "About Cesar Paublini," Facebook, https://www.facebook.com/cesar. paublini.1/photos?lst=641387816%3A1134620178%3A1511016970& source_ref=pb_friends_tl.

6   Authors' interview with Jeannette Moran, September 30, 2017.

CHAPTER 11: "TELL THE DEA I WANT THIS DONE F—ING NOW!"

1   Authors' interview with Jeannette Moran, September 30, 2017.

2   Authors' interview with Kevin Stanfill, August 30, 2017.

3   Authors' interview with confidential informant, September 14, 2017.

4   Authors' interview with Kevin Stanfill, August 30, 2017.

5   http://ftw.usatoday.com/2015/08/cris-carter-told-nfl-rookies-to-get-a-fall-guy-in-case-they-get-in-trouble.

6   Authors' interview with Jeannette Moran, September 30, 2017.

7   Salvador Hernandez, "O.C. Doctor Pleads Guilty to Smuggling, Distributing Steroids," *Orange County Register*,

June 5, 2009, https://www.ocregister.com/2009/06/05/oc-doctor-pleads-guilty-to-smuggling-distributing-steroids/.

8   Authors' interview with Penny Payne-Korte, November and December 2017.

9   Tim Brown and Jeff Passan, "Ryan Braun Listed in Records of Alleged PED Clinic; Says He Used Anthony Bosch as Consultant," Yahoo! Sports, February 6, 2013, https://sports.yahoo.com/news/ryan-braun-s-name-listed-in-biogenesis-clinic-records-235650670.html.

10 Authors' conversation with Rob Manfred.

11 Authors' interview with Kevin Stanfill, assistant special agent in charge of the Biogenesis case for the Miami DEA, August 30, 2017, phone interview, and in Miami, September 28, 2017.

12 Authors' interview with Tony Bosch, Miami, October 2, 2017.

13 Christian Red and Michael O'Keeffe, "Alex Rodriguez Called Anthony Bosch While Yankees Faced Tigers in 2012 ALCS: Report," Daily News [New York], June 18, 2013, http://www.nydailynews.com/sports/i-team/report-a-rod-called-bosch-alcs-article-1.1376388.

14 Authors' interview with Jay Reisinger, December 20, 2017.

15 Authors' interview with Pat Sullivan, 2017.

CHAPTER 12: HACKER

1   Authors' interview with Lazaro Collazo at his home in Miami, October 2, 2017; Julie K. Brown, Hardball: When Major League Baseball Investigators Came to Town," Miami Herald, October 5, 2013, http://www.miamiherald.com/news/local/community/miami-dade/article1955929.html.

2   Authors' interview with Lazaro Collazo, Miami, October 2, 2017.

3   Michael O'Keeffe and Christian Red, "Yankees Slugger Alex Rodriguez Sued by Former Miami Pitching Coach Lazaro Collazo as Biogenesis Scandal Won't Go Away," Daily News [New York], June 13, 2015, http://www.nydailynews.com/sports/i-team/yankees-a-rod-sued-miami-pitching-coach-collazo-article-1.2256794; authors' interview with Lazaro Collazo, Miami, October 2, 2017.

4   Authors' interview with Frank Quintero Jr., September 29, 2017.

5   Authors' interview with Lazaro Collazo, Miami, October 2, 2017.

6   Authors' interviews with Jeannette Moran, September and October 2017.

7   Authors' interview with Kevin Stanfill, August 30, 2017.

8 Steve Eder, Serge F. Kovaleski, and Michael S. Schmidt, "In Rodriguez Arbitration, Two Sides Play Hardball," *New York Times*, November 3, 2013, http://www.nytimes.com/2013/11/04/sports/baseball/in-rodriguez-arbitration-two-sides-play-hardball.html.

CHAPTER 13: JUSTICE

1 Fredric Horowitz arbitration ruling in January 2014, which was attached to Alex Rodriguez's lawsuit against MLBPA et al, which was filed January 2014.

2 Teri Thompson and Christian Red, interview with Jay Reisinger, telephone interview, December 2017.

3 Authors' interview with Tony Bosch, Miami, October 2, 2017.

4 Buster Olney, "A-Rod Missed Change to Cut a Deal," ESPN, January 3, 2014, http://insider.espn.com/blog/buster-olney/post/_/id/4427/a-rod-missed-chance-to-cut-deal-with-mlb?addata=2013_insidertwitter_ARodMissedChanceBlog_social.

5 Teri Thompson, Bill Madden, Michael O'Keeffe, Christian Red, and Nathaniel Vinton, "Alex Rodriguez Was Set to Quit Baseball Until Former Drug Mole and Ex-convict Desiree Perez Convinced the Yankees Slugger to Fight MLB over PED Suspension," *Daily News* [New York], May 18, 2014, http://www.nydailynews.com/sports/i-team/babe-ruthless-rod-shady-lady-article-1.1796578.

6 http://www.nydailynews.com/sports/baseball/yankees/a-rod-tweets-cleared-play-article-1.1382509.

7 "Galea, Anthony Michael (CPSO#: 59671)," College of Physicians and Surgeons of Ontario, December 6, 2017, http://www.cpso.on.ca/DoctorDetails/Anthony-Michael-Galea/0042993-56971.

8 http://www.nydailynews.com/sports/i-team/weiner-warns-drug-cheats-face-major-road-block-article-1.1401845.

9 http://www.nydailynews.com/sports/baseball/yankees/a-bomb-a-roid-alex-homers-rehab-game-suspension-looms-article-1.1416459.

10 MLB press release, August 5, 2013.

11 http://www.nydailynews.com/sports/i-team/a-rod-mlb-211-game-drug-suspension-article-1.1418060.

12 Authors' interview with Anthony Bosch, October 2, 2017.

13 NYDN Oct 19, 2013, "Alex's Payoff Pitch" http://www.nydailynews.com/sports/i-team/a-rod-shelled-305g-evidence-linking-doping-source-article-1.1490193.

14 From transcripts of Alex Rodriguez 2013 arbitration, September 30, 2013 to November 21, 2013.

15 Authors' interview with Anthony Bosch, October 2, 2017.

16 From transcripts of Alex Rodriguez 2013 arbitration, September 30, 2013 to November 21, 2013.

17 https://www.youtube.com/watch?v=xkV9CSPSTuw.

18 Teri Thompson, Michael O'Keeffe, Christian Red, and Nathaniel Vinton, "Alex Rodriguez Walks Out of MLB's Arbitration Hearing, Slams Bud Selig on Mike Francesa's Radio Show," *Daily News* [New York], November 21, 2013, http://www.nydailynews.com/sports/i-team/a-rod-walks-arbitration-hearing-calls-process-farce-article-1.1523436.

19 http://www.nydailynews.com/sports/i-team/judge-denies-a-rod-reguest-seal-horowitz-ruling-article-1.1578058.

20 https://www.cbsnews.com/news/the-case-of-alex-rodriguez/.

CHAPTER 14: "QUEEN FOR A DAY"

1 Authors' interview with Jeannette Moran, August 30, 2017.

2 Authors' interviews with Jeannette Moran, September and October 2017.

3 Authors' interview with Kevin Stanfill, August 30, 2017.

4 Authors' interview with Jeannette Moran, September 30, 2017.

5 Steve Eder and Michael S. Schmidt, "Baseball Shakes Up Its Investigative Unit," *New York Times*, May 1, 2014, https://www.nytimes.com/2014/05/02/sports/baseball/major-league-baseball-shakes-up-its-investigative-unit.html.

6 Authors' interview with Jeannette Moran, September 30, 2017.

7 Ibid.

8 Authors' interview with Kevin Stanfill, August 30, 2017.

9 Authors' interview with Jeannette Moran, September 30, 2017.

10 http://www.nydailynews.com/sports/i-team/mlb-hires-new-top-ties-washington-article-1.1927209.

11 Christian Red, Michael O'Keeffe, and Teri Thompson, "Alex Rodriguez Peed on Our House! . . . 'He Is the Devil . . . He Is Evil,' Says Cousin Yuri Sucart's Wife Carmen as She Fires Back at Tarnished Yankees Slugger," *Daily News* [New

York], November 14, 2014, http://www.nydailynews.com/
sports/i-team/a-rod-devil-cousin-yuri-wife-carmen-article-1.2001588.

12 ICSS brochure from the conference "Securing Sport," November 3–4,
2015. International Centre for Securing Sport.

CHAPTER 15: "THIS TOWN IS A HUSTLER'S TOWN"

1 Email to *Daily News* reporter, December 13, 2017, from Charles
Scheeler, Mitchell Report investigator.

2 http://ftw.usatoday.com/2015/06/
mlb-commissioner-rob-manfred- cardinals-hacking-astros-probe-fbi.

3 Authors' interview with Anthony Bosch, October 2, 2017.

4 Authors' interview with Frank Quintero, attorney for Biogenesis
defendant Lazaro Collazo; Tim Elfrink, "Tony Bosch Lived on Fisher
Island, in Luxury Downtown Apartments on MLB's Cash," *Miami
New Times*, March 4, 2015, http://www.miaminewtimes.com/news/
tony-bosch-lived-on-fisher-island-in-luxury-downtown-apartments-
on-mlbs-cash-7530933.

5 Authors' interview with Anthony Bosch, October 2, 2017.

6 George J. Mitchell, *Report to the Commissioner of Baseball of an
Independent Investigation into the Illegal Use of Steroids and Other
Performance Enhancing Substances by Players in Major League
Baseball*, December 13, 2007, http://files.mlb.com/mitchrpt.pdf,
SR-28.

INDEX